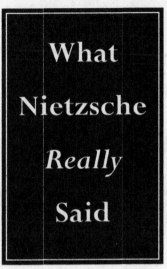

What

Nietzsche

Really

Said

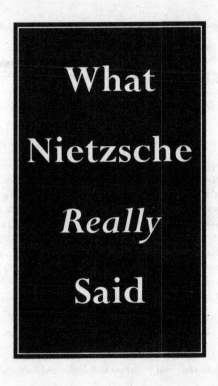

What Nietzsche *Really* Said

ROBERT C. SOLOMON

and

KATHLEEN M. HIGGINS

SCHOCKEN BOOKS
NEW YORK

Grateful acknowledgment is made to the following for permission to reprint previously
published material: *Viking Penguin:* "Twilight of the Idols," "The Antichrist" and "Thus
Spoke Zarathustra" by Friedrich Nietzsche, and "Nietzsche Contra Wagner" by Friedrich
Nietzsche, edited by Walter Kaufmann, from THE PORTABLE NIETZSCHE, edited and
translated by Walter Kaufmann. Translation copyright © 1954 by The Viking Press,
renewed 1982 by Viking Penguin Inc. Reprinted by permission of Viking Penguin, a
division of Penguin Putnam Inc. · *Random House, Inc.:* Excerpts from THE GAY SCIENCE
by Friedrich Nietzsche, translated by Walter Kaufmann. Copyright © 1974 by Random
House, Inc.; excerpts from ON THE GENEALOGY OF MORALS by Friedrich Nietzsche,
translated by Walter Kaufmann. Copyright © 1967 by Random House, Inc. Reprinted
by permission of Random House, Inc.

Library of Congress Cataloging-in-Publication Data

Solomon, Robert C.
What Nietzsche really said / Robert C. Solomon and Kathleen M. Higgins.
p.   cm.
Includes bibliographical references and index.
ISBN 978-0-8052-1094-1
1. Nietzsche, Friedrich Wilhelm, 1844–1900. I. Higgins, Kathleen
Marie. II. Title.
B3317.S6155 2000
193—dc21   99-33796
CIP

for Frithjof Bergmann
and Karsten Harries

Contents

Acknowledgments

We would especially like to thank Cecilia Cancellaro for encouraging us to take on this project and for her support throughout. We want to thank Jennifer Turvey for seeing the book through in its final stages and our agent Melanie Jackson for her continuing advice. We would also like to thank our various editors and publishers who have allowed us to pillage our previous and present writings on Nietzsche, in particular, Richard Schacht and Terry Moore at Cambridge University Press (Richard Schacht, ed., *Nietzsche's Postmoralism,* New York: Cambridge University Press, 1999), Richard Schacht again, *Nietzsche, Genealogy, Morality: Essays on Nietzsche's On the Genealogy of Morals* (Los Angeles: University of California Press, 1994), Bernd Magnus and Cambridge University Press again (*The Cambridge Companion to Nietzsche,* ed. Bernd Magnus and Kathleen Higgins), and Tom Rollins at The Teaching Company (*The Will to Power: The Philosophy of Friedrich Nietzsche,* 24 video/audio lectures, 1999). We would like to thank Random House and Viking for their kind permission to quote from Walter Kaufmann's translations of Nietzsche's central texts.

Nietzsche's Works

* In second edition (1886) title changed to *The Birth of Tragedy, or Hellenism and Pessimism.*
** Date of publication; written in 1888.
*** Edited by others; published posthumously.

Introduction:
"How to Philosophize
with a Hammer"

Regarding the sounding out of idols, this time they are not just idols of the age, but eternal idols, which are here touched with a hammer as with a tuning fork; there are altogether no older, no more convinced, no more puffed-up idols—and none more hollow. That does not prevent them from being those in which people have the most faith . . .

—from *Twilight of the Idols*[1]

HERE AT THE END of the twentieth century, Friedrich Nietzsche has become one of the most talked about philosophers in history. Unfortunately, he has not also become one of the best understood. Myths and rumors continue to swirl around his legacy, some of them concerning his sex life, his politics, his mental health, many of them supposedly cutting to the heart of his philosophy—the "will to power," his attack on religion and morality, and the infamous *Übermensch* (super-man). What

Nietzsche really said gets lost in a maze of falsehoods, misinterpretations, and exaggerations. But he is such an exciting and insightful thinker, not to mention a mesmerizing writer, that it is well worth our while—and a treat—to really understand him.

Getting down to what Nietzsche really said, however, is no simple matter. He was not one of those philosophers who set out with a carefully plotted plan and pursued it faithfully to its completion. He was not a systematic philosopher: he railed against the attempt to make philosophy into a system, calling it "a lack of integrity." We cannot squeeze all of Nietzsche's varied observations and insights into a single coherent mold without losing not just the charm but the essence of what he was trying to do. Nietzsche wrote in aphorisms, short paragraphs, and cryptic allegories, carefully arranged but nevertheless disjointed and purposively disorienting. He wanted to shock us, surprise us, make us see matters from different angles, different perspectives, in different ways. Much of his writing consists of quick guerrilla-style attacks on a broad variety of established positions—moral, metaphysical, social, and religious—and some of the leading figures of both his past and present. Nietzsche aims in different directions, now attacking this position, now attacking its opposite. Such strategies may look like contradiction, but they are not. These multiple campaigns represent the many different "skirmishes of an untimely man," as he describes his onslaughts in *Twilight of the Idols*.

Michel Foucault, one of the more illustrious Nietzscheans of this century, insisted that there was no single Nietzschean philosophy, and that our question should be, "What serious use can we make of Nietzsche?" The word *serious* is an attempt to close off frivolous misinterpretation and prevent the careless pillaging of Nietzsche's texts. Nevertheless, Foucault's point is that there is no single consistent account to be given of what Nietzsche really said without consideration of the various uses we make of him. But even when we agree that use shapes interpretation, that does not mean that we should not try to be faithful to Nietzsche's words, his stated intentions, his ambiguities, even his inadequacies.

Therefore we will not attempt in this book to squeeze Nietzsche into a suit that does not fit him. We would like to dispel the myths and rumors, present some helpful hints and guidelines for reading his works—a delightful but also difficult and dangerous adventure. We want to suggest, at least, the complex, subtle, and sometimes genuinely ambivalent nature of Nietzsche's various campaigns against the monumental forces of Christianity and morality and his various attacks on such individuals as Socrates, Schopenhauer, and Wagner. We will bring in some of Nietzsche's heroes and nemeses to show how this self-consciously eccentric and "untimely" thinker placed himself in the long history of Western thought. But, most important, we want to emphasize Nietzsche's affirmative philosophy, his positive suggestions, along with his famously misunderstood doctrines and his enthusiasms. To think of Nietzsche as nothing but negative, "the great destroyer," is to misunderstand him profoundly. Nietzsche himself would insist that the essential thing is to say *yes* to philosophy, and to life.

Nietzsche wrote many books. Which of those many books one chooses to emphasize will skew one's interpretation considerably. For example, the relatively philological and aesthetic content of his early *Birth of Tragedy*, the conscientious polemic of

On the Genealogy of Morals, and the intentionally blasphemous *The Antichrist* of Nietzsche's later years all present very different Nietzsches. "What Nietzsche really said" depends in part on what one reads and how one interprets what one reads. (Nietzsche insists: "There are only interpretations.")

Nietzsche also wrote many notes, most of which he never published, nor intended to publish. If one focuses on these unpublished notes (as Martin Heidegger, for example, chose to do), one can come up with a very different Nietzsche than the one that emerges from the works Nietzsche himself intended to present to the world. Nietzsche scholarship has gone through many fads of interpretation, with the focus ranging from his scattered comments on women to his supposedly monolithic preoccupation with "the will to power." Nietzsche's unpublished early essay "On Truth and Lie in a Nonmoral Sense" has come to assume definitive importance in postmodernist literary criticism, and Nietzsche's unpublished plans for a systematic work have stimulated many imaginative but farfetched "reconstructions."

Nietzsche's life, like that of the earlier "existentialist" Søren Kierkegaard, was illustrious only in his soul, his mind's interior, and in what he produced. His life, the actual day-to-day details of how he lived and suffered, strikes virtually every reader as unenviable, even miserable. Nietzsche was born on October 15, 1844 in a small German town, Röcken. His father, a Lutheran minister, died when Nietzsche was only four years old. He was raised by his mother, grandmother, and two very religious maiden aunts. As a student, Nietzsche displayed obvious brilliance, even genius (a term much abused in the nineteenth century). He was made a professor of philology (classics) in the university at Basel at the age of twenty-four, served briefly as a medical orderly in the Franco-Prussian War in 1870, and resigned his university post after little more than a decade of teaching because of poor health. He spent the rest of his life largely alone, perched in some of the most spectacular landscapes in Europe.

Nietzsche never married. He suffered from excruciating headaches and chronic insomnia. Nevertheless, he started writing and publishing his remarkable books in the early seventies and despite his infirmities reached a veritable writing frenzy in his late thirties, finishing several books in his last productive year. In 1889, while in Italy, he collapsed on the street in a deranged mental state and suffered the first of a debilitating series of seizures and strokes. This ended his writing career, at the age of forty-four. He lived another decade, at first under the tender care of his mother, but later subject to the manipulative management of his proto-Nazi sister, Elisabeth. He died in August of 1900, in the first summer of the new century.

In large measure, Nietzsche's life was his work. As one prominent commentator has written, his life *is* literature.[2] To be sure, Nietzsche the man created Nietzsche the author, but it is the author who is most real to us. In what follows, accordingly, we will not be concerned with Nietzsche's life except by way of refuting some of the most scandalous myths and rumors about him (in chapter 1, "Rumors: Wine, Women, and Wagner"). What will concern us are his guiding themes and campaigns and his published books (which we will introduce in modest detail in chapter 2, "Faced with a Book by Nietzsche").[3] Chapters 3 and 4 concern two of Nietzsche's most notorious and persistent campaigns, against Christianity (although we will argue that Nietzsche's position is considerably more nuanced than a simple rejection) and against Judeo-Christian morality. Chapter 5 takes a look at one of Nietzsche's more outrageous rhetorical devices, his use of the *ad hominem* argument—that is, an argument directed against the person and the person's character and circumstances as a way of understanding (or undermining) his or her philosophical doctrines. We catalogue, in the form of two "top ten" lists, Nietzsche's heroes and role models on the one hand, and his favorite targets on the other. In chapter 6, we consider Nietzsche's own character, or at least the character of the person he wanted to be (and urges us to be). We interpret Nietzsche's philosophy as a version of "virtue ethics," and so, accordingly, we consider Nietzsche's virtues. Finally, Nietzsche's philosophy is so often presented as mere critique—as purely critical and destructive—that we close the book with a discussion of Nietzsche's affirmative philosophy and his insistence on "saying yes to life." Chapter 7 develops a detailed presentation of some of his more positive and enthusiastic ideas: for example, his celebration of fate (*amor fati*) and his now famous conception of eternal recurrence. The conclusion summarizes Nietzsche's influence and legacy. In an appendix ("Nietzsche's Bestiary") we present some of Nietzsche's most striking images.

What
Nietzsche
Really
Said

Rumors:
Wine, Women, and Wagner

NIETZSCHE IS NOW the most often cited philosopher in the Western tradition. His name gets dropped in novels and movies, from Hermann Hesse's *Steppenwolf* and Milan Kundera's *The Unbearable Lightness of Being* to *Blazing Saddles* and *A Fish Called Wanda*. The literature about and against Nietzsche is voluminous, but despite a great deal of good scholarship in the past half century, old myths and prejudices remain prominent in the public consciousness. The infamous *ad hominem* argument, "Nietzsche was crazy, so don't take anything he wrote seriously," can still be heard in some philosophy seminars. Nietzsche's supposedly right-wing political views continue to be cited and abused in intelligent street conversation, and Nietzsche's supposed hatred of women is so well established as a bulwark of patriarchy that it is accepted even by those who should know better. Nietzsche's alleged affiliation with Hitler and the Nazis survives fifty years after Walter Kaufmann debunked that vile association; and Nietzsche's imagined love of raw, brute power remains a staple of quasi-philosophical college lore.

In order to even begin to make some headway into the question of what Nietzsche really said, it is first necessary to say with some confidence what he did *not* say, what he did not do, what did not motivate him, what he did not think. We begin, therefore, with thirty rumors about Nietzsche, many of them prominent mainly among those who condemn him without reading him, but others common even among his more enthusiastic readers. Let us begin with:

Rumor # 1. Nietzsche Was Crazy

It is true that Nietzsche suffered from mental illness at the end of his life. For his last ten years, from 1889 until his death in 1900, he was utterly incompetent (in the clinical sense), and during this time he did not write at all. Some scholars claim to detect some craziness in his last book, *Ecce Homo,* but what is interpreted as impending insanity (and the key word here is *impending*) is much more convincingly understood as ironic, self-mocking genius. Those who attempt to make the case that Nietzsche was already mad typically interpret Nietzsche's hyperbole and bombast as indications of delusions of grandeur. For example, Nietzsche entitles the chapters of *Ecce Homo,* "Why I Am So Wise," "Why I Am So Clever," "Why I Write Such Excellent Books," and "Why I Am a Destiny." But Nietzsche was a masterful and uninhibited wit, and irony as a form of philosophizing had its precedents. Socrates, considering the oracle's pronouncement that he was the wisest man in Athens, announced to everyone who would listen (including the jury that would condemn him) that he was the wisest only because he knew that he was completely ignorant. Nietzsche's implicit comparison with Socrates is hardly modest, but pseudo-self-aggrandizement hardly counts as "crazy."

Nietzsche, while in Turin, in January 1889, is said to have "collapsed" into madness when he saw a horse being beaten by its driver. He walked up to the horse, attempted to protect it by hugging it, and lost consciousness. After he was taken back to where he was staying, Nietzsche wrote some peculiar letters to friends, who, consequently, became worried about his sanity. The letter that resulted in his institutionalization was written to Jakob Burckhardt, who had been Nietzsche's colleague while he was a classics professor in Basel. This letter, dated January 6, 1889, began.

> Dear Professor:
>
> In the end I would much rather be a Basel professor than God; but I have not dared push my private egoism so far as to desist for its sake from the creation of the world. You see, one must make sacrifices however and wherever one lives. . . . [1]

Nietzsche's writing in the voice of God the Creator, who has restrained his egoism enough to be content in that role, distressed Burckhardt. He showed it to another of Nietzsche's friends, Franz Overbeck, who had also received a letter from Nietzsche, this one signed "Dionysus" and claiming "I am just having all anti-Semites shot." [2] Overbeck went to Turin and took Nietzsche to a nursing home in Basel, eventually arranging for his hospitalization in an asylum in Jena (in the eastern part of

Germany). Nietzsche was released a short while later into the care of his mother. After her death responsibility for him fell to his sister Elisabeth, who moved him to Weimar and quite literally put him on display for visitors in her efforts to develop a cult around him and his philosophy. These efforts were sufficiently successful that she later got Hitler interested in Nietzsche's writings.

Nietzsche may have been "crazy," in the vernacular sense, in the last years of his life, but this does not mean that he was mentally ill before 1889. But even if he displayed symptoms of mental disturbance (and how many of history's great philosophers have not been neurotic, at least?), one must nevertheless admit that much of what he says, though often extreme, is hardly insane.

Rumor # 2. Nietzsche Hated Women

Nietzsche's alleged misogyny is still the target of routine feminist attacks, but the truth is that Nietzsche struggled with many of the same ideas feminists today have been grappling with. He recognized the importance of education in determining the specifics of gender roles, for example, and he suggested that men and women have different perspectives that affect their understanding of the world. Because he shares a number of concerns with our era's feminists, a number of feminist thinkers are currently reinvestigating Nietzsche's ideas about sex and gender.

It is certainly true that Nietzsche shared at least some of the male chauvinism of his times, and he was no doubt influenced by his mentor Arthur Schopenhauer, who made many disparaging comments about women. Nietzsche's personal relationships with women were complex, but they do not betray signs of hatred so much as confusion. Twice he proposed marriage to women so early on in the relationship that he could not reasonably have expected an acceptance. A more likely diagnosis is that he panicked, that he sought relief rather than acceptance, that he did not really want to get married.

Despite his romantic record and his largely solitary lifestyle, Nietzsche was close friends with several women of exceptional talent. One of his would-be fiancées, Lou Andreas-Salomé, was an accomplished writer and critic in her own right, and the two developed an intimate friendship of great significance to both of them, although the romance itself lasted only a few months. In a famous photograph with Nietzsche and their mutual friend (and Nietzsche's rival) Paul Rée, Lou is perched in a wagon, holding a whip over the two men. This picture is often "Exhibit A" in the case against Nietzsche for his sexism. But Nietzsche himself posed the picture, and we should not forget who holds the whip, nor the joking spirit in which the picture was made.

The photograph with Lou may have added a dimension of private humor (most likely black humor) to a scene in *Thus Spoke Zarathustra* that Nietzsche wrote shortly after their estrangement. This scene presents Nietzsche's protagonist Zarathustra's reporting of a conversation with an old woman, which concluded with her comment, "You are going to women? Don't forget your whip."[3] As in the photograph, the whip is introduced here by a woman, and the scene is far more complex than the usual out-of-context quote would reveal. Given that Zarathustra has been rhapsodizing about his own fantasies of heterosexual love, the old woman's suggestion hints that she does not think that women will participate so readily. Far from endorsing the naturalness of male control, the old woman presents the sexes as engaged in a power struggle that the male is by no means assured of winning.

Rumor # 3. Nietzsche Was a Nazi

First, the obvious: Hitler did not form the Nazi party (National-sozialistische Deutsche Arbeiterpartei) until 1919 and he did not ascend to power with it until 1933, several decades after Nietzsche's death (in 1900). In the plainest sense, therefore, Nietzsche could not have been a Nazi. Nevertheless, there is a famous photograph ("Exhibit B") of Hitler staring eyeball-to-eyeball at a bust of Nietzsche in the Nietzsche Archive in Weimar in 1934. But let us remind ourselves that there is little to support such suspicions of "backward causation." Even if Hitler did accept or adopt some ideas of Nietzsche's (and we have no evidence that he actually read much of Nietzsche's work) it does not follow that Nietzsche is responsible for what Hitler did with those ideas. (Likewise, a philosopher such as Hegel is not responsible for the use of some of his political ideas by the Italian dictator and former philosophy professor Benito Mussolini, as Karl Marx was not responsible for the Soviet monster Joseph Stalin). To be sure, monstrous use was made of some of the ideas that Nietzsche defended—for example, eugenics, the project of manipulating human reproduction to produce the most desirable characteristics. But almost every intellectual of the period took eugenics seriously (including

George Bernard Shaw in England). Hitler's use of the gas chamber in the service of his own perverse plan to shape the species was not a strategy Nietzsche either suggested or imagined.

Nevertheless, it can be argued that even if Nietzsche was not a member of the Nazi party, many of his ideas and attitudes prefigured the views of the Nazis—notably, his more general views about race and human inequality, his celebration of power and "might makes right," his championing of the *Übermensch* (superman) and "master morality," and his condemnation of the weak. But few of these doctrines, as they were presented by Nietzsche, mean anything like what the Nazis took them to mean. Nietzsche expressed his views on race, like his views on just about everything, in an uncensored fashion. He did believe that many character traits were inherited, including some that were acquired by generations of one's ancestors adopting a certain way of life or developing a particular diet. But what he praised most was miscegenation, the mixing of the races, not the "racial purity" idealized by the Nazis. And although he thought the desirability of genetic endowments varied across the species, Nietzsche went out of his way to ridicule the Germans and their "Aryan" pretensions to racial superiority. The "blond beast" he famously refers to is just that—a lion, the "king of the jungle," not the blond-haired German soldier of Nazi iconography. Whatever else he might have thought of them, Nietzsche did not think the Germans were either super-men or masters.

We will discuss Nietzsche's supposed celebration of power shortly, but let us say firmly here that it has nothing to do with the infamous "might makes right" argument that is put forward by Thrasymachus in Plato's *Republic* and is often associated with Niccolò Machiavelli, the sixteenth-century polemicist and consultant to princes. Nietzsche famously criticizes weakness, but it is mainly spiritual weakness that he has in mind, not political powerlessness.

Perhaps most important of all in the list of differences between Nietzsche's views and the Nazis' was the fact that Nietzsche was no anti-Semite. Indeed he became an *anti*-anti-Semite. (Consider the flamboyant letter to Overbeck when his sanity broke.) Nietzsche's sister, Elisabeth, is the manipulative presence behind the Nietzsche-Nazi myth. She was indeed sympathetic to the growing fascist cause and married to a notorious anti-Semite of whom Nietzsche thoroughly disapproved. (He had even refused to attend their wedding.) It was she, years after her brother's death, who invited Hitler for his "photo-op" at the Nietzsche Archive. Elisabeth took over Nietzsche's literary estate after his incapacitation, and she even published apocryphal books and "editions" of Nietzsche's notes under his by-then famous name. With her husband, Bernhard Förster, she tried to found a "pure" Aryan colony in the jungles of South America. (It failed.)

Unfortunately, Elisabeth's political views became firmly attached to Nietzsche's name, and the association survived even the exposé of her forgeries and misappropriations of Nietzsche's works. Yet we can say with confidence, that Nietzsche was no Nazi and that he shared virtually none of the Nazis' vicious ideas about the "ThousandYear Reich" and the superiority of the German race. Indeed, Nietzsche famously declared himself "a good European" and lamented the fact that his native language was German. He spent virtually his entire adult life, from his professorship in Switzerland through his voluntary exile in and around the Alps, until his last moments of sanity in northern

Italy, outside of Germany. Throughout his career he ridiculed the folly of taking German military victories as signs of cultural superiority. The fact that many German soldiers in World War I carried Nietzsche's *Zarathustra* in their backpacks is a great and tragic irony.

Rumor # 4. Nietzsche Hated Jews

Germany has a long history of anti-Semitism, dating back (at least) to the Middle Ages. Jews were the target of hostility from the Christian majority long before Hitler and his concentration camps. It is much to Nietzsche's credit, then, living where he did and surrounded by anti-Semites, that he refused to share their intolerance and came to openly denounce anti-Semitism.

Nevertheless, Jews were the subject of many of Nietzsche's reveries. For a German Christian to speak of Jews, especially when his tone is so often ironic and cutting, is to invite charges of anti-Semitism. Nietzsche's mistaken reputation as a Nazi and a fascist aggravates the complaint, and the fact that Nietzsche is so often quoted out of context provides evidence for those who would claim that he, like many Germans of his time, hated Jews.

In fact, many of Nietzsche's comments stemmed from his scholarly, historical interests. As a philologist, he was interested in both the origins of Christianity in Judaism and the complex relation between the Jews and the Greeks, particularly around the time of Philo of Alexandria and Saul of Tarsus (Saint Paul). As a student of what we would now call anthropology, he was also interested in the comparison of societies, the "Jewish race" included. As a moral historian he was deeply interested in the role of the Jews in the development of Western morality.

Nietzsche did have mixed feelings about Jews, as he did about most peoples, including the Germans, the English, and most Christians. We should remember, however, that he often characterizes Christianity as an offshoot of Judaism. What he finds objectionable in the Jewish moral outlook he usually finds in the Christian perspective as well. Some of his seemingly negative comments about Jews can be seen as barbs aimed at Christian anti-Semites, Nietzsche turning their own slurs back on them. For example, he describes Jesus as "too Jewish," since he failed to recognize that "if God wished to become an object of love, he should have given up judging and justice first of all. . . . The founder of Christianity was not refined enough in his feelings at this point—being a Jew."[4]

In the first book of *On the Genealogy of Morals,* similarly, he criticizes Judaism while describing Christianity as derivative and less creative. Nietzsche unmistakably refers to Jews when he introduces the idea of resentment (he uses the more general French term, *ressentiment*) giving birth to "slave morality." "All that has been done on earth against 'the noble,' 'the powerful,' 'the masters,' 'the rulers,' fades into nothing compared with what the *Jews* have done against them." Theirs is "an act of the *most spiritual revenge.*"[5] Nietzsche grudgingly praises this boldly "creative" act, and he notes that any such race "is bound to become *cleverer* than any noble race." And if the Jews are viewed as the defenders of "the people" (or "the slaves," "the herd," or "the mob"), Nietzsche writes, dripping with irony, then "no people ever had a more world historical mission."[6]

Nietzsche is sharply critical not only of Judaism but of the entire sweep of Western history that followed. For Jews them-selves, Nietzsche shows not malice but a strange fascination:

> The Jews [as compared to the Romans] were the priestly nation
> of *ressentiment par excellence,* in whom there dwelt an unequaled
> popular-moral genius; one only has to compare similarly gifted
> nations—the Chinese or the Germans, for instance—with the
> Jews, to sense which is of the first and which of the fifth rank.[7]

If one is looking for anti-Semitism in Nietzsche's life, one need not look far. His sister and brother-in-law of course, but also Nietzsche's early hero, Richard Wagner—all were anti-Semites. And in Wagner's case this was one of the reasons why Nietzsche turned against him.

Rumor # 5. Nietzsche Favored Eugenics

Again, if it were not for the Nazis, eugenics—the selection of "desirable" human characteristics for reproduction and the exclusion of "undesirable" characteristics—would probably not be a matter of ferocious debate. Among the nineteenth century's proponents of eugenics were numbered virtually all the progressive thinkers of Europe, as we have mentioned; and the actual practice of eugenics, in the sense of choosing a mate with some thought toward the traits of one's offspring, has taken place ever since men and women first noticed the connection between sex and babies. Of course, like any gain of human control over natural and hitherto uncontrollable processes—the prolongation of life, the preselection of sex in pregnancy, the ability to clone and artificially reproduce in laboratory conditions—it has its dangers and the potential for abuse. Yet the idea of minimizing debilitating and lethal birth defects and improving general intelligence and well-being is, except in deranged political agendas and extreme *laissez-faire* theologies, beyond rebuke, and current scientific research continues to make steps toward realizing such goals. Yes, Nietzsche favored breeding a race that was more intelligent, free-thinking, creative, and less resentful than the folks he saw all around him, but he had few practical ideas about how this would be implemented. Being childless, he obviously did not engage in the practice himself.

Rumor # 6. Nietzsche Was a Fascist

Nevertheless, even if Nietzsche was not a Nazi or an anti-Semite (so the argument goes), he was certainly a fascist. He attacked democracy and ridiculed the idea of equality. He believed in government by the strong (whether or not he would have claimed that "might makes right") and he praised some of the most notorious tyrants in Western history, Napoleon for one, Cesare Borgia for another.

In fact, Nietzsche was apolitical, if "political" has to do with endorsing social movements, parties, or causes. He described political parties as a manifestation of humanity's "herding" tendencies, and as being only negligibly distinct from one another. His "praise" for the cruel Borgia was an ironic put-down of Wagner's character Parsifal, the "holy fool" who seeks the Holy Grail, and his comment deliberately outrageous: "Those to whom I said in confidence that they should sooner look even for a Cesare Borgia than for a Parsifal, did not believe their own ears."[8] Napoleon, we tend to forget, was chastised as a dangerous *liberal* in Germany, not as an autocrat. Several distinguished authors have labored to show that Nietzsche was in fact a political thinker, but the range of their views, from liberalism to authoritarianism, shows, even more clearly than the absence of any identifiable political doctrines in Nietzsche's texts, that no coherent political viewpoint emerges from his work. Nietzsche attacks democracy and socialism, but he attacks with equal ferocity autocracy, tyranny, oligarchy, theocracy, nationalism, militarism, racism, intolerance, and political stupidity of all kinds. If he defends any kind of political notion, it is aristocracy, "the rule by the best," a notion he shared, ironically, with his favorite target, Socrates. Also like Socrates, Nietzsche abjured personal involvement in politics and paid full attention to the question of individual virtue, what Socrates summarized as "the good of one's soul."

Nietzsche was interested in individuals and their self-realization, and he is concerned with great states, as he puts it, only insofar as they are capable of producing (a few) great individuals. The virtues Nietzsche praises are not political virtues, and it is of little interest to him whether they have political consequences. A philosopher who praises solitude and artistic creativity is not likely to have a sympathetic ear for the fascist rant of submerging one's individuality in the State and conforming to its laws as a matter of spiritual necessity.

In line with his emphasis on individual self-realization, Nietzsche does have some socially relevant ideas, for example, about the nature of education and child rearing (although he had no children himself and spent very little time with any). He had harsh words for democracy, but so did Plato. His comments are not very different in their tone or temper from the routine complaints we hear today (from democrats) about uneducated and ignorant voters who are easily led astray by demagogues, about the irrationality of making delicate and important strategic decisions by majority vote, about the need for leadership and wisdom at the top rather than simply a popular mandate through polls. Yet despite his opposition to democracy, Nietzsche was the very opposite of a fascist. He was a true believer in individual initiative and originality, and if he believed in any politics at all it was a politics in which there would be no need to be "political."

Rumor # 7. Nietzsche Adored Power

One of the best-known phrases from Nietzsche's philosophy is "the will to power" (*der Wille zur Macht*). Nietzsche coined this expression as an alternative to pessimistic philosopher Arthur Schopenhauer's "will to life," the alleged motive of self-preservation that explained all beings' continued efforts in life, despite the suffering involved. Nietzsche's seeming celebrations of "will to power" are typically at the expense of Schopenhauer. As opposed to the pessimistic vision associated with "will to life," Nietzsche posits that life is "will to power," the enthusiastic drive to enhance vitality to act on the world (rather than reacting to it).

Not at all a modest author, Nietzsche often praised himself for discovering that human behavior is motivated by the desire for power. He did not, however, praise either the mechanism or many of its expressions, much less raw instances of power-mongering. Indeed, he claims, "Power *makes stupid*."[9] We might note that the German word for "power" is *Macht,* not *Reich,* indicating something more like personal strength than political might. One might think that Nietzsche's own lack of political power suggests he would not have been familiar enough with it to adore it, but as Nietzsche would have been the first to point out, those without power are among the most likely to praise it and crave it.

Nietzsche's "will to power" is not about political maneuverings but a psychological hypothesis about what drives human (and animal) behavior. He rejects what he sees as the rampantly hedonistic theory of his English (and some German) counterparts, their idea that people (and animals) are universally motivated by the pursuit of pleasure and the avoidance of pain. Throughout his works Nietzsche insightfully catalogues cases of human behavior that cannot be explained by the hedonist paradigm. Heroes and martyrs accept the most excruciating pain and an agonizing death, not to gain pleasure or avoid worse pain but to prove something, to make a point, to win a great victory.

None of this points to anything resembling political power, or, for that matter, power over other people. Indeed, what Nietzsche most often celebrates under this rubric is self-discipline and creative energy, and it is not so much *having* power or even *feeling* power that Nietzsche cites as the motivation of our behavior as the need to increase one's strength and vitality to do great things—for example, to write great books in philosophy.

Rumor # 8. Nietzsche Believed That "All Is Permitted"

Nietzsche's remark "God is dead" [10] is often conflated—or simply confused—with Ivan Karamazov's desperate statement in Dostoyevsky's *The Brothers Karamazov,* "If God does not exist, then all is permitted!" But Nietzsche, unlike Dostoyevsky, never thought that values come from God. Some values are part of our biological makeup, the premium we place on health, for example. Others are socially constructed, and still others emerge from the creative activity of robust individuals who formulate their own judgments, independent of any social or religious sanctions. It is true that Nietzsche predicts that with "the death of God" (that is, as people come to realize that belief in God no longer constrains their behavior), people will come to doubt their previous values and even doubt that values are possible. But this is a diagnosis, not a proclamation, and Nietzsche anticipates the coming of such a world, already in evidence, with proper horror. Even if Nietzsche thinks it desirable that the death of God will lead to the dismantling of old moral codes, he is far from thinking that it does not matter how one lives. To the contrary, if there is no God and no afterlife, *this* life is all that matters.

Rumor # 9. Nietzsche Was a Nihilist

Given the horror with which Nietzsche predicted the coming of nihilism in Europe and the vehemence with which he denounced the nihilism he saw as inherent in the Judeo-Christian tradition, it is surely a misunderstanding to say, as so many do, that he himself was a nihilist. His mouthpiece, Zarathustra, does indeed declare. "What is falling, we should still push,"[11] but it is amply clear that the purpose of destroying some already rotting structures (and beliefs) is to make room for building new ones.

"Nihilism" was a relatively new concept in Europe in Nietzsche's time. It was invented by the generation of Russian writers that included Ivan Sergeyevich Turgenev (1818–1883), who in his novel *Fathers and Sons* used the term to refer to the rebellious younger generation who rejected their parents' conservative values. Nietzsche defines nihilism in his notes with the cryptic remark *"the highest values devaluate themselves."*[12] But it is clear in everything he says about nihilism that he sees it as a sign of decadence and is in no way in favor of it.

Even some of his admirers claim that Nietzsche's philosophy is completely destructive, or deconstructive, that he has nothing positive or affirmative to tell us. But Nietzsche's philosophy is nothing if not affirmative, even if he does spend an enormous amount of time and energy criticizing and lambasting those people and ideas who oppose or undermine the positive vision he embraces. Nietzsche is not merely a destroyer, a nihilist who undermines everything. Paraphrasing Gordon Gekko in Oliver Stone's *Wall Street,* who claims, "I am not a destroyer of companies," Nietzsche might well say, "I am not a destroyer of the virtues, I am a *liberator* of them."

Rumor # 10. Nietzsche Admired Barbarians

One of the best-known figures in Nietzsche's philosophy, in part due to the lavish parody by George Bernard Shaw in his popular play *Man and Superman* (subtitled: *A Comedy and a Philosophy*) is the *Übermensch,* the "overman" or, in the more comical and ordinary translation, "the Superman." Although Shaw's rendition of the *Übermensch* pictured him as a sophisticated and philosophically suave defender of the "Life Force" that drives the universe (Shaw's own philosophy), subsequent references have only heightened the image of the *Übermensch* as some sort of crude barbarian, culminating, not surprisingly, in Arnold Schwarzenegger's characterization in the 1982 film *Conan the Barbarian*. This cartoon image of the *Übermensch,* which Nietzsche does not forestall in his brief and cryptic announcements in *Zarathustra* ("Man is a rope, tied between beast and over-man"[13]), makes a mockery of much that Nietzsche valued—aesthetic sensitivity, humor and even self-mockery, creativity, and, despite his reputation, social grace and courtesy.

Another basis for the rumor that Nietzsche admires barbarians is his preference for the morality of the "masters" of ancient Greece over the "slavish" morality of the modern world. Although Nietzsche clearly includes in this allusion the less than fully civilized heroes of the Trojan War (1200 B.C.E.), these were not simply barbarian warriors fighting over captive slave girls. Primarily, Nietzsche was referring to the creative and sophisticated Greeks of the Golden Age of Pericles (fifth century B.C.E.). They were distinguished by their "nobility," by which Nietzsche means not privileged birth but style and refinement. In *Daybreak* he explicitly associates the position of the "masters" with cultivated manners; he observes that a person who is aware of having power becomes "very fastidious and noble in his tastes."[14] Nietzsche urges his contemporaries in *The Gay Science* to aspire, in the fashion of such "masters," to " 'give style' to one's character—a great and rare art!"[15] For the barbarians of his own time (Otto von Bismarck, for example) Nietzsche had nothing but scorn.

Rumor # 11. Nietzsche Drove Students to Murder

In 1924 two exceptional students at the University of Chicago, Nathan F. Leopold and Richard A. Loeb, plotted the gratuitous murder of a child named Bobby Franks, supposedly thus demonstrating their status as *Übermenschen,* after reading Nietzsche. I hope that we need not make the point here that they seriously misunderstood Nietzsche. But the legend has been passed down since their trial, popularized in the novel *Compulsion* by Meyer Levin and dramatized first as a play and then a movie in 1959 (with Orson Welles playing the boys' defense lawyer, Clarence Darrow). The legend has been supplemented by a number of other deranged criminal acts in which Nietzsche and other exciting philosophers were said to have influenced overly suggestible sociopaths who sought something other than their bad brain chemistry to blame for their atrocities. Once again, we want to proclaim, rather indignantly, that an author is not responsible for vile misreadings of his works.

Nevertheless, Nietzsche's inspirational effect on students cannot be denied; and while most of the time their Nietzschean rebelliousness takes on forms no more dangerous than a couple of extra beers or a rude English composition essay, there are some very real dangers in Nietzsche's militant prose. All the more reason, then, to try to understand and get across what Nietzsche really meant, which was not ruthlessness but a soul-searching appreciation for those values that might make life more vigorous and healthy. More than any other philosopher, Nietzsche is reknowned for urging that we affirm life. "My formula for greatness in a human being is *amor fati* [literally, "love of fate," the embracing of one's fate]: that one wants nothing to be different, not forward, not backward, not in all eternity. Not merely bear what is necessary, still less conceal it . . . but *love* it."[16] How tragic, then, that murder has ever been committed in his name.

Rumor # 12. Nietzsche Was a Drunk, and He Took Drugs

This much is true: Nietzsche spent most of his adult life sick and in pain. He had great difficulty sleeping and suffered terrible headaches that limited his daily writing time to a few hours (on good days). Accordingly, he kept something of a pharmacy on hand, including some powerful painkillers and sedatives to allow him a few pain-free hours of sleep. When he finally went mad, he no doubt did at first appear to be drunk, hugging a horse and then collapsing in the street. But Nietzsche, unlike some of his French contemporaries (notably Baudelaire), had no use for recreational or inspirational drugs, and he generally avoided alcohol. Ironically, however much Nietzsche praises Dionysus, the Greek god of wine, intoxication, and frenzied group behavior, little of the fermented grape ever passed his lips.

Rumor # 13. Nietzsche Could Not Dance

Nietzsche talks a lot about dancing, but there is no evidence that he did very much of it, at least while mentally competent. (Apparently he was given to outbursts of expressionistic dancing while in the asylum.) For a thinker who so celebrated the Dionysian, it is sad but true that Nietzsche seems not to have had many experiences of being possessed by the Dionysian impulse to dance. His health was fragile throughout his life, and his energy was limited. It is easy to imagine that he would have loved to dance and that he liked to think about dancing. Dancing is one of the defining characteristics of Dionysus (as of Shiva in Hinduism), and it is Nietzsche's continuing metaphor for how to do philosophy. "Thinking wants to be learned like dancing, *as* a kind of dancing."[17] Nietzsche's relative solitude, however, was not conducive to much ballroom dancing. If Nietzsche had been more of a dancer, however, would we have as much of his philosophy?

Rumor # 14. Nietzsche Had No Sex Life

Interest in the sex lives of the rich and famous has always been a popular entertainment in the lives of the not so rich or famous, and as Nietzsche's fame has increased, so has interest in his sex life. Unfortunately for the voyeurs, but perhaps fortunately for the speculating rumor-mongers, Nietzsche was extremely discreet in his personal life—no matter how many personal observations and details spill into his writings—and so we have no idea what his intimate life was like. Krell and Bates report that while Nietzsche was a student at Bonn, his cohorts in the fraternity Franconia "proclaimed him a man 'untouched by woman.' "[18] Nietzsche's own report of a visit to a brothel is that he preferred the piano to any of the women present. Nevertheless, Joachim Köhler has amassed considerable evidence to support the conclusion that Nietzche was gay, which might explain his reticence about his own sexual life despite his use sometimes of highly charged sexual metaphors. The juxtaposition of erotic prose and a seemingly sexless personal life is suggestive, but what we can conclude from it remains speculative, at best.

Rumor # 15. Nietzsche Had Syphilis

The diagnosis given when Nietzsche entered the asylum in Jena in 1889 was dementia praecox (syphilitic paralysis and chronic inflammation of the brain and major membranes of the nervous system, causing progressive insanity). This diagnosis has been disputed, sometimes because Nietzsche had aberrant symptoms (for example, he did not suffer from general paralysis) sometimes on the grounds that if Nietzsche had congenital syphilis he would have gone mad much sooner, while if he was infected in adulthood, we do not know where Nietzsche would have contracted the disease. Nietzsche's discretion in his sex life is in keeping with his refined manners. While we have no direct evidence regarding Nietzsche's sexual encounters, he allegedly visited prostitutes in his youth. Nietzsche also announced in the asylum that he had infected himself twice, but it is hard to know how to regard statements made in that context. In his last decade, Nietzsche suffered a series of debilitating strokes. Pneumonia and a final stroke killed him in the summer of 1900. Most scholars conclude, however, that syphilis played an important role in his deterioration.

Rumor # 16. Nietzsche Hated Christianity

Nietzsche clearly disliked some things about Christianity, but we should be very careful about making the blanket statement that Nietzsche hated Christianity *as such*. Nor is it at all true to say that he hated Christians *as such*. Like his near-contemporary Kierkegaard, Nietzsche had many words of contempt for "Christendom," "the Christian mob," those unthinking conformists who superficially accepted the words of the Gospel without believing them in any deep sense or living their lives according to them. Yet Nietzsche admired those exceptional Christian souls who really lived and suffered what they believed, Jesus in particular. Nietzsche himself was raised a Lutheran, and his father and grandfathers were all Lutheran ministers.

What he disliked—is *hated* too strong a word?—about Christianity was its "nihilism," its disdain and contempt for the things of this world in favor of the "next world." He despised and ridiculed the Christian denial of the flesh and its nervousness about the body more generally, and he certainly despised Christian hypocrisy, especially in the realm of morals. Christian morality is nihilistic, he insisted, because it refuses to see man as he is rather than through the lens of a ridiculous, life-denying ideal. It refuses to honor the instincts and appetites because it refuses to accept human *nature*. Nevertheless, Nietzsche is a firm defender of the spiritual, so long as this notion is not etherealized and rendered otherworldly. Spirituality, for Nietzsche, is heightened aesthetic awareness, a keen sense of life and destiny, the "love of fate" and a sense of the magnificence of nature—human nature included.

Rumor # 17. Nietzsche Was an Atheist

In his last, very tongue-in-cheek, semiautobiographical book, *Ecce Homo,* Nietzsche declares that he was an atheist "from instinct." In the same passage, he claims that "God" was one of those concepts (together with "immortality of the soul" and "redemption") to which he never devoted any attention or time, "even as a child," adding "perhaps I have never been childlike enough for them?"[19] But in other instances Nietzsche talks a lot about God, and he admits that as a youth he was so convinced of God's power that he concluded that God must be the origin of evil as well as good.

In most of his later works, what Nietzsche says about God is even less worshipful and often abusive. He complains that God has been turned into a petty and pathetic being, who has nothing better to worry about than the trivial prayers and fickle faith of his followers. "God is a gross answer, an indelicacy against us thinkers—at bottom merely a gross prohibition for us: you shall not think!"[20] In *Genealogy,* Nietzsche makes it clear that God is the hope of the hopeless, the sweet promise of a better life to those who have too little to live for. As such, God serves as crutch for the weak and power for the resentful.

Nietzsche pointedly juxtaposes the Christian God to the pagan gods of Greece and Rome, commenting that the conception of gods as such "need not lead to the degradation of the imagination," and that there are "nobler uses for the invention of gods than for the self-crucifixion and self-violation of man in which Europe over the last millennia achieved its distinctive mastery."[21] Nietzsche is not a typical atheist, in the sense of rejecting the very notion of a deity, but one would be hard put to say that he is any sort of "believer" in the usual sense either. Indeed, he thinks that his era, like him, has in practice moved beyond the issue of whether the Judeo-Christian God exists or not, and seeks instead to explain how humanity came to believe in such a deity.

Historical refutation as the definitive refutation.—In former times, one sought to prove that there is no God—today one indicates how the belief that there is a God could *arise* and how this belief acquired its weight and importance: a counter-proof that there is no God thereby becomes superfluous. . . . In former times . . . atheists did not know how to make a clean sweep.[22]

Rumor # 18. Nietzsche Condones Cruelty

Nietzsche often makes points in striking ways, and one of the most upsetting or unsettling ways in which he attacks the overly benign view of human nature promoted by many philosophers is by pointing out the prevalence of cruelty in human history. In *Genealogy,* he famously discusses the "voluptuous pleasure" that the semipowerful enjoy in punishing the powerless, "a delicious morsel, indeed as a foretaste of higher rank." He describes how the moral world begins "like the beginnings of everything great on earth, soaked in blood thoroughly and for a long time. And might one not add that, fundamentally, this world has never since lost a certain odor of blood and torture?" ("Even in good old Kant," he adds, "the categorical imperative smells of cruelty.") Indeed, he concludes, "Without cruelty, there is no festival: thus the longest and most ancient part of human history teaches—and in punishment there is so much that is festive!"[23]

What are we to make of such passages? To be sure, *Genealogy* is forthrightly presented as a "polemic" and much of what Nietzsche says is ironic and not to be taken at face value. But it would be as much of a mistake to simply dismiss such passages as mere outrageousness as it would be to take them literally as a defense (or celebration) of cruelty. Remember, Nietzsche spent his last ounce of strength trying to save a horse from its cruel master.

In *The Gay Science,* Nietzsche tells a story about "*holy cruelty.*" A man holding a horribly crippled child approaches a holy man for counsel, not knowing what to do. "Kill it!" shouts the holy man, and he tells the man to hold the dead child for three days to create a memory that will dissuade him from again begetting a child this way. The story concludes, "When the man heard this, he walked away, disappointed, and many people reproached the holy man because he had counseled cruelty. . . . 'But is it not crueler to let it live?' asked the holy man."[24]

This story will not warm the hearts of those who believe that any life is a life worth living, but it illustrates rather well the overall point that Nietzsche wants to make. Cruelty and suffering are part of life, and what counts as cruelty depends on how one thinks of suffering and its place in life. Against those many thinkers who would deny the reality of suffering or dismiss it as insignificant in the light of eternal salvation, Nietzsche, like the Buddha in his first Noble Truth, insists on recognizing that life *is* suffering. The question is only, what are we to do about it.

The ancient Greeks, Nietzsche says, turned their suffering into something beautiful. Their famous tragedies, accordingly, were cruel simply because they recognized that life itself is cruel. Christianity, by contrast, ostensibly seeks salvation from suffering, but in an afterlife, not in this world. Implicitly, then, Christianity also recognizes the cruel character of life, seeing this as an objection to life on this plane. By emphasizing the role of suffering in human affairs Nietzsche wants to jolt us back into the recognition that not only do we suffer, but we quite consciously cause and even enjoy the suffering of others. This is no less true in Christianity than elsewhere. Nietzsche reminds us of Tertullian, a Father of the early Christian Church, gloating over the tortures of the damned.

So what are we to say about Nietzsche's seeming celebration

of cruelty? Not that it is not serious, but that it has an ulterior, benign purpose. Nietzsche tries to force us to look at life as it is, not as we might fantasize it to be, to get us to accept and celebrate life, even at its ugliest, to get us to face ourselves and our own darkest pleasures and motives. But what Nietzsche really celebrates, in the passages that follow his treatment of suffering, is *justice,* conceived not as the fair distribution of punishments but as "love with open eyes," in the words of Zarathustra.[25] Nietzsche sees real justice as involving a largeness of spirit that considers all forms of punishment petty, and which does not feel lessened by showing mercy.

What Nietzsche offers us is not celebration of cruelty. Instead, his accounts provide a mirror in which we can see ourselves, ideally without hypocrisy. He aims to spur us into a different way of facing life, without resentment and vengefulness, but he argues that this requires, first of all, an honest assessment of what we are.

Rumor # 19.
Nietzsche Was a Frustrated Composer

As a young man, Nietzsche aspired not to be a great philosopher but rather a great musician. He played the piano and seems to have been at least an entertaining improvisationalist. From his teens, he attempted composition in various traditional forms, writing mostly for piano. He also wrote many *Lieder* (songs) and choral works, and composed a duet for piano and violin. After he became personally acquainted with Wagner, Nietzsche wrote a number of longer works, a particularly ambitious accomplishment given that he was simultaneously writing his first book and beginning his career as a university professor.

This flurry of compositional activity, beginning in 1871, came to a halt in 1874. After that, Nietzsche did not write any entirely new compositions, although he later revised several of his earlier ones. Nietzsche may have been dissuaded from further pursuing a musical career by the unflattering assessment of conductor Hans von Bülow, who described Nietzsche's "Manfred Meditation" as "the most fantastically extravagant, the most unedifying, the most anti-musical thing I have come across for a long time in the way of notes put on paper."[26] This blow may have been somewhat cushioned by some encouragement from Liszt and Wagner. In that von Bülow complains that Nietzsche lacks traditional training and uses Wagnerian technique as a foundation, Nietzsche might also have suspected that von Bülow was venting his hostility toward Wagner, who had run off with the conductor's wife, Cosima (whom he later married).

Whatever the reason, Nietzsche's later artistry is expressed mainly through writing. Nietzsche's indications that he considers his writing style "musical" may suggest that he consciously considered his literary work a continuation of the same ambition that he had earlier pursued as a composer. Whatever his own assessment, his critics concur in assessing this shift as a sound decision. Nietzsche's music is best described as undistinguished, while he continues to be rightly regarded as a master of German literature and philosophy.

Rumor # 20.
Nietzsche Was in Love with Wagner's Wife

Cosima Wagner was the daughter of the great Hungarian composer-pianist Franz Liszt and the mistress and then wife of Nietzsche's one-time hero, Richard Wagner. She was beautiful and talented, and Nietzsche considered her the epitome of refinement. He describes her in his autobiography as "by far the first voice in matters of taste that I have ever heard."[27] She was also unconventional, having left her first husband, Hans von Bülow, to live with Wagner, with whom she had three children before she and von Bülow divorced.

Unlike Wagner, who was literally the age of Nietzsche's father, Cosima was closer to Nietzsche's own age. At the high point of Nietzsche's friendship with the Wagners, she corresponded with Nietzsche more often than did Wagner himself, and at times the tone is like that of two enthusiasts, almost worshipful in their mentions of "the Master." Nietzsche certainly felt close to her. He made presents of some of his creative work to her, including five prefaces for prospective books which he dedicated to her as a Christmas present in 1872. She did not see this gesture as romantic in nature, however. Instead, she was annoyed with him for not coming to spend Christmas with her and the Master, and wrote a peevish letter telling him so. The Wagners seem both to have been extremely temperamental, with the consequence that Nietzsche was often required to avert offending them with gestures that would suit a comedy of manners. For example, Wagner, unwilling to share acclaim with any other living composer, threw a tantrum when Nietzsche brought a Brahms score to Wagner and spoke favorably of Brahms. Nietzsche turned down an invitation to visit Greece from the son of Felix Mendelssohn-Bartholdy, fearing that he would offend the Wagners if he kept company with a Jewish member of a rival's family. These were not Nietzsche's most willful years.

Some of Nietzsche's remarks at the time of his breakdown suggest that Cosima had been an object of his long-term fantasies. In his flurry of final missives, he wrote her a one-line letter, "Ariadne, I love you. Dionysus."[28] (Nietzsche's sister, Elisabeth, apparently jealous of all the women with whom he was infatuated, makes a dubious point of denying that the several references to Ariadne in her brother's writings referred to Cosima.) Nietzsche also announced in the asylum, "My wife, Cosima Wagner, has brought me here."[29] We have no evidence, however, that Cosima ever recognized any romantic feelings on Nietzsche's part. He may have harbored amorous longing for Cosima throughout their acquaintance, but if so, he was characteristically discreet about them.

Rumor # 21.
Nietzsche Was in Love with Wagner

A very different interpretation of Nietzsche's mad claim that Cosima Wagner was his wife is that he had come to identify with Wagner. If Cosima was a figure of fantasy for Nietzsche, Wagner was apparently much more so. In the years after his break with Wagner, he revisits the relationship in his writings numerous times. In his last year of writing, he wrote *The Case of Wagner* and assembled *Nietzsche contra Wagner,* both apologies, in a sense, for the end of his friendship with the composer. The fact that the latter was Nietzsche's final work before he was overtaken by insanity suggests the importance he placed on this relationship throughout his productive life (if not beyond).

Nietzsche was already a fan of Wagner's music during his university years and was invited to meet him while the latter was secretly visiting his sister and her husband, who lived in Leipzig. Wagner's sister was a friend of the wife of Nietzsche's adviser, Professor Albrecht Ritschl; and when Ritschl's wife mentioned to Wagner that she and her husband had been introduced to his music by Nietzsche, Wagner asked to meet the young man.

Nietzsche and Wagner hit it off, particularly when they discovered their common admiration for Schopenhauer. Wagner invited Nietzsche to come visit, which he had ample opportunity to do when he was appointed to the faculty at the University of Basel a few months later. Wagner's villa in Tribschen was not far from Basel. Nietzsche became very close to the Wagners, even doing some of Cosima's Christmas shopping for her in addition to more scholarly chores (like proofreading) for Wagner. The visits to Tribschen were conducive to the development of Nietzsche and Wagner's intellectual friendship. Referring particularly to this period, Nietzsche writes in his autobiography, "I would let go cheap the whole rest of my human relationships. . . . I call Wagner the great benefactor of my life. . . . I have loved Wagner." [30]

Nevertheless, the friendship with Wagner was unstable, and eventually it collapsed. One factor in the break, operative from the start, was that Wagner regarded Nietzsche as the junior member of the friendship, while Nietzsche considered the relationship a true meeting of equals. Wagner's anti-Semitism became increasingly distasteful to Nietzsche, as did the smug superficiality of the audiences that Wagner attracted. The latter became painfully obvious to Nietzsche when he went to Bayreuth for the inaugural festival of Wagner's newly constructed theater. Nietzsche considered the audience a group of unmusical philistines, "truly a hair-raising lot."[31] The end of the friendship was definite when Wagner sent Nietzsche a copy of his music-drama *Parsifal*, which promoted religious sentiments that Nietzsche considered unsavory and (in Wagner's case) hypocritical.

Wagner was born in the same year as Nietzsche's father, whom Nietzsche idealized after his death, when Nietzsche was only four years old. Some scholars have speculated that Nietzsche responded to Wagner as a father figure, and felt ambivalent Oedipal feelings for him. If so, a break with Wagner might have been psychologically necessary for Nietzsche as a means of asserting his autonomy, regardless of the particular events that actually provoked it. The break signaled a new and highly original turn in Nietzsche's thought.

Rumor # 22. Nietzsche Was a Relativist

Nietzsche certainly did defend a view which has since been dubbed *perspectivism*. One of Nietzsche's most prominent innovations, providing a bridge to the twentieth century, is his insistence that there is no absolute knowledge that transcends all possible perspectives: knowledge is always constrained by one's perspective. In the natural sciences, for example, knowledge depends on one's intellectual setting, on the nature of one's apparatus, and on the problems that have been posed. In modern-day terms, we might say that Nietzsche strongly anticipated the American pragmatists William James and John Dewey in his emphasis on the practical presuppositions and provisional nature of knowing.

Nietzsche rejects Immanuel Kant's notion of the world's existence "in itself," independent of our knowing faculties. Such an idea, according to Nietzsche, is absurd and superfluous. If there were such a world, we could not know it, nor could we even know *of* it (a conclusion that Kant himself comes close to accepting). Anything we do know we know from a certain perspective, and that perspective depends on our physiological constitution, our skills of inquiring and interpreting, our culture, and our language. Nietzsche was ahead of his time in realizing the extent to which language determines our beliefs about the world, the way in which grammar sets the stage for metaphysics. "I am afraid we are not rid of God because we still have faith in grammar," he says, in one of his strongest declarations of that view.[32] He suggests that the very linguistic structures that require a subject for every predicate encourage us to look for some person or agent as the cause behind the active flux of the world.

But does Nietzsche's perspectivism amount to a commitment to what is variously and usually disdainfully referred to as *relativism*? Perspectivism is generally accepted as part and parcel of the scientific world view, and it is accepted by most ecumenical thinkers as the watchword of religious tolerance. There are different perspectives on the world, and this is a good thing. Relativism, by contrast, has been generally condemned and disowned even by those philosophers whom we would expect to be most committed to it. On one account, relativism is the thesis that every view is as good as any other—no better, no worse. For obvious reasons, this is anathema to any thinking person. It is an invitation to stupidity, and negates any warrant for pursuing the truth, or even plausibility, right from the outset. Given how often Nietzsche lambastes views for their falsehood or stupidity, it is clear that he is not a relativist in this sense.

But relativism has also been defined more sensibly as the view that all views are *relative to* a particular framework, an outlook, a culture, a time and place. Thus the early Medievals honestly thought, in the light of the available evidence, that the earth was flat and stationary, the center of their universe. Subsequent science showed them to be mistaken, yet it would have been a rational belief to hold, say, in the year 799. The problem comes in when one tries to say that that thesis about the earth *was true for* the Medievals, rather than simply false but justifiable given the available evidence then. If a "true" belief is one that corresponds to the facts, this doesn't make sense. Nevertheless, it is clear enough what one might mean, if one considers a "true" belief to be one that is warranted on the basis of available evidence. Given the plausible supposition that all knowledge is provisional and that our most firmly held scientific beliefs, like so many scientific beliefs of the past, may someday be shown to be false or inadequate, then we should admit that "true" for us, too, must always be provisional and admitted to be relative to our perspective. Relativism, defined this way, looks very much like Nietzsche's perspectivism.

Nietzsche recognizes the awkwardness of his being a relativist on one view and a nonrelativist on another. He confronts this tension head-on, and in some of his more outrageous pronouncements declares "there is no truth." Many readers take such claims to be an endorsement of relativism in an extreme sense, implying that we should abandon all hope of learning the truth and simply regard ourselves as condemned to ignorance and falsehood. But this is not what Nietzsche meant. Here again, he is attacking the presumptuous belief that we can get at the truth "in itself," free from any conditions or perspectives, a world "behind" the mere appearances of everyday and scientific experience. Nietzsche retorts, "The 'apparent' world is the only one: the 'true' world is merely added by a lie."[33] If relativism means "relative to our experience, and the best we can come up with given what we know so far," then it is hard to see how anyone would resent Nietzsche's perspectival relativism, except for the dogmatists he attacks.

Rumor 23. Nietzsche Was an Egoist

Nietzsche was indeed an egoist (also an egotist, but that is another matter). "Egoism" is a term for the twin views that we (a) do or (b) ought to look after our own interests. Some egoists accept both of these views, while others accept only one of them. Nietzsche would be hesitant to accept either as a universal principle. According to Nietzsche, we each have an impulse to seek to enhance our own power, but this does not always involve looking after our own interests. In some cases, people risk all they have, even their lives, for power. Moreover, Nietzsche would differentiate among individuals, considering the interests of certain exceptional individuals as more important than those of the majority. His first question, to a defender of universal egoism, would be, "*Whose* interests?" "*Whose* ego?"

Nietzsche also raises questions about what a person's real interests might be. Socrates obeyed the laws of Athens and gave himself up for execution, claiming that he did so not so much because it was the right thing to do but rather because it was "good for his soul." Was that selfish? Does it make any sense at all to say that his was a selfish course of action? A soldier on the battlefield suddenly "finds himself" charging up a hill against machine-gun fire to save a buddy who has just been wounded. Asked about it later, he claims he "just had to do it. I couldn't have lived with myself otherwise." Is he selfish? Nietzsche wrote great philosophy books, not because he was imbued with an altruistic spirit, but because he loved what he was doing; in the preface to *Twilight of the Idols* he calls writing that book "a recreation, a spot of sunshine." [34] Was he just being selfish?

What Nietzsche does for us, among many other things, is to call into question our facile use of such notions as selfishness, self-interest, egoism, and their opposites, altruism and self-sacrifice. Noble actions are both for the sake of the actor and serve some larger purpose. To force an "either/or" opposition onto our behavior——asking, for example, "Is this self-serving or is this altristic?"——is to distort and cripple the complex (and often unknown) motives that go into every significant action. A saint may be egoistic when he faithfully serves his God. A hero may be avoiding a display of cowardice when he fights bravely by the side of his comrades. The honest grocer that Kant and Adam Smith both consider may well be acting *both* out of a concern for his good reputation and integrity *and* in order to keep his customers coming back to spend more.

On the other hand, Nietzsche would join us in criticizing petty egoism, the inconsiderate, childish, meaningless, competitive effort to get more than one's proper share or to appear more important than other people. Nevertheless, even then, Nietzsche would say that the egoism of such behavior will usually be among the least of our concerns. Rather, it is the pettiness, the childishness, the rudeness and lack of perspective. Egoism *as such* is not the problem.

Rumor # 24. Nietzsche Praised War

Nietzsche loved to use warrior imagery. Despite his antimilitarism and short military service, he retained a love for military discipline, formality, and precision. Nietzsche often describes his own philosophical campaigns as declarations of war (for example, the preface to *Twilight*) and like his ancient ally, Heraclitus, celebrates war as the ultimate *agon* (contest) of human experience. (Heraclitus: "War is father and kin of all.") In part, no doubt, such metaphors were compensation for his own poor health. He often talks about regaining his health in military terms, most famously in the passage, "Out of life's school of war: Whatever does not destroy me, makes me stronger."[35] The military imagery is also a reflection of his fondness for and fantasies of the Homeric Greeks and his contempt for the meek self-righteous pacifism of some of his contemporaries. Then again, warrior imagery was also the *macho* literary currency of Nietzsche's times, and in this respect he was merely doing what was fashionable. Hegel had similarly described war in terms of the ultimate solidarity of the state in his *Philosophy of Right*.

We should remember, however, that for Europe the nineteenth century was one of the longest protracted periods of peace in memory. The only notable exception was the Franco-Prussian War, in which Nietzsche served as a medical orderly and saw some of the devastating effects of war firsthand. Like most people with any sense, he found the actual ravages of battle grotesque and terrible, and it would be misreading the man if not so obviously his books to understand him as a warmonger. We should remember, too, that war had not yet taken on the aspect of gruesome wholesale mechanical slaughter invented in the twentieth century. When he speaks admiringly of wars in which people are willing to risk their lives for their ideas, he is not envisioning nuclear or contemporary biological warfare.

Nietzsche loved the good fight, the *agon,* but the primary struggle in Nietzsche's mind was his own struggle within himself, with his health, with his Christian bourgeois upbringing, with his own feelings of meekness, pity, and resentment. There he was indeed a trooper, if not exactly a warrior. All the rest, we can charitably but cheerfully say, was mere metaphor.

Rumor # 25. Nietzsche Was a (Pre-)Postmodernist

In recent years Nietzsche has been widely interpreted and celebrated as a postmodernist, or at least as the single most important precursor of twentieth-century postmodernism. This is not the place to try to define postmodernism—a minor academic industry in itself. We can, however, readily spot some themes that would make Nietzsche attractive to such people as Jacques Derrida, Gilles Deleuze, Michel Foucault, Julia Kristeva, and Luce Irigaray (all of whom have written a book about him or claim to have been heavily influenced by him).

The first is Nietzsche's radical critical stance, his searching for flaws in the very origins of things, which naturally allies him with what is now known as "deconstruction." Second is his fascination with and attention to language, or "discursive practices," always a favorite focus of the linguistically minded poststructuralists. Third is Nietzsche's penchant for flamboyant proclamations. His claims that there is no truth and that there are "only interpretations" warm the cockels of the "nothing but the text" generation. Fourth is Nietzsche's rejection of much of the tradition of philosophy since Plato (and Socrates), a favorite stance borrowed by the postmoderns from Heidegger. Fifth are Nietzsche's various assaults on the self and the notion of agency, much in tune with the "fragmentation of the subject" and "death of the author" fixations of the current French academic scene.

Nevertheless—let's just say it—Nietzsche is no postmodernist. He would have little sympathy for the irresponsible "play" that passes for serious philosophy these days. Maudemarie Clark has shown in considerable detail how false are some of the readings of Nietzsche that would render him an ally of postmodernism. True, Nietzsche adopted a critical or perhaps even "deconstructive" stance, *but only in order to promulgate a more vigorous, positive philosophy.* He rejected the notion of truth and insisted on the importance of interpretation not in order to undermine science but rather because he agreed with its empiricist aims and methods. Furthermore, although Nietzsche was trained as a philologist rather than as a philosopher, his writings (like those of Heidegger) are steeped in the philosophical traditions of the West. Nietzsche demolishes certain views of the self and subjectivity only to make room for a very different notion of agency, and with it a very different notion of self. This great individualist cannot be conscientiously read as dispensing with the self and its unique perspectives.

Rumor # 26. Nietzsche Argued Fallaciously

We began this chapter by entertaining the dismissive *ad hominem* argument "Nietzsche was crazy, so don't take anything he wrote seriously." Since we do take Nietzsche seriously, such arguments are something of a joke, not to mention the fact that Nietzsche, as we have argued, was not crazy when he created his works. Nevertheless, Nietzsche himself often uses arguments that look very much like this one. Indeed, *ad hominem* arguments, which criticize the person instead of the works, seemed to have special appeal to Nietzsche. In *Twilight of the Idols* he argues notoriously that we should be suspicious of Socrates' teachings because Socrates was ugly! Such an argument is an offense to philosophers everywhere (some of whom are not so good-looking themselves). We should ask ourselves, Why does Nietzsche so flagrantly violate such a crucial canon of professional courtesy, that one may attack the position, the argument, or the philosophy but not the philosopher?

The first part of the answer is that Nietzsche insisted that the philosopher should be an example of his own teachings. Nietzsche recognized that Socrates would not have been a very effective or influential teacher of virtue if he had not been seen as an exemplar of virtue himself. And Jesus, whatever his divine status, would surely have been a fraud if he had taught meekness and compassion but demonstrated nothing but personal combativeness and insensitivity.

One might well object, as many have, that Nietzsche, "the miserable little man" who suffered so many sleepless nights and never had a proper girlfriend, put on a fairly poor performance when judged against this criterion, however brilliant his writing.[36] On the other hand, if what Nietzsche *lived for* was his devotion to and the production of his work, then the objection may not have such a devastating impact. He was indeed an example to us all, of true philosophical originality, dedication, and enthusiasm.

Nietzsche's *ad hominem* arguments are of many kinds. Sometimes, they concern a whole people, as in his treatment of the Jews in *Genealogy* and of the Germans in many contexts. ("How much *beer* there is in the German intelligence!"[37]) In *Genealogy* Nietzsche clearly intends to show how whole moralities follow from certain attitudes and character, which in turn develop in response to certain ways of life and social circumstances— a particularly important example of the perspectivism that pervades Nietzsche's views of values, as well as of knowledge. In such cases, where the target of attack is collective, one is less likely than in attacks on individual targets to simply dismiss *ad hominem* arguments as mere fallacies. Such discussions force us to pay closer attention to what philosophers often seek to ignore, the concrete social and psychological situations out of which ideas, ideologies, and whole philosophies are born.

Ad hominem arguments are not the only examples of "informal" logical fallacies that can be found in Nietzsche. Appeal to emotion (as opposed to "reasoning") is another of those offenses beginning students are regularly warned against. But throughout his work, Nietzsche appeals to the emotions, to contempt and disgust as well as outrage and his always present sense of humor. Nietzsche often employs circular reasoning, even "begging the question," for the sake of rhetorical flourish, usually because he is convinced that repeating a bad thesis will display its limitations in a more devastating manner than would engaging in an outright refutation of it. He attacks straw men left and right, although, as so often, there are very real targets hiding behind the straw men. A philological genius, Nietzsche often plays with the various meanings of a term, sometimes shifting back to ancient or archaic etymology to make a point. He delights in slippery-slope arguments; his conclusions are often ambiguous or unclear; he delights in hyperbole and overstatement; he often substitutes boisterous assertion for real argument; and he is often willing to tolerate ambiguity, incoherence, and even contradiction.

However, as Nietzsche's American hero Ralph Waldo Emerson wrote in one of his best known essays ("Self-Reliance"), "a foolish consistency is the hobgoblin of little minds. With consistency a great soul has nothing to do. . . . To be great is to be misunderstood."[38] What Nietzsche does, to the horror of logicians and English composition teachers, is to call on us to rethink what we mean by "logic" and what we condemn as "fallacy." To argue fallaciously is sometimes just to argue with conviction and more convincingly than one does when one has nothing but a good argument on one's side.

Amusingly, Nietzsche turns *ad hominem* against himself on this very point. As a child and grandchild of Lutheran clergymen, he must have himself in mind when he remarks:

> The sons of Protestant ministers and school teachers may be recognized by their naive certainty when, as scholars, they consider their cause proved when they have merely stated it with vigor and warmth; they are thoroughly used to being believed, as that was part of their fathers' job. [39]

Rumor # 27. Nietzsche Sees the *Übermensch* as an Evolutionary Goal

Nietzsche was an ambivalent follower of Darwin, who had published his great *Origin of Species* in 1859 and *Descent of Man* in 1871. On the one hand, there was a great deal in Darwin that Nietzsche clearly accepted with enthusiasm: his stark naturalistic thesis, the continuity of man and ape, the concepts of "natural selection" and "fitness," at least in their general outline. But Nietzsche read (or misread) Darwin in a number of less agreeable ways, for example, as a teleologist who believed that man emerged as the highest creature. To this view Nietzsche provided an alternative: human beings are not the "end" of Nature; the *Übermensch* [sometimes translated "the overman" or "the Superman"] may follow the human species on the evolutionary ladder. But Nietzsche suggests that this is far from an inevitability.

Lest anyone imagine that the *Übermensch* is an assured stage of evolution, Zarathustra contrasts the *Übermensch* with the Last Man, the person who is too risk-averse to pursue any aim beyond comfort, and who consequently avoids starting a new generation. He is utterly unadventurous, incapable of self-criticism, wholly caught up in his own petty pleasures, his contentment, his "happiness." The Last Man is clearly presented as a dolt, the ultimate couch potato, and Nietzsche suggests this as a warning. If we do not aspire to be "higher," this is what we shall become. But whereas Nietzsche clearly intended the *Übermensch* as a fiction, the likelihood of the coming of the Last Man, he thought, was all too real. (When Zarathustra announces this vision to the people of the town, for example, Nietzsche has them all cheer and demand, in effect, that they be made Last Men now.) Zarathustra presents the *Übermensch* and the Last Man as two alternative possibilities, asking modern individuals which mode of existence their own lives promote.

The *Übermensch,* moreover, seems to be the ideal aim of spiritual development more than a biological goal. In *Ecce Homo,* he scoffs at the "scholarly oxen" who "have suspected me of Darwinism" in connection with this concept.[40] In *Zarathustra,* the only text in which the *Übermensch* is discussed at any length, Nietzsche's fictional hero presents the idea in images, describing this *Übermensch* as devoid of human timidity, continually aspiring to greatness and living life as a creative adventure. A person who embodied these ideals would be an improvement on the contemporary human being; but Nietzsche does not think that natural selection will produce such a type. Instead, we should reconsider our own way of living, redesigning it to aim in the direction of the *Übermensch,* even if this ideal is too extreme to be fulfillable.

Rumor # 28.
Nietzsche Was an Irresponsible Historian

In *On the Genealogy of Morals,* Nietzsche presents his most protracted version of a historical ("genealogical") argument, one
that he both anticipates and refers to in many of his other
works. The argument consists of a sociological-psychological
analysis of the nobility and the poor in the ancient world. Nietzsche sometimes makes specific reference to particular epochs in
Greek and Roman history but just as often provides only
generic portraits of the pyramidal structure of most ancient
societies, a small number of rich and powerful men at the top
and the great mass of ordinary subjects down below. Intermin-
gled with this, and throughout Nietzsche's works, are detailed
references to the history of Christianity. From these descriptions, Nietzsche makes bold claims about the nature of morality
and religion, the natural structure of society and the ways in
which language expresses status and values even when it seems
to be purely descriptive. These claims are controversial enough
in themselves, but what further fuels the controversy is Nietzsche's history. His story reads more as allegory than history, and
there are, needless to say, respectable alternative accounts in
which Christianity and Christian morality, in particular, come
out looking far more attractive.

What are we to make of Nietzsche's historical analyses? He
was a skilled philologist and a keen reader of history, but even
his readings of the ancient world are contentious and against the
grain of the dominant scholarly convictions of his time. They are
often biased, and his targets are often snatched from historical

context and thus not presented historically at all. But, of course, Nietzsche presents history to make polemical points, and he himself would probably say that the literal truth of his story is not what is at issue. Instead the question is: Does it capture the psychological essence of what has happened?

We will not make any defense of Nietzsche's history here, much less try to give any detailed support for his specific historical claims. Nevertheless, as a perspective on history, a perspective that inverts the usual readings of Christianity as a civilizing influence on pagan barbarism and the Judeo-Christian tradition as the sole repository of what is best and highest in the human spirit, Nietzsche's genealogy and its accompanying observations serve an important purpose. They provoke us to think and see differently, to see the deficits as well as the blessings of our heritage, and perhaps to get ready to try something different for a change.

Rumor # 29.
Nietzsche Wrote Only in Disorganized Aphorisms

In his "middle," or "experimental," period—in his books *Human, All Too Human; Daybreak;* and *The Gay Science*—Nietzsche experimented with short bursts of prose, each of them a distinctive (and often ambiguous) insight. But even in those books, in *The Gay Science* in particular, there are often substantial prose paragraphs that develop several thoughts together, and in all of these books the arrangement and composition of the short segments is as important as the insights themselves. Nietzsche's strategy is juxtaposition, following one sort of thought with another, manipulating moods and expectations (and sometimes thwarting them).

Nietzsche's works are not all aphoristic. In his earlier works (notably *The Birth of Tragedy*) and his later ones (for example, *On the Genealogy of Morals*) he writes, if not in standard essay form, in continuous prose and polemic. The aphorism is only one among many unorthodox philosophical styles Nietzsche adopts to get across his most unorthodox philosophy. Even more strikingly, he employs nursery rhymes (in *The Gay Science*), songs (in *Beyond Good and Evil*) and a faux-Biblical style (in *Zarathustra*)— whatever it takes to get the point across.

Rumor # 30.
Nietzsche, Who Insisted That the Philosopher Should Be an Example, Was Himself a Pathetic Example

It is not clear that Nietzsche would come off at all well as a philosophical example. He was lonely, desperate, and occasionally embarrassing in his behavior, not to mention in some of his published writings. He was incompetent to the point of humiliation with women, and his friendships were turbulent. He did no great deeds. Unlike his imaginary *alter ego* Zarathustra and his one-time mentor Wagner, he addressed no crowds, turned no heads, confronted no enemies. Nietzsche was sickly all his life, and yet he was one of the few philosophers who celebrated *health* as a philosophical ideal. He died badly; indeed, he was perhaps the worst imaginable counterexample to his own wise instruction, "Die at the right time." He lingered on in a virtually vegetative state for a full decade, sometimes cared for by a sister who would use him to promote views he despised. He railed throughout his career against pity, an emotion that, according to those who knew him, was one of the most prominent features of his own personality. Marie von Bradke, who knew Nietzsche in Sils Maria, describes him in the summer of 1886 as follows: "The inner struggle with his pathologically delicate soul, overflowing with pity, was what led him to preach, 'be hard!' "[41] But for Nietzsche, it is hard for us not to feel pity. (How he would have hated that!)

Like his near-contemporary in Copenhagen, Søren Kierkegaard, Nietzsche did not have an externally dramatic life. For Kierkegaard, it was the "inner life," "passionate inwardness," that counted. But, we should certainly ask: Can virtues be entirely "internal," even "private"? In what sense is a rich inner life an admirable life, a virtuous life? By Nietzsche's own standards, the inner life is hardly sufficient. One should not just be inward but be "fruitful" as well, striving for greatness whenever possible. As an example, Nietzsche is more plausibly viewed as a play of opposites. Like Rousseau's, his advice might be best understood to say, "Admire people most *unlike* yourself." But then again, there are those great works and words. From that perspective, what philosopher's life has been more exemplary?

Faced with a Book
by Nietzsche

NIETZSCHE'S IDEAS cannot be distilled from the brilliant prose in which he expressed them without great loss, so a book such as this demands that the reader also confront Nietzsche's own books, face to face. In a passage entitled "Faced with a Scholarly Book," Nietzsche describes his own reaction to a particular reading experience "just now as I closed a very decent scholarly book—gratefully, very gratefully, but also with a sense of relief." The relief was a reaction to leaving the "closet air, closet ceilings, closet narrowness" of the book.[1]

We can confidently predict that Nietzsche's own books will not inspire this reaction. Yet Nietzsche's books are very far from easy reading. They are engrossing, but often hard to follow. Nietzsche did not try to be accommodating. He even took some pride in being difficult. "It is not by any means necessarily an objection to a book when anyone finds it impossible to understand: perhaps that was part of the author's intention—he did not want to be understood by just 'anybody.' "[2]

One might read this statement as a display of Nietzsche's "sour grapes" attitude toward his readers. Indeed, his books did not sell well, and he was often distressed by what some readers made of his writings. More positively, however, Nietzsche's comment indicates that he did expect to find readers who could grapple with his ideas. He hoped for a meeting of minds with readers who could appreciate his concerns, get his jokes, share his sense of mission to address the modern world's spiritual crisis. Readers of this sort would be active readers. They would not merely follow Nietzsche's drift, but be inspired to their own original thinking. They would be Nietzsche's companions in thought.

Nietzsche therefore leaves a great deal for his readers to do. He challenges them to reconsider their standing beliefs and to take fresh views of their circumstances. He chooses strategies as a writer that will further these efforts. In order to incite his readers to reevaluate their own views and values, he does not dictate doctrines. Instead, he makes jokes and startling observations. He leaves it to his readers to glean the implications of such comments. His preference for aphorisms reflects his goals, as his character Zarathustra indicates.

Whoever writes in blood and aphorisms does not want to be read but to be learned by heart. In the mountains the shortest way is from peak to peak: but for that one must have long legs. Aphorisms should be peaks—and those who are addressed tall and lofty.[3]

Nietzsche attempts nothing less than a personal, even intimate relationship with his reader. He is like an engaging conversationalist, who both invites and requires the interlocutor to respond. Much of the fun of the encounter is its interactive nature. Nietzsche's styles and formal strategies ask the reader, "What do *you* think?" They also allow Nietzsche to confide his own way of thinking—not just the content, but the whole experience of thought. Nietzsche often compares his writing to music. He wants his reader to experience along with him, much as one shares experiences with musical performers by listening actively, or by dancing. "Thinking wants to be learned like dancing, *as* a kind of dancing."[4] Nietzsche sees literary style as a tool for such learning by doing. "To communicate a state, an inward tension of pathos, by means of signs, including the tempo of these signs—that is the meaning of every style. . . ."[5]

The difficulty of Nietzsche's works is not due to murky writing. His statements are highly polished, exemplars of exactitude and nuance. Nietzsche disdains opaque expression. He bears in mind his own admonition: "Those who know they are profound strive for clarity. Those who would like to seem profound to the crowd strive for obscurity. . . ."[6] Nietzsche knew he was deep, and so strove for clarity.

The difficulty of Nietzsche's prose is that he packs so much into terse and elegant formulations. He wants his statements to brim with hints and intimations, to reward being taken to heart. "It is my ambition to say in ten sentences what everyone else says in a book—what everyone else does *not* say in a book."[7] Nietzsche's education in theology and philology offered models for his rich formulations. He was taught how to probe the full scope of passages from Scripture and the classics of antiquity. He attempted himself to write passages that would merit such interpretive care.

Another consequence of Nietzsche's extensive education is that he was learned across the humanities. He makes allusions to the classics of philosophy and several European literary traditions. Nietzsche's wit often draws from his erudition. This, too, causes problems for readers. Those who have not read as broadly as Nietzsche will miss some of his jokes. Fortunately, his favorite sources for allusions remain well studied. The best-known passages from the Bible, Plato, and Kant, are regular reference points for Nietzsche, as are the most popular works of Shakespeare and Goethe.

So how should we approach a book by Nietzsche? Most importantly, we should be open-minded. Besides forgetting the rumors about Nietzsche, we should forget what we expect of philosophical writing. We will not find the typical fare of philosophical essays, which focus steadily on a topic and present a logical sequence of arguments in support of a particular view. Nietzsche does not tell us what he's going to say, then tell us, then tell us what he's told us. Summary statements are rare in his writings. We will not find him often reviewing the literature or anchoring views with a pile of footnotes. We will find some outlandish images, and sometimes jokes that at first look quite somber. Perhaps most disorienting, Nietzsche sometimes seems to contradict himself, and quite blatantly, in consecutive passages.

An acquaintance with the typical format of scholarly writing will certainly not help to orient us in Nietzsche's writings. We can gain our bearings, however, by facing his books with our own questions. The following are often especially useful:

- *Is Nietzsche making a consistent case, or is he contradicting himself? If the latter, is contradiction a deliberate strategy?*

Sometimes Nietzsche offers sustained analysis. *The Birth of Tragedy*, although written to engage our attention, unfolds a theory about the origin and purpose of Athenian tragedy, with only a few digressions, at least until he turns to the broader implications of assessments of cultures, particularly of the modern age. *The Antichrist* similarly varies pace and format to captivate readers, yet it offers a sustained attack on Christianity as an institution and a moral worldview.

In many of his writings, however, especially the "aphoristic" works, Nietzsche moves quickly from one topic to another, or moves from one view of a topic to another view of it, often returning to themes after much has intervened. In these works a reader is likely to observe tensions or outright incompatibilities between two "takes" on a topic. The most likely explanation is that these contrary views reflect Nietzsche's perspectivism, his view that knowledge and insight are always relative to a given point of view, and that points of view vary among individuals and even among different moments in the same individual's experience. Nietzsche rejects the common objective in Western philosophy of formulating statements that are "true" under all circumstances. He insists that rigid statements do not reflect our world's reality. Any statement is at best provisionally useful for navigating our experience, and any statement held as dogma is really a prejudice, more misleading than enlightening.

Nietzsche tries to disabuse us of the hope of finding perfectly secure beliefs, but he suggests that this should not discourage us. If we shift from dogmatism to perspectivism, we will understand our world much better. Perspectivism, in other words, is an epistemological tool, enabling us to arrive at a more nuanced awareness of the world. The possibility of doing a double take that increases and focuses our awareness depends on perspectivism, according to Nietzsche, and therefore so does the possibility of really learning from experience. Perspectivism allows us to take account of things from various viewpoints, to appreciate a situation in some respects despite misgivings from other viewpoints. Nietzsche's seeming contradictions remind us that even illuminating statements fail to tell us the entire story. It is always worth our while to reexamine, to see if we may have missed some feature of value in an object, a person, or a situation. As temporal beings, we can revise our assessments of things. What sounds like contradiction is actually a sign of our ongoing engagement with reality.

• *Is Nietzsche juxtaposing several lines of thought?*

Nietzsche's aphoristic works, particularly, zip from one topic to another. The reader comes to expect a shift beginning with each new section. What can look like fits and starts, however, are often subtle manipulations of the reader's awareness. Nietzsche took considerable care in organizing the sequence of aphorisms. He moves from topic to topic with the aim of manipulating and motivating the reader's own discoveries.

For example, the early aphorisms of *Daybreak* (subtitled *Thoughts on the Prejudices of Morality*) make a number of claims about social customs and also a number of statements about morality. By juxtaposing reflections on these two categories, he prompts the reader to notice similarities between the two.

Nietzsche does not say outright that much of morality is cultural habit; but by showing it, he comes so close to saying it that the reader will probably draw this conclusion.

In addition, the pace of changing aphorisms sets up a rhythm. Nietzsche orchestrates like a musician, including the reader's own movement along with the beat. When this happens, the reader's mind internalizes the rhythm, and ideally responds with its own conjectures. The rhetorical force of this strategy is powerful. Conclusions that we reach by ourselves are more powerful than those handed to us. Insofar as Nietzsche tries to motivate our abandonment of dogmas, his juxtapositions offer hints of other ways to think, while letting the reader make the decisive, liberating step. The rhythmic movement also induces us to a pace of shifting gears. The aphoristic momentum takes over once the reader begins interacting with the text, propelling a flow of reflection.

• *Is Nietzsche mimicking other writers? If so, is this a lampoon, an homage, or both?*

Nietzsche seems to enjoy writing parodies, best of all when he splices two or more together. *Thus Spoke Zarathustra*, Nietzsche's only extensive foray into fiction, conjoins many parodic elements. The opening passage makes simultaneous allusions to the New Testament account of Jesus' life and to Plato's famed Myth of the Cave. In the latter, a society trapped in a cave sees only shadows, and it takes these and themselves to be the totality of existent things. When one person is able to leave the cave and discover the sun and the world beyond, he wants to share his discovery with others. This parable of the philosopher's mission compares to the Scriptural mission of Jesus, who longs to bring the Good News to others. Both stories take tragic turns. The cave society concludes that their benefactor has ruined his eyes, and when he insists on his claims they want to kill him. Jesus, too, attracts enemies, who ultimately succeed in having him crucified.

The opening of *Thus Spoke Zarathustra* describes its hero, the Persian religious innovator Zarathustra (or Zoroaster, 628–551 B.C.E.) leaving his mountain cave to bring good news to his society. Zarathustra had left his home to reflect in solitude at the age of thirty, the age when Jesus went to the desert. Details that associate Zarathustra with Jesus and Plato's philosopher begin to accumulate, but so do some points of contrast. Jesus leaves his desert after forty days to begin his mission; Zarathustra lives in solitude for ten years before returning to human society. Like Plato's philosopher, Zarathustra returns by descending, but he goes down to a valley with the news of what he learned in a cave, the realm of individual awareness and personal insight, reversing the Platonic valuations of inner and outer world.

The combination of similarities and dissimilarities between the models and the new text is inherent in the project of parody. It is also an indication of Nietzsche's complex responses to his models. While critical of the Christian and Platonic worldviews, he sees their founders as turning points of history, admirable for the force of their individual visions, even if those visions should now be transcended. Nietzsche poses Zarathustra as a comparable alternative to Jesus and Socrates, the Platonic philosopher par excellence.

His use of parody does not necessarily indicate Nietzsche's hostility toward a predecessor; it is also an acknowledgment, even a gesture of admiration while moving onward. Being alert to Nietzsche's parodies, then, makes us aware both of the traditions Nietzsche honors as our heritage as well as of new possibilities for the way our continuing story may unfold.

A corollary question asks if Nietzsche makes any allusions to a well-known text or saying. His penchant for punning and scholarly witticisms makes this question worth asking, even if we acknowledge that these may not all speak to us. When an allusion is recognized, it is worth probing and is often extremely amusing.

For example, Zarathustra is asked by one of his auditors about a speech he made some time before: "Why did you say that the poets lie too much?" Zarathustra begins his answer by saying that the reasons for his previous statement may not remain valid today, and he adds, "But Zarathustra too is a poet. Do you now believe that he spoke the truth here? Why do you believe that?"[8] The claim that the poets lie too much is a paraphrase of a famous claim by Socrates in Plato's *Republic,* a claim that he uses as a rationale for claiming that poetry should be distrusted and censored. Nietzsche's allusion, coupled with Zarathustra's further comment about himself, draws attention to Plato's inconsistency in writing his philosophical works in literary form (dialogues) while having his main character cast aspersions on the "lies" of literary form.

Zarathustra's remarks also raise questions about how we are taking Zarathustra's own speeches. Are we taking them to be gospel truth? If so, are we not contradicting the spirit of Zarathustra's message? One might also reconsider Nietzsche's double parody in this light. Does Plato not contradict the philosophical independence preached by his teacher, Socrates, by constructing a character whose words may well be taken as absolute truth by his readers? Could one not read Scripture similarly, asking whether Jesus' disciples have not distorted the existential import of his message by insisting that they be interpreted in an orthodox manner and taken as absolute truth? (Chapter 3 includes a more in-depth discussion of the ways in which Nietzsche thinks that Jesus' disciples distorted his teachings.) On the other hand, why should we take Zarathustra's comments seriously, if he admits that he is a lying poet? Is he unusually honest, or is he merely joking?

• *What metaphors are prominent?*

Metaphor is one of Nietzsche's suggestive strategies, designed to prompt his readers' reflection and interpretive imagination. He favors metaphors with long histories of symbolic resonance. Among these are images of height, of health and disease, of animal species, and of times of the day (such as daybreak and twilight). Some of his metaphors are virtually cartoons. His Zarathustra describes, for example, a giant ear on the horizon, which turns out to have a tiny human being dangling from it like an earring. This comical picture pokes fun at those who are admired for a single talent that may have truncated their persons as a whole.

When we make note of Nietzsche's favorite metaphors in the Appendix ("Nietzsche's Bestiary"), our aim is not to preempt our own readers' speculations. In some cases, however, those who read Nietzsche in translation are likely to miss the ways in which he adds to his metaphors' force by engaging in plays on words. His notebooks reveal how much he enjoyed punsical word play—for example, the note fragment in which he cites "the intellectual dessert for many: Gorgon-Zola."[9] The sound is the name of a cheese, and a smelly one. But in its written form, a hyphen conjoins the name of a mythical monster, the Gorgon, and that of Émile Zola, the French novelist who specialized in realistic depictions of the underprivileged. The word splice clearly reflects Nietzche's contempt for the novelist and is far more devastating than a wordy "critical review." (Perhaps he still has cheese in mind when he remarks in *Twilight of the Idols*, "*Zola:* or the delight in stinking.")[10] As this example suggests, Nietzsche enjoys a degree of self-indulgence in his wordsmanship. Fortunately, in his published works, most of his allusions are publically accessible, even when they are also private jokes.

• *Is Nietzsche praising anyone? If so, what is he praising? Is his praise ironic, for shock effect?*

One should never put irony past Nietzsche. Apparent praise or criticism should be taken in context. Sometimes Nietzsche's praise is loaded with sarcasm. Similarly, his self-assertions can be aggressively ironic (for example, in his autobiography, where he titles chapters "Why I Am So Wise" and "Why I Am So Clever"). In one passage where he criticizes Wagner as writing music that jangles the nerves, he mentions that a Wagnerite once told him, "Then you really are merely not healthy enough for our music."[11] A man of chronic illness, Nietzsche may seem to be letting Wagner off the hook with this comment. After all, Nietzsche was *not* healthy enough for much of anything. However, the Wagnerite comes off as a true believer, assuming that if Nietzsche isn't one of them, the fault must lie with him. Once again, Nietzsche lets us draw our own conclusion, but there is little doubt what he thinks.

Nietzsche's praise is often genuine. When this is so, he usually has some reason to think it worth reporting. Rarely does Nietzsche simply add his vote to the popular opinion. He shares a few of his heroes with contemporaries. Goethe is a striking case in point; however, when Nietzsche praises Goethe, he praises him for reasons rarely noted (Goethe's "Dionysian" character, for instance). Another mode of Nietzsche's praise is the genuine but shocking. Nietzsche might describe some admirable feature of someone history sees as a monster—the Emperor Tiberius, for example. Occasionally, he reiterates others' shocking admiration, as when he praises Shakespeare's Brutus, as some French literary critics had done.

The shocking tribute is another expression of perspectivism. It is also a demonstration of moving "beyond good and evil" in moral assessment. Even perpetrators of infamy are not devoid of merit. By viewing them with some degree of sympathy, we practice the art of idealization, an outlook that Nietzsche associates with theater. Through theater we learn to appreciate others' characters and motivations, and thus also to appreciate our own. This more artistic way of looking at things is not malicious; nor does it encourage self-hatred or viciousness. Through these outlooks, we become more humane, and we can start to overcome moral judgmentalism.

• *Is Nietzsche using hyperbole?*

Nietzsche often sounds like an extremist. He doesn't merely criticize Christianity, he "condemns" it. He is not a mere critic of tradition; he tells us "I am dynamite."[12] However polite he may have been as a person, Nietzsche as a writer is not known for his tact, nor is his Zarathustra. "What? does life require even the rabble? Are poisoned wells required, and stinking fires and soiled dreams and maggots in the bread of life?"[13]

To some extent, Nietzsche is quite judgmental, exemplifying the moralism he attacks. Although unbridled in this respect, he is not inconsistent. He suggests that one's moral background poisons one's outlook, a phenomenon he knows well. On the other hand, the extremity of Nietzsche's statements is often a rhetorical device, not a measured reflection of his views. He exaggerates, like a stand-up comedian, drawing our attention to problems we have failed to notice by making statements that are excessive—though not so excessive as we might like to think.

• *Who are Nietzsche's targets?*

Nietzsche is hardly secretive. He usually opts for direct attacks. He relishes the *ad hominem,* the attack on the person and not just the view. Many logic texts cite the *ad hominem* argument as an informal fallacy, insisting that the merits of a view should not be assessed on the basis of the person who holds it. Nietzsche, by contrast, urges this as a very good test of a view. He does not consider it the only test; but he thinks we should ask, "What kind of person would believe this?" Opinions are often fronts for the motives that prompt them. A sour view held by a sick person may serve as a symptom, and a reason to discount it. Nietzsche's *ad hominem* case against Socrates, for example, explains Socratic rationalism as a symptom of decadence. If

Western thought has embraced it, maybe it, too, is sick, or sickened by it.

Although Nietzsche is direct and sometimes hyperbolic toward his targets, he does not always mention them specifically. Thus, while Nietzsche takes Saint Paul's teachings and temperament as the epitome of what is deplorable in Christianity, he does not always single out Paul when he attacks the Christian worldview. It is therefore worthwhile to take notice of those individuals whom he takes as exemplars of objectionable outlooks. Nietzsche tries to avoid global moral pronouncements. Not every Christian is attacked when he attacks Christianity. If we recognize his specific targets, we can also recognize the characteristics that he finds especially objectionable, as well as those individuals in whom he sees much to admire, despite some blame. (We will consider some of Nietzsche's targets below, in chapter 5, "Nietzsche *Ad Hominem*.")

With such questions in mind, let us now turn to the peculiarities of Nietzsche's particular books.

The Birth of Tragedy, Out of the Spirit of Music

Nietzsche was already an associate professor of philology at the University of Basel when he published his first book, *The Birth of Tragedy* (1872). The book offered a speculative theory of the nature and purpose of Greek tragedy. As he did not observe the developing conventions of scholarly writing, which required extensive references to earlier philological literature and the use of footnotes, the reception by Nietzsche's academic colleagues was largely unfavorable. The book was better appreciated by Wagner, for it described Wagner's music dramas as a revival of the spirit that had motivated tragedy. This discussion of popular developments in contemporary music was a further basis for scholarly disdain. One member of Nietzsche's professional peer group, Ulrich von Wilamowitz-Möllendorff, wrote a sneering pamphlet against Nietzsche's contribution, calling it "*Zukunftphilogie*" ("philology of the future") and lampooning Nietzsche's admiration for Wagner's efforts to create a "*Kunstwerk der Zukunft*," or an "artwork of the future."

Nietzsche analyzes Athenian tragedy as a synthesis of two artistic principles that agree with the respective religious outlooks celebrated by the gods Apollo and Dionysus. Apollo, as the sun god who mythically gave light to the world, was the patron of order and illuminating clarity. Nietzsche described artistic images that featured beautiful form and clear structure, accordingly, as Apollonian. He considered sculpture to be a paradigmatic example of an Apollonian art. Dionysus, by contrast, was the originally foreign god of wine, sexual abandon, loss of self in the frenzy of group experience, and other forms of excessive behavior. Nietzsche considered music, which intoxicates the listener and breaks down divisions between individuals, as the quintessentially Dionysian art. Nietzsche's Apollonian principle conforms with the classical ideal for art in the aesthetic tradition of Kant, in which a well-formed image is an object of disinterested contemplation. Nietzsche's emphasis on the importance of the Dionysian principle, therefore, represents an implicit critique of that tradition—that it fails to recognize the role of passion and engagement in great art, and fails, also, to appreciate the importance of passion in living a meaningful life.

Greek tragedy achieved a balance of these artistic principles.

According to Nietzsche, the value of this achievement was not simply a formal artistic achievement, but a spiritual accomplishment as well. Tragedy provided the Athenians with an opportunity to address the central religious problem, the problem of evil: How can human life be meaningful if human beings are subject to undeserved suffering and death? The plots of Athenian tragedy were stories that poignantly raised this question. The Apollonian beauty of the tragic drama was one response to the question of meaning. Human life becomes meaningful through the transformation of distressing material into objects of beauty. This would be hollow comfort, however, if not for the tragedy's simultaneous evocation of the Dionysian effect, the intoxication of the audience with a sense of participation in something larger than the individual self. The tragic chorus, captivating the spectator with music, caused one to remember that just to be part of the roaring flow of life was so powerful and joyous that life was unquestionably worth its susceptibility to suffering, the price of admission. Nietzsche contends that this is the only adequate solution to the problem of evil. "It is only as an *aesthetic phenomenon* that existence and the world are eternally *justified*."[14]

Unfortunately, even the Athenians lost sight of this solution. Socrates, with his insistence on consistency and rational comprehension of all things, popularized a worldview that left little room for Dionysian experience. The tragic drama itself, in the plays of Euripides, began to observe Socratic injunctions. *The Birth of Tragedy* is the first of Nietzsche's many works that criticize the Western philosophical tradition. He subjects Socrates, usually considered that tradition's founder, to critical reassessment, suggesting that Socrates' rationalistic optimism, his view that all flaws in human experience are correctable, promoted a conception of life that is dangerously false and psychologically unhealthy. Nietzsche also criticizes the modern, scientific worldview, which he sees as the latest version of the Socratic faith in reason's omnipotence. He suggests that our worldview ignores the murky Dionysian side of experience and leaves us ill-prepared to confront the irrational side of our natures.

Untimely Meditations

The series of essays that followed *The Birth of Tragedy* were, in Nietzsche's own words, "untimely," "unmodern," "unfashionable." Each provides a nonstandard assessment of a recent phenomenon, expressing opinions that went against the grain of contemporary thought. The first of these, "David Strauss, the Confessor and the Writer" (1873), was an attack on theologian David Strauss. Strauss was a pioneer in historical criticism of Scripture, which attempted to ascertain and assess the historical facts of the Bible's construction and of the life of the real person Jesus. In light of Nietzsche's own later complaints that the Christian Church distorted the facts of its origins, his vituperative account of David Strauss is perplexing; it certainly shocked Strauss himself, who mused that he could not understand such hatred from a man who had never met him. The explanation is that Nietzsche made this assault on behalf of Richard Wagner, who had previously been denounced by Strauss.

The essay is also a manifestation of Nietzsche's ambivalence toward demythologizing strategies, despite his own many efforts to debunk the moral tradition, and despite his own admiration for Strauss's early analysis of the historical Jesus. But now Strauss had written an unscholarly book called *The Old and the New Faith*, which struck Nietzsche as a banal defense of cheap patriotism and scientific materialism. Strauss appeared to him a bit like Euripides, as one whose efforts to explain away the irrational undercut his society's mythic heritage without any concessions to the genuine psychological needs that prompted them. The simplistic optimism Strauss encouraged was, in Nietzsche's opinion, an aggravation, not a solution, to the problems of the age.

Nietzsche's second *Untimely Meditations,* "On the Uses and Disadvantages of History for Life" (1874), more directly considers his era's outlook, in particular its enthusiasm for historical knowledge. Nietzsche challenges the view that historical accuracy is intrinsically good, suggesting that history is valuable only when it assists the main project of the current age, that of living well in the present. According to Nietzsche, three approaches to history are beneficial to contemporary society. Monumental history, which commemorates great accomplishments, is useful because it helps us to appreciate what human beings can do. Antiquarian history takes a reverential view of the past, and it provides the living with a sense of gratitude and of the resources that inhere in their own way of life. Critical history attempts to learn from history, using its assessments of previous conditions as a basis for critically reassessing the present.

Despite the many benefits of historical knowledge, Nietzsche thinks that history can diminish the present. This happens when historical knowledge is treated as valuable for its own sake, without much thought about what use we will make of this knowledge. Too often, the accumulation of facts about the past convinces the living that humanity's great periods lie behind them or that present efforts make little difference when considered in the sweep of history. Historical scholarship should not be allowed to encourage people to belittle their present lives or to adopt a cynical attitude toward their own endeavors.

Modern society should also be aware that history is not the only lens through which we should observe our experience. Art and religion serve as antidotes to the tendency to visualize every human enterprise as slipping away; they provide an impression of stable foundations for the projects that we mount within the fluid of history. We should also allow ourselves to consider our efforts within the framework of the limited horizons of given projects. We should certainly attempt to rid ourselves of the fantasy that history places determining constraints on the human capacity for greatness. Human greatness is not a function of historical progress. Instead, it is possible at all times, and society should make efforts to organize its institutions, particularly its educational institutions, to foster the development of great individuals whenever they arrive on the scene.

The most obvious target of Nietzsche's attack on contemporary approaches to history is Hegel, and in this he follows his philosophical hero, Arthur Schopenhauer. The third of the *Untimely Meditations*, "Schopenhauer as Educator" (1874), presents Schopenhauer explicitly as the kind of educator that might inspire others to overcome their sense of ineffectualness in the face of history and to aspire to greatness on their own terms. Strangely, the essay does not say much about Schopenhauer's thought. Schopenhauer is presented as a genius, an original human being who serves as an example to others precisely because he is so completely an individual. As Nietzsche later said of Wagner, "his life . . . shouts at every one of us: 'Be a man and do not follow me—but yourself! Be yourself.' "[15] This essay endorses the sentiment expressed in one of Nietzsche's favorite slogans, borrowed from the Greek poet Pindar, "Become who you are." Schopenhauer's greatness was that he lived by this motto.

"Richard Wagner in Bayreuth" (1876) was the fourth and last of the *Untimely Meditations*. Although Nietzsche set out to write a kind of homage to the composer, growing strain in the two men's friendship affected the essay that emerged. Wagner's treatment of Nietzsche as a junior partner was one factor. More substantially, however, Nietzsche was becoming increasingly disturbed by what he saw as Wagner's willingness to compromise too much for the sake of theatrical effects. Yet, on balance, the essay is still favorable. It presents Wagner as a man of his time, embodying both its virtues and its vices. Nietzsche allowed, for the moment, that Wagner remained true to his ideals, but he did not maintain this assessment much longer. Many later works attempt psychological and cultural analyses of Wagner, but never again with so much effort to be sympathetic.

Nietzsche originally intended to write thirteen *Untimely Meditations,* but he published only these four. During the period of writing them. Nietzsche also wrote a number of drafts and partial manuscripts that he did not publish, one of which has attracted much scholarly attention in recent years. "On Truth and Lies in a Nonmoral Sense" (1873) is a suggestive essay in which Nietzsche considers the ways in which language imposes its own shape on our experience, with the effect that it does not accurately reflect the world as it is. Our experiences are unique, but language makes experiences labeled with the same words appear to be the same. Language is inherently metaphorical, translating phenomena into images that are more standardized, and more anthropomorphic, than reality justifies, but we usually forget this fact. We imagine that we have penetrated appearances to something secure when we claim we have reached a "truth." Nietzsche makes similar claims in later works, but this essay is noteworthy for some expressive images. "Truths are illusions which we have forgotten are illusions; they are metaphors that have become worn out and have been drained of sensuous force, coins which have lost their embossing and are now considered as metal and no longer as coins."[16] Nietzsche suggests that the modern era should reassess its commitment to truth at any price, much as it should reassess its aspiration to historical knowledge.

Human, All Too Human, A Book for Free Spirits

Human, All Too Human (1878) initiates a new phase in Nietzsche's thought. He had lost faith in both Wagner and Schopenhauer. In a later preface to the book, he describes his condition in writing it: never, he claims, had he felt so alone. But his loneliness only spurred his independence of thought, and it is this independence that the book celebrates. In contrast to his earlier emphasis on metaphysical approaches to the meaning of life and on mythic responses to the tragic human condition, Nietzsche now displays enthusiasm for science and naturalistic explanation. Many passages consider the causal determinants of how things appear to us and of why people think and behave as they do.

Human, All Too Human is the first of Nietzsche's "aphoristic" works, with numbered aphorisms and short discussions, but without explicit transitions connecting one to another. Nietzsche's migraine headaches and eyestrain had something to do with this form: he could dictate short discussions even when he was suffering. But he soon came to appreciate the power of the aphorism and came to prefer this format. It provided a literary expression for his claim that every description of the world and its phenomena is shaped by the perspective of the interpreter. This "perspectivist" position is the basis for many of Nietzsche's critiques in *Human, All Too Human* and later works. In particular, Nietzsche criticizes the moral outlook associated with Christianity as motivated by (and as reinforcing) a perspective that is inherently unhealthy.

In 1886, Nietzsche published a second edition of *Human, All Too Human* which included the entire first edition and two aphoristic works that he had written subsequent to the first edition. These were *Assorted Opinions and Maxims* (1879) and *The Wanderer and His Shadow* (1880). In large measure they deal with the same themes as the first volume but show greater mastery of succinct statement.

Daybreak, Thoughts on the Prejudices of Morality

Nietzsche makes his first sustained assault on the Christian moral worldview in another aphoristic work, *Daybreak* (1881). The book's extensive psychological analyses suggest that the motives behind Christian virtue are far from savory. By postulating that our moral nature is corrupt, the Christian account uglifies its believers' impression of themselves. Consequently, Christians are motivated to look for ways to improve their extremely judgmental self-assessments. The most straightforward way to accomplish this is to see other people as at least as bad as oneself, and, optimally, far worse. In this way, the Christian moral framework motivates contemptuous outlooks on others, despite its professed celebration of "love of neighbor." This framework encourages both vilification of our natural instincts and harmful efforts to rid ourselves of our appetites. Presented as the cure for our moral failings, this framework is what causes us to think ourselves "ill" in the first place, according to Nietzsche. He envisions a transformed perspective that would reenchant us with ourselves and the natural world.

The Gay Science

Nietzsche's *The Gay Science* (1882) continues his exploration of what might restore a sense of innocence to our natural experience, now focusing on our modern intellectual outlook and the grim scholarship (*Wissenschaft,* or science) that it produces. Nietzsche calls for a new lightheartedness, in the manner of the Provençal courtiers, who abandoned traditional moral conventions in favor of devotion to beauty. Nietzsche continues his psychological analyses of the mechanisms involved in Christian morality, attempting to demonstrate that ostensibly self-sacrificing values are often veiled efforts to assert control over others.

The Gay Science introduces some of Nietzsche's most well-known ideas. One of these is the shocking announcement that "God is dead." The God-centered worldview that once grounded the Western way of life, Nietzsche tells us, is no longer real for most Westerners. Instead, most modern Europeans base their lifestyle on scientific materialism, which is not well suited to establish values. The consequence is modern nihilism, the sense that life has no purpose. Nietzsche does not propose that "God" be resuscitated. Instead, he provides suggestions throughout *The Gay Science* as to how a modern person might develop a naturalistic sense of meaning. Much of the work might be considered practical advice for the spiritually sensitive atheist.

Nietzsche recommends two more of his most celebrated ideas, the ideal of *amor fati* (love of fate), which is an appreciative acceptance of one's life in all its circumstances, and the vision of *eternal recurrence*. The latter notion postulates that time is cyclical, reiterating the same sequence of events over and over again. If one can face such a prospect with enthusiasm, one has successfully found meaning in life. In this light, eternal recurrence can be seen as an indicator of the extent to which one has overcome nihilism.

Thus Spoke Zarathustra, A Book for All and None

Nietzsche's *Thus Spoke Zarathustra* (1883–85) is probably his most famous work. It is a fictional account of Zarathustra (Zoroaster), the great Persian prophet, whom Nietzsche introduces at the end of *The Gay Science* (in its first edition, before a fifth part was added). Like the historical prophet, Nietzsche's Zarathustra is a sage with a message, but his message is addressed to modern Europe and its contemporary crisis of nihilism. The book includes multiple parodies, with references to Plato's dialogues and the New Testament. Zarathustra, these parodies suggest, is akin to Socrates and Christ in offering a fundamentally new way of approaching human life.

Zarathustra preaches on a wide spectrum of philosophical ideas, including the "will to power" and the idea of eternal recurrence. Zarathustra also presents the idea of the *Übermensch* (the super-man), the ideal aim of human development, although such a being transcends human capacities. In particular, the *Übermensch* is devoid of human timidity. The *Übermensch* aspires continually to greatness, living a life of creative adventure. Zarathustra contrasts the *Übermensch* with "the Last Man," his caricature of a person who is too risk-averse to pursue any aim beyond comfort, to such an extent that even procreation is too exerting. Zarathustra poses these as two alternative goals, asking modern individuals which mode of existence their own lives embody and promote.

Beyond Good and Evil, Prelude to a Philosophy of the Future

Beyond Good and Evil (1886) begins a new phase of Nietzsche's work, focusing on the "revaluation of all values" and an explicit "critique of modernity." The book attacks the dogmatism that has afflicted philosophy so far, particularly regarding the nature of truth and morality. Philosophers' pretense to objectivity is just a pose. In fact, any philosophy or morality is an "unconscious and involuntary memoir" of the person who presents it.[17]

Accordingly, we do well to ask ourselves, when confronted with any viewpoint, the question Nietzsche asks with respect to Kant's categorical imperative: "What does such a claim tell us about the man who makes it?"[18]

Nietzsche calls for "new philosophers" who would create new values through a process of open-minded experimentation. The philosopher, accordingly, has a significant political role, directing cultural development. Nietzsche urges philosophers to articulate an outlook that is "beyond good and evil," in other words, beyond the simplistic, judgmental moral categories employed as basic terms in the Christian worldview. While the articulation of new values is a challenging ambition, it is not an impossible dream. Moral values have already historically changed along with circumstances, so they are clearly malleable.

Nietzsche offers us a "natural history of morals." The currently reigning moral outlook is a form of "slave morality," which devalues any behavior that is assertive and self-assured. More wholesome is "master morality," which takes one's own way of living as the standard of goodness. (Nietzsche acknowledges that an individual person's morality may be a combination of the two, but he tends to see one or the other as characteristic of a society, or of a faction within a society.) Better than master morality would be subtle discernment in judging, "to be able to see with many different eyes and consciences, from a height into every distance, from the depths into every height."[19]

Of Nietzsche's published writings, *Beyond Good and Evil* provides the fullest descriptions of the "will to power." Nietzsche postulates a fundamental drive to ever greater vitality and life-enhancement, and suggests that this characterizes not only human motivation but the behavior of all that lives. "[L]ife itself is *will to power*; self-preservation is only one of the indirect and most frequent *results*."[20] Nietzsche's Zarathustra makes a similar point: "The most concerned ask today, 'How is man to be preserved?' But Zarathustra is the first and only one to ask, 'How is man to be overcome?'"[21] The psychological motivations of morality that Nietzsche so aptly describes are, on this account, all expressions of will to power. Nietzsche contends, however, that such expressions are not equally healthy. He also denies that people are equal in value, proposing instead that they naturally fall into "rank order." The highest human beings are the goal of the species, but they are necessarily quite rare.

On the Genealogy of Morals, A Polemic

On the Genealogy of Morals (1887) continues Nietzsche's analysis of the origin of moral values. By contrast with his aphoristic works, *Genealogy* is composed of three focused inquiries. The first pursues the development of master and slave moralities. Master morality is the orientation of those who are masters of their own lives, like the free Athenians of antiquity. They do not question the value of their own way of living. They simply consider those who are not masters to be base, or bad. Many of these people are (literally) enslaved by the masters, and they are consequently discontent with their own conditions. They resent the masters who oppress them. Their primary moral judgment is motivated by this hostility, and it deems the masters and everything they stand for as "evil." Nietzsche's formula "beyond good and evil" proposes the rejection of such resentful judgments, in favor of a less reactive, more self-assertive way of life.

The book's second essay seeks the origins of "bad conscience" and the associated concept of guilt. Their basis, claims Nietzsche, is cruelty, a natural human disposition that is displayed unabashedly in punishment. Bad conscience is the same cruelty turned inward. Although the person afflicted with bad conscience suffers, this suffering is mingled with self-satisfaction about causing and enduring such pain. The Christian saga of sin and atonement plays on these feelings. Moreover, the very notion of God's justice ascribes our own cruel psychology to God. God is interpreted as being vindictive about slights to his honor and demanding the satisfaction of seeing the most perfect human being tortured, in the form of Jesus' death on the cross.

The third essay asks how ascetic (self-denying) ideals developed. If vitality, the love of life, and self-enhancement are basic motives, what could motivate the ideal of self-denial in Christian and other moral worldviews? Nietzsche answers that this ideal is only apparently life-denying. It actually promotes life in its own devious way. Ascetic ideals are also more widespread than is usually believed. They are not just restricted to monks and hermits. The scientific quest for truth is also ascetic. The dogged pursuit of science sometimes betrays itself as an evasion of life. Indeed, the psychology of asceticism shapes our secular world as well as the great religions of the West. The person who works constantly and is thus unable to enjoy the fruits of this labor is a paradigm case of the ascetic, in Nietzsche's sense.

The Case of Wagner: A Musician's Problem and *Nietzsche contra Wagner: Out of the Files of a Psychologist*

The trauma of ending his friendship with Wagner plagued Nietzsche for many years, as is evident in these two works, both written in 1888. In *The Case of Wagner* (1888) Nietzsche analyzes Wagner as an emblem of his decadent culture. He describes Wagner's style as a "chaos of the atoms," geared to stimulating the nerves without liberating the spirit.[22] About Wagner, Nietzsche no longer states his points politely. "He has made music sick."[23] The book was not designed to please Wagner enthusiasts, and it provoked a hostile response. *Nietzsche contra Wagner* (1895), the last work before the Turin collapse, is a short anthology of passages on Wagner that appear over the span of Nietzsche's writings. *The Case of Wagner* was his most uninhibited, but his qualms about Wagner had been surfacing over the years.

Twilight of the Idols, or How One Philosophizes with a Hammer

The title of Nietzsche's 1889 book *Twilight of the Idols* (*Götzendämmerung*) puns on the title of one of Wagner's operas, *Götterdämmerung* (*Twilight of the Gods*). At the same time, it casts Nietzsche as one who, following Francis Bacon, exposes the deceptive "idols" of philosophy and culture. The subtitle, *How One Philosophizes with a Hammer*, reinforces this pose. Nietzsche describes himself in the preface as using a hammer to "sound out" idols, to determine whether they were hollow. But the connotation of a hammer as a harsh and destructive instrument cannot be denied.

The "revaluation of all values" is another of Nietzsche's characterizations of his aim in the book. However, his primary targets are people, not values as such. Much of the book consists of *ad hominem* attacks upon Socrates, Kant, and a large number of contemporary as well as traditional writers. He describes many of these assaults as the "skirmishes of an untimely man," suggesting once again that his views are unfashionable. He also reintroduces Dionysus, now associating him with eternal recurrence, described as life's cyclical renewal.

The Antichrist

The Antichrist (1895) is, as one might expect from the title, the most conscientiously blasphemous of all of Nietzsche's books. It offers a historical and psychological account of the development of Christianity. Despite the title, Nietzsche's portrait of Jesus is essentially positive. Jesus is presented, in Gary Shapiro's phrase, as a free spirit who is "blissed out" by the immanent presence of God here and now.[24] The book's villain is Paul, the main organizer of the Church, and the inventor of the interpretation of Jesus' death as an atonement for humanity's sins. Against the judgmentalism of Christianity, Nietzsche pronounces his own judgment: "I *condemn* Christianity. . . . I call Christianity the one great curse, the one great innermost corruption . . . the one immortal blemish of mankind."[25]

Ecce Homo, How One Becomes What One Is

Ecce Homo (1895) is Nietzsche's autobiography, begun on his forty-fourth birthday. Its title is Pontius Pilate's statement made when he presented Jesus to the crowd that was calling for his crucifixion, *"Ecce Homo"*—"Behold the man" (John 19:6). Besides comparing himself to Jesus, Nietzsche casts himself as Socrates, the Delphic oracle's "wisest man in Athens," when he ironically titles his chapters "Why I Am So Wise" and "Why I Am So Clever." Nietzsche goes so far as to claim that he is "a destiny." Some commentators conclude that Nietzsche was already mad when he wrote this book, but they miss its dark ironic humor. Soon after completing this summary volume, however, Nietzsche's working life came to an end.

The Will to Power

A curious perversity in Nietzsche scholarship is that some commentators have preferred Nietzsche's scrambled notes to his masterful publications. The "book" known as *The Will to Power* is actually a compilation of materials from Nietzsche's notebooks (the *Nachlass,* or "leftovers"). Speaking of this compilation, Martin Heidegger, one of Nietzsche's most influential interpreters, claims that Nietzsche's greatest work was one that he never completed. Nietzsche's sister, Elisabeth, is responsible for giving this dubious, posthumous volume the title *The Will to Power,* a title that Nietzsche had once envisioned but had never yet used when he collapsed. Elisabeth Förster-Nietzsche was the original editor of this volume, which she produced with the help of several assistants, organizing Nietzsche's notes around themes that suited her political agenda ("breeding," "power," "race"). Scholars have attempted to undo Elisabeth's handiwork, and most now make an effort to corroborate claims in Nietzsche's notebooks with statements in his published works. In other words, they treat the *Nachlass* as an alternative source of juicy one-liners, but hardly a "book," let alone a masterpiece.

Nietzsche Said,
"God Is Dead"

ALTHOUGH INFAMOUS for his rejection of the Christian religion, Nietzsche writes about Christianity as an insider. Beginning life in a parsonage, Nietzsche was immersed in Christian sermonizing from his earliest years. In his childhood his demeanor was so much in keeping with this environment that other children called him "the little minister." His childhood prose (such as we find in his journal and an autobiography written when he was thirteen) is full of sentimental pieties. When he entered the university, he planned to study theology as well as classical philology.

It was during his student years that Nietzsche broke with his religious upbringing. One of his influences was Schopenhauer, the pessimistic German philosopher whose nontheistic metaphysical views Nietzsche first encountered as a college student. Another cause of his religious disaffection was his growing sense that the values of the ancients—the focus of his philological studies—were not entirely consistent with those promoted by Christianity. Pride, for example, while a virtue for the ancient Greeks, was considered the deadliest of sins in Christianity. Perhaps most crucial for Nietzsche's decision was his exposure to historical theology, which sought to construct a historically accurate account of the development of Christianity and its Scripture. Such studies tended to naturalize stories that had traditionally been approached as miraculous or as having supernatural significance. Nietzsche, like many others, came to see this approach as undermining the very faith that motivated theological study in the first place.

Nietzsche's early adherence to the faith that he later rejected is important for our understanding of his anti-Christian writings. Although one might complain that what he attacks is a caricature of Christianity, one certainly could not attribute this to Nietzsche's ignorance of the religion. He was very well informed as to Scriptural detail, historical theology, and doctrinal subtleties.

Nietzsche's account of Christian psychology is similarly affected by his own life experiences. He sometimes presents his psychological portraits of the typical priest, the believer, and important figures in Christian history as if these were objective analyses, but mostly he criticizes Christianity for its effects on the individual believer. We might reasonably question whether the effects Nietzsche blames on Christianity are as widespread as he suggests. Perhaps, at least some of the time, he tells us more about himself than about "Christians" in general.

Finally, Nietzsche's background makes sense of his conviction that the loss of faith in God is a calamitous cultural crisis. Although writing as one who has lost faith and who sees his own religious tradition as having many pernicious effects on its adherents, he experienced the loss of faith as a personal trauma. He was shocked that others seemed to throw off their religious backgrounds so casually, and he eventually concluded that many of his contemporaries had not really shed their religion but instead continued their old habits in disguised forms. Because he was convinced that the Christian worldview had harmful psychological effects, he endeavored to show how such damage continued to affect his contemporaries who maintained the habits of the old worldview, even though they no longer endorsed it.

We see Nietzsche not as the "atheist by instinct" he claims to be in his autobiography but as a religious *desperado*. If one understands by "religious" the effort to integrate one's life with what is larger than oneself, Nietzsche rejects Christianity for religious reasons. His many complaints about the ideology that the Christian Church has foisted on its members express his conviction that it harms our ability to love and to be responsive to others in the world and to nature. If a critic, he is also a seeker, and he believed that his society was in desperate need of a new spiritual focus. He advances some positive suggestions for helping to construct this new focus and to restore harmony to our sense of ourselves in the world.

Why Nietzsche Condemns Christianity

One of the texts that Nietzsche studied closely while a student of theology was Ludwig Feuerbach's *The Essence of Christianity*. Feuerbach, an outspoken atheist, argued that God is the projection of human characteristics onto something external, outside the self. In particular, human beings dissociate themselves from their own powers to think, to take action, and to love, attributing these powers to God instead of to themselves. Fear is the motivation for this projection. By projecting and exaggerating human abilities onto a supernatural personage, believers can imagine themselves as protected by a power that far exceeds that of any threatening person or natural force.

The problem with this human creation of God is that it depends on human self-denigration. Attributing human traits to God, human beings have disowned their own powers and accordingly have lost awareness of how to use them. Human beings have become estranged from themselves. Feuerbach urges that we rediscover our own capacities and reinternalize our projected powers. Until we do so, we will continue to be victims of our own conviction that we ourselves are powerless and utterly dependent.

Although Nietzsche rarely writes about Feuerbach directly, he often employs Feuerbachian statements and images. He urges us to imagine our transformed situation should we cease "to *flow out* into a god."[1] He compares the Judeo-Christian projection of human powers onto a supreme God to a self-sabotaging political maneuver.

The Jews' enjoyment of their divine monarch and saint is similar to that which the French nobility derived from Louis XIV. This nobility had surrendered all of its power and sovereignty and had become contemptible. In order not to feel this, in order to be able to forget this, one required royal splendor, royal authority and plenitude of power without equal to which only the nobility had access. By virtue of this privilege, one rose to the height of the court, and from that vantage point one saw everything beneath oneself and found it contemptible. . . . Thus the tower of the royal power was built ever higher into the clouds, and one did not hold back even the last remaining stones of one's own power.[2]

Nietzsche's case against Christianity depends in large part on his basic acceptance of Feuerbach's view that human beings invented God by divesting themselves of any sense of their own powers. Through this operation, Nietzsche insists, believers exchange an active stance toward their environment for the reactive stance of a pet or a victim. Instead of actively engaging with their problems, they treat their lived experiences like hieroglyphics whose real significance is decipherable only on a different—supernatural—plane. Nietzsche contends that this shift of focus amounts to a complete falsification of our actual circumstances.

In Christianity neither morality nor religion has even a single point of contact with reality. Nothing but imaginary *causes,* "God," "soul," "ego," "spirit," "free will"—for that matter "unfree will," nothing but imaginary *effects* ("sin," "redemption," "grace," "punishment," "forgiveness of sins").[3]

For Nietzsche, this outlook is damaging to one's ability to function and flourish in one's life. It obstructs one's view of the real world, addles one's ability to see the real forces at work in one's life, and destroys one's ability to recognize how best to address them. The imaginary scheme implicit in the Christian worldview is also dangerous for another reason. It interprets suffering as punishment. Suffering allegedly entered the world as God's retaliation for Adam and Eve's sin. Nietzsche complains in *Daybreak* that "Only in Christendom did everything become punishment, well-deserved punishment: it also makes the sufferer's imagination suffer, so that with every misfortune he feels himself morally reprehensible and cast out."[4]

With its supernatural scheme as the real determinant of the success or failure of one's life, Christianity encourages believers to feel that mistakes they have made have catastrophic effects. If one has ever seriously erred, one deserves eternal damnation. One's only hope is that God will be merciful and disregard what one truly deserves.

And yet Christianity provides mixed messages about God's mercy. God is supposed to be a loving father, but also a wrathful judge. God's tendency to retaliate for sins, which he takes as insults to his honor, is evident in the doctrine of atonement: that God could only be appeased if a divine human being were brutally tortured and killed on the cross. The supremacy of God and his insistence on homage strikes Nietzsche as a projection of some of humanity's own less admirable traits.

The Christian presupposes a powerful, overpowering being who enjoys revenge. His power is so great that nobody could possibly harm him, except for his honor. Every sin is a slight to his honor . . . and no more. Contrition, degradation, rolling in the dust—all this is the first and last condition of his grace: in sum, the restoration of his divine honor. . . . Sin is an offense against him, not against humanity. Those who are granted his grace are also granted this carelessness regarding the natural consequences of sin. God and humanity are separated so completely that a sin against humanity is really unthinkable: every deed is to be considered *solely with respect to its supernatural consequences* without regard for its natural consequences; . . . whatever is natural is considered ignoble.[5]

Christianity's repudiation of nature, particularly human nature, is a further target of Nietzsche's attack. According to Nietzsche, Christianity interprets our natural appetites as dangerous temptations. The body is viewed as a source of sin that must be subdued, even if this requires harming it. Fasting is a slow method for undercutting one's health and thereby diminishing the force of one's drives. Christian moralizers are willing to urge even more aggressive measures for silencing the instincts.

> The most famous formula for this is to be found in the New Testament, in the Sermon on the Mount, where, incidentally, things are by no means looked at from a height. There it is said, for example, with particular reference to sexuality: "If thy eye offend thee, pluck it out." Fortunately, no Christian acts in accordance with this precept.[6]

Nietzsche believes that, in addition to encouraging the believer to despise the body's demands, the Christian worldview encourages the idea that our psychological makeup, which naturally seeks self-assertion and self-enhancement, is pernicious. The hostility of Christianity to our physical and psychological natures is evident in the list of sins that it considers most "deadly"—pride, envy, greed, gluttony, sloth, lust, and anger. These sins are all expressions of natural instincts, presented in their ugliest form. Instead of providing techniques for developing self-control in the expression of these urges, Christian morality urges their obliteration.

One cannot destroy one's instincts, however, without destroying oneself. Nietzsche anticipates that most people will be unable to eliminate their instincts and passions—a natural result, but in the Christian worldview a failure. The upshot of Nietzsche's analysis is that Christianity encourages self-hatred. If we vilify the essential urges and instincts that underlie our physical and psychic health, we cannot regard ourselves with satisfaction; instead, we feel we should be at war with fundamental components of our being and we consider ourselves failures for having human constitutions. The war between the flesh and the spirit, of which Luther makes so much, strikes Nietzsche as an indication of the degree to which Christianity promotes inner conflict and makes unfulfillable demands. The person who seriously accepts the Christian vision of the human being is bound, in Nietzsche's view, to develop a degraded vision of him- or herself.

Because Nietzsche thinks that "will to power," or the impulse to enhanced vitality, is basic to the human makeup, he does not think that our psyches will simply accept this self-denigrating vision without struggle. Indeed, Christian faith *depends* on the believer's inability to live comfortably with this account. Once one internalizes a view of oneself as having depraved impulses and as deserving damnation, one is desperate to vindicate oneself. The Church and its various practices are appealing precisely because believers seek alternatives to their damaged self-assessment and the Church stands ready to "solve" the problems it has created. The Church assures them that what it offers will put things right on the supernatural plane. This claim is unfalsifiable (neither provable nor disprovable), but nevertheless, once it has inculcated self-disgust, the Church then claims the power to improve believers' views of themselves.

Nietzsche also criticizes Christianity for encouraging believers to see others in a negative light. In order to improve one's own self-assessment, one need only look at others with a keen eye for human flaws. Observing the small sins of others, one feels less sinful. Moreover, in the quest for moral superiority, one *seeks out* sinful behavior in others, taking mere foibles for crimes against God. In this way, then, the Christian outlook, in effect, creates a popular appetite for sensational scandals, which provide assurance that even if one is depraved, one is still clearly better than certain notorious characters.

Nietzsche does not think that Christianity's doctrine of "love of neighbor" compensates for this drive to find fault with others. Nietzsche thinks that "love of neighbor" is merely a hollow slogan to "cover" one's indifference to the particular psychologies of real people, encouraging one to treat others with an indiscriminant superficial kindness. Love of neighbor thus becomes a means of using others to improve one's impression of oneself. Not caring whether one's gestures actually help or harm another, one performs symbolic acts of kindness for one's own benefit, to convince oneself that one is virtuous after all.

What Nietzsche Admires in Christians

A corollary of Nietzsche's perspectivism is that one should not rest content with dogmatic, unscrutinized, one-dimensional judgments, whether positive or negative, and Nietzsche is consistently perspectival in his approach to Christianity—at least until his late, polemical writings. He often complicates his critical assessment of Christian ideology by acknowledging that over its history, Christianity has nurtured admirable abilities and cultivated real heroes. We have already observed that Nietzsche admired Jesus, if not his Church-organizing disciples. Nietzsche also expresses admiration for certain individual Christians who pursued the religious life. He describes "the figures of the higher and highest Catholic priesthood" as "the most refined figures in human society that have ever yet existed"[7] and expresses admiration for the "self-overcoming every individual Jesuit imposes upon himself."[8]

Nietzsche also admits that religions of all sorts, Christianity included, offer a vision that at least superficially improves life for the believer. Religious interpretations transfigure life, making it appear as a manifestation of the highest values, and thus tremendously meaningful. In light of Nietzsche's critique of the imaginary character of the supernatural dimension, he may seem to be inconsistent. But he is considering the evolution of Christianity over time and suggests that its impact on believers changed as it became a powerful institution. As we will see in the discussion of master and slave morality in the following chapter, Nietzsche contends that early Christianity was popular among the powerless because it represented a healthy gesture of self-assertion, if only inwardly. However, this improvement developed potentially dangerous psychological mechanisms that flourished when Christianity itself became a pervasive and powerful social institution, undermining the healthy self-assertion that earlier it had promoted.

Nietzsche consistently encourages modern society to move beyond the Christian worldview, but he acknowledges that Christianity historically nurtured and promoted some valuable human abilities. Nietzsche credits even the turning of aggressive instincts inward and the potential for inner conflict, which Christianity has fostered, to have been "something so new, profound, unheard of, enigmatic, contradictory, and *pregnant with a future* that the aspect of the earth was essentially altered."[9]

One of Christianity's great virtues, from Nietzsche's point of view, is its commitment to honesty. In this respect, Christian values made way, however unintentionally, for the development of knowledge.

> Christianity, too, has made a great contribution to the enlightenment, and taught moral skepticism very trenchantly and effectively, accusing and embittering men, yet with untiring patience and subtlety; it destroyed the faith in his "virtues" in every single individual. . . . In the end, however, we have applied this same skepticism also to all religious states and processes. . . .[10]

Christianity's encouragement of honesty as a virtue promoted, ultimately, an alternative, more scientific way of seeing the world, according to Nietzsche. It also led ultimately to its own demise. Eventually, those trained in the Christian virtue of honesty felt the demand for truthfulness even in those cases where it personally pained them. They directed their inquiry at Christianity itself, and discovered that they could not honestly sustain their belief.

You see what it was that really triumphed over the Christian god: Christian morality itself, the concept of truthfulness that was understood ever more rigorously, the father confessor's refinement of the Christian conscience, translated and sublimated into a scientific conscience, into intellectual cleanliness at any price.[11]

Confronting the Shadows of God

Nietzsche's striking and ambivalent report of the death of God tells of a madman who appears in the marketplace and cries, "I seek God! I seek God!" The crowd mocks him, apparently considering themselves too "modern" to have any thought of God. The madman challenges them.

"Whither is God?" he cried; "I will tell you. *We have killed him—* you and I. All of us are his murderers. But how did we do this? How could we drink up the sea? Who gave us the sponge to wipe away the entire horizon? What were we doing when we unchained this earth from its sun? Whither is it moving now? Whither are we moving? Away from all sun? Are we not plunging continually? Backward, sideward, forward, in all directions? Is there still any up or down? . . . How shall we comfort ourselves, the murderers of all murderers? What was holiest and mightiest of all that the world has yet owned has bled to death under our knives: who will wipe this blood off us? What water is there for us to clean ourselves? What festivals of atonement, what sacred games shall we have to invent? Is not the greatness of this deed too great for us? Must we ourselves not become gods simply to appear worthy of it?"

His audience remains unresponsive, and the madman concludes that he has come too early. The awareness of the great deed of killing God has not yet dawned on those who have perpetrated it. Still, he himself feels the need to honor both the dead God and the event of his passing. Nietzsche continues:

> It has been related further that on the same day the madman forced his way into several churches and there struck up his *requiem aeternam deo*. Led out and called to account, he is said always to have replied nothing but: "What after all are these churches now if they are not the tombs and sepulchers of God?"[12]

This story reflects an aspect of Nietzsche's view of the death of God that is often ignored. Nietzsche is far more concerned about spirituality than most of his educated contemporaries, who do not consider religion to be very important. Nietzsche presents the madman as sincerely religious and concerned for the modern world's spiritual condition. The madman's audience, his contemporaries, who pride themselves on having renounced religious superstition, are out of touch with the brewing crisis. They do not imagine that they have lost anything by arranging their lives around entirely secular goals. They do not notice, in part because they have maintained the habits that religion fostered, particularly the habit of faith. They have replaced faith in God with faith in science.

This new faith, Nietzsche thinks, is no improvement over the old. Nietzsche couples his statement that "God is dead" with a critique of modern faith in scientific materialism. Intellectuals imagine that they have replaced fables with facts, but Nietzsche sees the dominance of scientific accounts as substituting one self-denigrating myth for another. If anything, the scientific myth is worse. Faith in God eroded confidence in our own human powers, but at least encouraged belief that we had dignity as creations of God whom God took seriously. The myth of science, by contrast, posits that our existence is an accident and that we are organisms on an obscure planet on the periphery of a universe of mostly dead matter. This vision builds on and reinforces the sense of worthlessness that grew from our projection of our powers onto God. Worse yet, in the light of a religious worldview that sees the goal of life as a blissful afterlife, the absence of any "beyond" in the scientific account is bound to frustrate our inherited expectations about what would make life meaningful. Unless we seek meaning from a different source, science is only going to promote nihilism, the sense that our world lacks value. Thus Nietzsche encourages his contemporaries to attack the "shadows of God," our residual religious expectations that are bound to be frustrated by a scientific-materialist outlook.

Nietzsche's Spiritual Alternative

Nietzsche hopes for a rebirth of spirituality. Crucial to this transformation would be a renewed appreciation of earthly life and nature. Nietzsche hints that he advocates a sense of sacredness in nature when he describes himself as a "disciple" of Dionysus and has Zarathustra preach "the meaning of the earth." The West's shift from a Christian to a secular culture came about in part because the Christian account became too abstract, too divorced from embodied experience. Indeed, it declared war on the body, denouncing the passions and appetites as sources of sin. Nietzsche calls upon us to "rechristen our evil as what is best in us."[13] Specifically, we should consider our bodies and instincts positively, as promising capacities and sources of meaning that are sometimes more subtle than the rather thin track provided by our intellectual consciousness. "I counsel the innocence of the senses," declares Nietzsche's Zarathustra.[14]

Nietzsche charges that one of the more unfortunate legacies of the Christian outlook is that we are dis-integrated beings. We experience our natural existence as inherently deficient, and we are driven to take revenge on ourselves and the world for own inabilities, real or imagined. Nietzsche urges a reexamination of our inner lives and a reassessment of our natures. "When will we complete our de-deification of nature? When may we begin to 'naturalize' humanity in terms of a pure, newly discovered, newly redeemed nature?"[15]

Seeking an alternative to the Christian outlook on nature, Nietzsche finds inspiration in the ancient Athenians. In the god Dionysus, the Athenians worshiped the lusty and wild side of our nature that Christianity denounces. Nietzsche stresses the contrast between Dionysus and Christ ("the annointed one" as interpreted by Saint Paul). The Pauline doctrine of sin and atonement is what Nietzsche sees as the vicious core of Christian ideology. This doctrine claims that human beings are so defective, so worthy of damnation, and that God is so cruel and vindictive, that the only way of redeeming our situation is for God to take human form and be tortured to death. As Nietzsche sees it, this account regards our very existence as natural beings as being cosmically objectionable.

Dionysus, by contrast, confers value on our natural characteristics by *living* them, rejoicing in them. Dionysus also represents a very different way of understanding human limitations. According to one version of the myth, Dionysus, like Christ, was a suffering god. Dionysus suffered dismemberment when, as a boy, he was torn to bits by the Titans. But whereas Christianity goes on to celebrate the individual soul, Nietzsche uses the Dionysus story to suggest that suffering comes about because we take our individual existence too seriously and usually fail to recognize our participation in the whole. Nietzsche describes the rebirth of Dionysus as the end of individuation. This "rebirth" contrasts with the Christian conception, in which the just will be "reborn" as embodied individuals, their personality made eternal.

"Have I been understood?" Nietzsche asks at the close of his autobiography—"*Dionysus versus the Crucified.*"[16] This formula conveys the focus of Nietzsche's attack on Christianity.

Nietzsche's vitriolic case against Christian doctrine is more famous than his recommendations for mending the spirit. Because he encourages experimenting with life and reasserting our individual virtues and powers, he offers hints, not formulas. Among Nietzsche's hints are images that might help us to contemplate the natural world in fresh ways. "I counsel the innocence of the senses," says Zarathustra. The "innocence of the senses" would involve delighting in our experiences of the world, approaching the world without the resentful project of trying to improve one's wounded sense of adequacy, but learning to love ourselves and the world on its own terms. A loving contemplation of all natural things *as natural* is a primary source of meaning in life.

Some of Nietzsche's images draw attention to time as being cyclical—as opposed to linear, like the Christian tightrope to salvation, from which we might fall before reaching our goal. If time is a cycle, it has no ultimate endpoint, nor do the successive moments of our lives lead to any goal that lies outside of time. Each moment has its own validity. Indeed, there is no time like the present: the present moment is uniquely significant, for it is the only moment of our personal trajectories in which we can assert our aliveness, take action, engage in our projects or change our direction.

Seeing our lives as limited to a finite span in this life need not be seen as an indication of life's ultimate worthlessness. We can find tremendous meaning and satisfaction in the finite endeavors in which we engage. In *The Gay Science,* Nietzsche compares the goal-directedness of ocean waves with that of human projects. Both have a kind of profundity.

> How greedily this wave approaches, as if it were after something! How it crawls with terrifying haste into the inmost nooks of this labyrinthine cliff! It seems that it is trying to anticipate someone; it seems that something of value, high value, must be hidden there.—And now it comes back, a little more slowly but still quite white with excitement; is it disappointed? Has it found what it looked for? Does it pretend to be disappointed?—But already another wave is approaching, still more greedily and savagely than the first, and its soul, too, seems to be full of secrets and the lust to dig up treasures. Thus

live waves—thus live we who will. . . . You and I—do we not have *one secret?* [17]

Nietzsche urges us to throw ourselves into life. We can take satisfaction in our undertakings much as we do in the sight of waves. We achieve something admirable when we pursue our endeavors with intensity and strive to give the process a well-wrought shape. Particular efforts may not always succeed, but failed undertakings allow one to learn and do better. Again, Nietzsche counters the formula of sin and Christ's atonement, suggesting that we can refine our abilities and redeem past failures through growing mastery. Zarathustra counsels us to forgive ourselves our pasts and engage in ongoing life. He also counsels us to take inspiration in the beauty of the natural world, the things we so easily take for granted and that Christianity too quickly demeans as "worldly." "Place little good perfect things around you. . . . What is perfect teaches hope." [18]

Nietzsche encourages a sense of gradual development, cultivation, and transformation. He suggests that our projects are provisional and revisable, and that many involve developing practices that are refined only through many repetitions. Countering the Christian notion that any serious past failure can earn one infinite torment, Nietzsche suggests that one can turn failure to one's advantage and enhance one's life by moving forward. He describes this through the metaphor of music and compares it to the subtle growth of love over time.

This is what happens to us in music: First one has to *learn to hear* a figure and melody at all, to detect and distinguish it, to isolate it and delimit it as a separate life. Then it requires some exertion and good will to *tolerate* it in spite of its strangeness, to be patient with its appearance and expression, and kindhearted about its oddity. Finally there comes a moment when we are *used* to it, when we wait for it, when we sense that we should miss it if it were missing; and now it continues to compel and enchant us relentlessly until we have become its humble and enraptured lovers who desire nothing better from the world than it and only it.

But that is what happens to us not only in music. That is how we have *learned to love* all things that we now love. . . . Even those who love themselves will have learned it in this way; for there is no other way. Love, too, has to be learned.[19]

Nietzsche contends that the Christian worldview and the scientific materialism that has in many quarters replaced it have both harmed our capacity for self-love, and therefore our capacity to love beyond ourselves. Nevertheless, he believes we can recover true love and with it the spirituality that was cultivated and promoted by Christianity (and other world religions). This means going beyond Christianity, but without thereby rejecting its inner truth, that the meaning of life is to be found in the enchantment of the world—but this world, our world, and not a heaven or a host beyond.

Nietzsche's
War on Morality

IN LILLIANA CALAVANI'S rather eccentric movie about Nietzsche, *Beyond Good and Evil,* the very charming mustached character who plays the leading role bursts out laughing in the midst of a dinner conversation, *"Morality——ha, ha!"* That captures as well as any "sound bite" could Nietzsche's often dismissive view of morality. But morality for Nietzsche was no laughing matter. He saw it as the ultimate and most successful expression of decadence and nihilism, no matter that the leading moralists would claim that it is only morality (with its accompanying religion) that protects us from the evil forces of decadence and nihilism.

But what exactly do we mean by *morality?* Before we go any further, it is important to make a careful distinction, between various moralit*ies,* that is, different "rank orders of value," and "Morality," in one particular sense that is characteristic of (but certainly not unique to) modern bourgeois society. The first sense of the word *morality,* as a genus in which there may be many species, is a concept in anthropology. Every culture, no matter how cosmopolitan or "primitive," no matter how single-minded or multicultural, has its values, its ideals, it taboos, its practical guidelines, its rules (which in some societies become laws). In this sense, to be human is to have a morality. Even a hermit, separated from society, necessarily lives according to some values (for example, maintaining solitude), ideals (perhaps personal enlightenment), taboos (don't eat the squirrels), practical guidelines (put enough wood on the fire before going to sleep), and even rules (sing every day at sunset). A morality is a collection of inherited, invented, or even instinctual practices (what Hegel famously called "*Sittlichkeit*"). As such, the concept contains no *specific* values, no concrete rules or prohibitions, no particular guidelines or philosophical orientation.

The second sense of the word (and we will continue to capitalize it, Morality, in this sense) is, by contrast, quite specific and particular, even if it is sometimes described in terms of very general, even "universal" rules or principles. The best-known illustration of such a formal code of Morality is the Decalogue, the Ten Commandments, delivered personally by God to Moses on Mount Sinai. They are quite specific. "Thou shalt not kill," "Thou shalt not steal," "Honor thy parents," and so on. They also have an authoritative source (namely, God himself) and a particular logical form (namely, as unconditional commands). Immanuel Kant captured this form in what he famously called "the Categorical Imperative." Kant denied that the necessity of Morality so conceived lies in its supposed Divine Origin and claimed it rather as a product of Practical Reason, but there is no doubt that what he is defending in the most sophisticated philosophical terminology is one and the same Morality that he learned as a pious child at his mother's knee.

It is this conception of Morality as something singular, as something categorical (as opposed to conditional on the particular circumstances and temperament of a people or a person), as something dictated by authority (whether by God or Practical Reason), as something largely prohibitive ("Thou shalt not . . . !") that Nietzsche rejects and against which he wages war. He does not—and this bears repeating—he *does not* in any way suggest or imply that we should feel free to kill or steal or go out of our way to offend or dishonor our parents. The attack on morality does not signify that "everything is permitted," and when Nietzsche presents himself as an "immoralist," we should not be misled by his schoolboy bravado. In his less flamboyant moments, he declares himself quite sensibly in favor of not only the customary virtues (courage, generosity, honesty) but even such a genteel virtue as courtesy. What Nietzsche rejects is neither moralities (in the general sense) nor the accepted rules of civilized behavior.

How, then, should we understand his war on morality? The watchword of Nietzsche's ethics comes, predictably, from the ancients, in this case from the Greek poet Pindar (522–438 B.C.E.). Nietzsche writes, over and over again, *"Become who you are!"* This sounds like an unhelpful, even vacuous, piece of moral advice, much like a parent's frustrating assurance to a confused teenager, "Just be yourself." In the case of the teenager, the problem is that it is just this self that is in question. But Nietzsche says "become," not "be," and in this small difference lies a whole philosophy. It is indeed the self that is in question, but not just a particular person's self-identity.

Each of us, Nietzsche says, has a unique set of virtues, but by thinking that what we really are is defined by a set of general rules or principles (categorical imperatives), we deny that uniqueness and sacrifice those virtues to the bland and anonymous category of "being a good person." It is not that Nietzsche wants to defend immorality but rather that he wants to defend the idea of human excellence that defines his ethics. We should become who we are—"Be all that you can be" to quote a recent U.S. Army recruiting slogan. And becoming our best generally (but not necessarily) leads us into agreement with the prohibitions of popular morality. ("Why should I steal when I can make it on my own?")

One way to understand Nietzsche's rejection of Morality is to put it in terms of a historical juxtaposition between two very different types of ethical theory. On the one hand, we have Kant, the exemplar of the moral philosopher who focuses on general rules and particular obligations. Kant proposed that we determine the morality of given actions on the basis of whether or not we could will that everyone act on them. If we could endorse the behavior in question as a general rule, then the action is morally acceptable. If not, if the generalization yields a logical contradiction, it is morally wrong. Kant argued that reason alone can determine right and wrong, and that the principles of morality are identical for all human beings.

On the other hand, we have Aristotle, an ancient philosopher who (like his teachers, Plato and Socrates) focused rather on individual excellence or virtue (*areté*). Aristotle never denied or ignored the social and political context in which excellence could be achieved. In fact, he assumed that it was only within certain social and political contexts that excellence could be achieved. ("To live a good life, one must live in a great city" was a platitude among the ancients.) But individual excellence is also defined by particular circumstances, by character, by one's role in society. And although the virtues can be generally described (courage, truthfulness, and so on), the focus, for Aristotle, remains on the individuals who exemplify and cultivate those virtues. General principles (for example, "Be courageous!") tend to be empty rhetoric. The proof is in one's behavior, not in the principles one follows or claims to follow.

Nietzsche, to put the matter simply, is more like Aristotle than like Kant. In contemporary terminology, he defends an ethics of virtue rather than an ethics of rational principles or obligations. (Aristotle defends a role for rational principles, but it is not obedience or respect for principles that motivates or justifies an action. So, too, the Greeks had a clear sense of *duty,* but duties followed from one's roles and responsibilities. They were not, as in Kant, derived from universal principles.) We should not take the comparison of Nietzsche and Aristotle too far, however. Nietzsche considered Aristotle, along with Socrates and Plato, to be "decadents," latecomers to the glory that was Greece. He accused them of nostalgically defending virtues that had already been lost in Athens, and, of course, he went much further than Aristotle in stressing the *uniqueness* of the individual.

Furthermore, while Nietzsche might have agreed that, ideally, a great society might be lush breeding ground for cultivating the virtues in its individual members, his own rejection of the society he lived in suggests that he separated individuality and community, virtue and good citizenship, in a way that would have horrified Aristotle. A philosophical hermit like

Nietzsche (and his fictional mouthpiece, Zarathustra) would have a better chance to develop his or her particular excellence when not enmired in bourgeois society. Indeed, being so enmired, thinking of oneself as a good citizen and following the general rules rather than one's own particular virtues, is what Nietzsche so often condemns as "*herd morality*," a morality for cows and not for creative human beings.

Master and Slave Morality

What Nietzsche sometimes condemns as "herd morality" he also describes as "slave morality," a morality fit for slaves and servants. Although there are strong suggestions of this view in some of Nietzsche's earlier works (*Daybreak* and *Human, All Too Human*), it is first fully stated in *Beyond Good and Evil,* and later more thoroughly worked out in *On the Genealogy of Morals.* In *Beyond Good and Evil* Nietzsche boldly announces that "wandering through the many subtler and coarser moralities which have so far been prevalent on earth . . . I finally discovered two basic types, . . . *master and slave morality.*" He immediately adds that these two usually intermingle and function together in all sorts of complex ways, and that they even coexist "within a *single* soul."[1] This simple dichotomy belies Nietzsche's own insistence on subtlety and complexity, to be sure, but in the *Genealogy* he makes it quite clear that what he is giving us is a "*polemic,*" an oversimplified but brutally thought-provoking way of looking at morality.

Morality, in the singular sense presented in the Bible and defended by Kant, is slave morality. In its most crude forms it consists of general principles imposed from above (by the rulers or by God) that yoke and constrain the individual. In its subtler and more sophisticated forms, that external authority is relocated internally—in the faculty of reason, for example. But what is most characteristic of Morality in either its crude or its sophisticated forms is that it is mainly prohibitive and constraining rather than inspiring. Kant may have been "awed" by "the Moral Law within," but the Categorical Imperative itself, as he spells it out in several general formulas, consists mainly of implicit "Thou shalt nots" ("Only act such that you would have others in the same circumstances act in the same way," "always treat people as ends and never as means only") The ultimate test of a maxim, according to Kant, is whether when universalized it is something that logically *cannot* be done. Nietzsche, of course, thinks that universalization is utterly irrelevant to virtue. Indeed, insofar as it can be universalized (or even generally described!) a virtue is diminished or destroyed.

Master morality, by contrast, is an ethics of virtue, an ethics in which personal excellence is primary. But personal excellence is not to be contrasted with (or set in opposition to) personal happiness, as obligation so often is. Achieving excellence is precisely what makes one happy, according to both Nietzsche and Aristotle. To grudgingly fulfill one's obligations, at some cost to one's own goals and satisfaction, makes one unhappy. (Righteousness is a poor substitute for happiness.) The "master" takes as his or her morality (in the anthropological sense) just those values, ideals, and practices that are personally preferable and suitable. The "master" is epitomized neither by the overly genteel Aristotelian gentleman nor by the overly brutal Homeric heroes but by the very civilized yet still sufficiently Dionysian Greeks of the Golden Age. Master morality takes as its watchword "Become who you are," and whether or not one turns out to be like anyone else, or even whether or not one is acceptable to others, are matters of no concern.

It is the masters, Nietzsche tells us, who establish the meaning of "good." The masters use this term to refer to what they see as admirable, desirable, satisfying, and, in fact, to refer to themselves. (The bombastic Roman general in the musical *A Funny Thing Happened on the Way to the Forum* sings out proudly. "I am my own ideal!") They thus recognize the distinction between what is good and what is bad, but the latter refers only to deficiencies of the good, what is frustrating or debilitating, to failure, or inadequacy, to what is *other* than themselves, their tastes, their virtues, and to others who fail or fall behind. No principles, rulers, or gods are necessary to make the distinction, which arises from the ideals and desires of the masters themselves. Putting it simply, one might summarize master morality as "being myself, and getting what I want," with the understanding that what one is and what one wants may be quite refined and noble. (To interpret "getting what I want" as an expression of *selfishness* reflects an impoverishment of desire, a sure sign of slave morality.) Not getting what one wants is bad, not necessarily in any larger sense (such as causing disastrous consequences for the community, or violating God's laws and inviting divine retribution) but simply because it falls short of one's own aspirations and ideals.

For the slaves, by contrast, getting what one wants is just too difficult, too unlikely, too implausible. Slaves do not like themselves, so the idea of becoming who you are is not particularly appealing. Slaves ultimately do not value getting what one wants but, in a perverse yet readily comprehensible sense, *not* getting what one wants. Their virtue lies not in being themselves but in *not* being the other, the master, the privileged, the oppressor. The masters see the slaves as pathetic, as miserable, as unhappy, both because they don't get what they want and because what they want is often so petty. But the slaves do not see themselves that way. They see themselves as *deprived*. They see themselves as *oppressed*. They see themselves, in modern terms, as *victims*. Nor do they see the masters as merely happy and fulfilled. The slaves see them as *oppressors,* as people with the wrong values, the wrong ideals, the wrong ideas about living.

Thus, in the long history of Morality there came about a most remarkable "revaluation of values," according to Nietzsche. First the ancient Hebrews, then the early Christians, turned master morality on its head, declaring that the very values and ideals that the masters took to be the heart of their ethics were in fact offensive, first to God, then secondarily to God's righteous believers. Getting what you want, rather than being the standard of ethics, is the root of all *evil*. In slave morality, the simple distinction between good and bad gets replaced by the *metaphysical* distinction between good and *evil*. The masters' distinction between good and bad simply refers to getting versus not getting what one wants, fulfilling versus not fulfilling one's aspirations. The slaves' distinction between good and evil refers, instead, to external and "objective" standards, God's will and principles of reason. Nietzsche sees in this reformulation of values an "act of . . . *spiritual revenge*":

It was the Jews who, with awe-inspiring consistency, dared to invert the aristocratic value-equation (good = noble = powerful = beautiful = happy = beloved of God) and to hang on to this inversion with their teeth, the teeth of the most abysmal hatred (the hatred of impotence), saying, "The wretched alone are the good; the suffering, deprived, sick, ugly alone are pious, alone are blessed by God . . . and you, the powerful and noble, are, on the contrary, the evil, the cruel, the lustful, the insatiable, the godless to all eternity, and you shall be in all eternity the unblessed, the accursed, and damned!"[2]

It is in contrast to the sometimes bloated pretensions of philosophy, theology, and metaphysical dogma that simple appeals to motives and emotion gain their force. In attacking Christianity and Judeo-Christian morality, Nietzsche does not remain on the same level of esoteric abstraction as his religious and moral antagonists. What he does instead is to *dig under them*. What could be more effective against the self-righteousness pronouncements of some philosophers and theologians than an *ad hominem* argument that undermines their credibility, that reduces their rationality and piety to petty personal envy or indignation? What could be more humiliating for a morality that incessantly preaches against selfishness and self-interest than the accusation that it is in fact not only the product of impotent self-interest but hypocritical as well? And what could be a more effective argument against theism than ridiculing the psychosociological ground out of which such a belief has arisen?

Such humiliation is Nietzsche's objective in his psychological guerrilla war against Christianity and Judeo-Christian bourgeois Morality. Nietzsche wants to shock us. He wants to offend us. He wants us to see through the rationalized surface of traditional Morality to its historical genealogy, the actual human beings who lie behind it. Like Hegel, his great misunderstood predecessor, he holds that one can truly understand a phenomenon only when one understands its origins, its development, and its overall place in human consciousness. But understanding a phenomenon, in this sense, does not always lead to further appreciation.

Nietzsche contends that what we call "Morality" originated among actual slaves, the miserable *Lumpenproletariat* of the ancient world (a term introduced by Marx to denote the lowest classes of society). Morality continues to be motivated by the servile and resentful emotions of those who are "poor in spirit" and feel themselves to be inferior. "Morality," however brilliantly rationalized by Immanuel Kant as the dictates of Practical Reason or by the utilitarian philosophers as "the greatest good for the greatest number," is, according to Nietzsche, essentially the devious strategy of the weak to gain some advantage (or at least minimize their disadvantage) vis-à-vis the strong. What we call Morality, even if it includes (indeed emphasizes) the sanctity of life, displays a palpable disgust for life, a "weariness" with life, an "otherworldly" longing that prefers some other, idealized existence to this one.

To describe this, of course, is not to "refute" the claims of Morality. Morality might still be, as Kant argued, the product of Practical Reason and as such a matter of universalized principles. Nietzsche concedes that it may in fact be conducive to the greatest good for the greatest number, the public good. But to recognize that such obsessions with rational principles and general welfare are products and symptoms of an underlying sense of inferiority is certainly to take the glamour and the seeming "necessity" out of Morality.

The great moral philosophers have given us visions of the perfect society (Plato), portraits of the happy, virtuous life (Aristotle), formal analyses of Morality (Kant), and impassioned defenses of the principles of utility and equality (Mill). Nietzsche, by contrast, offers us a diagnosis, in which morals emerge as something mean-spirited and pathetic. The basis of slave morality, he tells us, is resentment, a bitter emotion based on a sense of inferiority and frustrated vindictiveness. It is a thoroughly *reactive* emotion, provoked by the successes of others.

The contrast between slave morality and master morality ultimately comes down to this emotional difference: that the slave nurtures resentment until it "poisons" him, while the master, noble and self-secure, expresses his feelings and frustrations. Although Nietzsche sometimes writes like an anthropologist, describing two alternative "perspectives" on life, his continuous condemnation of resentment leaves little doubt as to which of the two "moral types" he finds preferable. Nietzsche's "genealogy" of morals is designed to make the novice reader uncomfortable with his or her own slavish attitudes, but it is also written to inspire a seductive sense of superiority, the urge to become a "master." These are dangerous attitudes, however, quite opposed to the edifying moral "uplift" we usually expect from ethical treatises.

Nietzsche's "genealogy" is, in fact, only partially a genealogy; it is much more a psychological diagnosis. It does include a very condensed and rather mythic account of the history and evolution of morals, but the heart of his account is a psychological hypothesis concerning the motives and mechanisms underlying that history and evolution. "The slave revolt in morality begins,"

Nietzsche tells us in *Genealogy*, "when *ressentiment* itself becomes creative and gives birth to values."[3]

Modern critics might well dismiss such speculation as yet another version of the "genetic fallacy." (That is, the question is not the genesis or the motivation of morals but rather the *validity* of our moral principles.) But even Kant himself insisted that one cannot evaluate the "moral worth" of an action without considering its intentions. An action performed out of noble sentiments is noble, even if the act itself is rather small and inconsequential. An action expressing vicious sentiments is vicious, even if the act itself turns out to have benign consequences. At least in part, ethics is made up of what one might generically call "feelings"—or, better, what Kant called the "inclinations"—which would include not only respect, a sense of duty, and the sweet (but suspicious) sentiments of sympathy and compassion, but also the nasty negative emotions of envy, anger, hatred, vengeance, and, especially, resentment.

The Many Faces of Resentment

Nietzsche's emphasis on nobility and resentment in his account of master and slave morality is an attempt to stress character, motivation, and virtue (and with them, tradition and culture) above all else in ethics. A master morality of nobility is an expression of good, strong character. An ethics of resentment is an expression of bad character—whatever its principles and their rationalizations. Nietzsche argues that Kantian universalizability and universal rules in general (for example, the

Ten Commandments) distract us from concrete questions of character.

Furthermore, such abstraction in morals provides not only a respectable façade for faulty character but an offensive weapon for resentment. Reason and resentment have proven themselves to be a well-coordinated team in the guerrilla war of everyday morality and moralizing. "A race of such men of *ressentiment* is bound to become eventually cleverer than any noble race; it will also honor cleverness to a far greater degree."[4] Similarly, Nietzsche submits,

> Suppose that . . . the meaning of all culture is the reduction of the beast of prey "man" to a tame and civilized animal, a *domestic animal,* then one would undoubtedly have to regard all those instincts of reaction and *ressentiment* through whose aid the noble races and their ideals were finally confounded and overthrown as the actual instruments of culture.[5]

Nietzsche insists that we overcome our childish, simplistic tendency to think of all valuation in terms of Manichean "opposite values," good and evil, but this rejection of "good and evil" does not entail the rejection of good and bad. There is the good life, well-lived, and there is the pathetic life, filled with resentment and impoverished in everything but its sense of its own righteousness.

The diagnosis of resentment and the pathology-laden language that surrounds slave morality tells us, in no uncertain terms, that slave morality is bad. So, too, master morality—albeit in refined and more artistic form, far from its primordial brutishness—is not only good but, in an important sense, natural. It does not depend for its value on God or gods or any transcendent realm. Yet however much he may have admired his uninhibited masters, Nietzsche realizes that "we cannot go back," that twenty centuries of Judeo-Christian morality have had their combined beneficial and deleterious effects. We have become more spiritual, more civilized, under the auspices of slave morality and Christianity. What we should aspire to, therefore, is no longer what Nietzsche described as "master morality," although it is notoriously unclear what his proposed "legislation" of morals for the future ought to look like. The *Übermensch* is clearly beyond us, and even the best of the "higher men" are still "human, all too human"—that is, caught up in the petty cycle of defensiveness and revenge. We seem to be both stuck in our slave morality and ready to transcend it.

Nevertheless, we can still distinguish between what is natural and noble and what is reactionary and born of *ressentiment*. Nietzsche makes it hard for us to avoid the uncomfortable acknowledgment that, yes, morality does protect the weak against the strong and, yes, it does sometimes seem to be the expression of resentment and, yes, it is often used to "put down" or "level" what is best in us in favor of the safe, the conformist, the comfortable. Given a masterly warrior perspective—the view that Nietzsche absorbed from the *Iliad*, and which so many American college students take away from Hollywood "action movies"—our everyday conception of morality does indeed seem limp and timid, conducive to civility perhaps but not to spontaneous self-expression, nobility, or heroism.

> While the noble man lives in trust and openness with himself . . . the man of *ressentiment* is neither upright nor naïve nor honest and straightforward with himself. His soul *squints*. . . .[6]

Although resentment is born of impotence, Nietzsche sees it as being concerned, even obsessed with *power*. It is not the same as self-pity, with which it often shares the subjective stage; it is not merely awareness of one's misfortune but involves a kind of blame and personal outrage, an outward projection, an overwhelming sense of injustice. But neither is it just a version of hatred or anger—with which it is sometimes conflated, for both of these presume an emotional and expressive power base, which resentment essentially lacks. Resentment is obsessive. "Nothing on earth consumes a man more quickly," Nietzsche tells us, yet his descriptions often employ terms denoting slow, lingering consumption, such as "smoldering," "simmering," "seething," and "fuming." Although quick to cause damage, resentment does not burn out.

Resentment is also notable among the emotions for its lack of any specific, positive desire. In this, it is not the same as envy—a kindred emotion—which has the advantage of being quite specific and based on desire. Envy wants, even if it cannot have and has no right to have. If resentment has a desire, it is the desire for revenge, but even this is rarely very specific. It often takes the form of an infantile nihilism, entertaining the abstract desire for the total annihilation of its target. So, too, resentment is quite different from spite, into which it occasionally degenerates, for resentment is nothing if not prudential, strategic, even ruthlessly clever. It has no taste at all for self-destruction; to the contrary, it is the ultimate emotion of self-preservation.

Resentment may be an emotion that begins with an awareness of its powerlessness, but by way of compensation, resentment has forged the perfect weapon—an acid tongue and a strategic awareness of the world, which provides parity if not victory in most social conflicts. Thus the irony, the dramatic reversal of fortunes, as defensive resentment overpowers defenseless self-confidence and the sense of inferiority overwhelms its superiors. The neo-Nietzschean stereotypes are too often portrayed in terms of the cultivated, noble master versus the miserable, illiterate slave, and the descriptions in Nietzsche's *Genealogy* certainly encourage such a reading. But the typology that counts in the genealogy of resentment and morals is the articulate slave and the tongue-tied, even witless, master. It is the slave who is sufficiently ingenious to do what Nietzsche wants to do; he or she invents new values. And it is the master, not the slave, who becomes decadent and dependent and allows him- or herself to be taken in by the strategies of resentment. Hegel had it right in the *Phenomenology of Spirit*: language may be the political invention of the "herd" (as Nietzsche suggests in *The Gay Science*) but it is also the medium in which real power is expressed and exchanged. Irony is the ultimate weapon of resentment, and as Socrates so ably demonstrated, it turns ignorance into power, personal weakness into philosophical strength. It is no wonder that Nietzsche had such mixed feelings about his predecessor in the weaponry of resentment who created the "tyranny of reason" as the successful expression of his own will to power. Nietzsche used irony and "genealogy" as Socrates used dialectic, to undermine and ultimately dominate others and their opinions.

Eagles and Lambs:
Metaphors of Strength and Weakness

What Nietzsche despises about resentment is its pathetic impotence, its weakness. But the criteria for strength and weakness are by no means obvious or consistent in Nietzsche, and it is not even obvious, for example, that weakness is a lack of strength. Sometimes, the descriptions in *Genealogy* suggest that social status and class alone determine strength and weakness; aristocrats, by virtue of their birth and education, are strong. Because of their servile role, slaves are weak, whatever physical or spiritual strength they might possess. Sometimes, Nietzsche seems to be using a quasi-medical ("physiological") criterion—*strong* means healthy, *weak* means sickly. But even this is by no means consistent, and some of what Nietzsche says would even imply that it is the slaves who are strong, not the masters.

More than anything else, Nietzsche seems to see strength and weakness in *aesthetic* terms, harking back, no doubt, to his famous injunction in *The Birth of Tragedy* that one should consider one's life as a work of art. Masters are a delight to behold; it would be even more of a delight to be one, to experience that sense of spontaneity and self-confidence. Slaves, to put it politely, are banal and boring. Their demeanor is servile and timid. They protect themselves with humorless, submissive smiles, without character. When their backs are turned, they snarl. It is Othello who provides the nobility in the play that bears his name. Iago provides the plot, by way of his scheming resentment. But then again, we should remember Simone

Weil's well-placed warning, "Imaginary evil is romantic and varied; real evil is gloomy, monotonous, barren, boring."[7] The banality of goodness on the stage is no argument against it.

What is "power"? What is "strength"? What is "weakness"? It is all too easy to think in Homeric warrior metaphors, the strength of an Odysseus or a Hercules, the broken servility of a captured slave. Of course, there were all of those Christian gladiators, and the Jews at Masada, and there were those several generations of effete and all-but-defenseless mutually resentful Roman emperors and aristocrats. (Poison isn't the weapon of choice for a warrior.) But physical and military prowess is not the "power" that Nietzsche is endorsing, and one of the most effective responses to Roman military might, it turned out, was the rather masterly practice of "turning the other cheek." In our own times, of course, we have seen the strategy of nonviolent "passive resistance" practiced by Gandhi and Martin Luther King, Jr.

The metaphors Nietzsche most often uses in talking about strength are medical metaphors, health and sickliness, "physiological" images. Master morality is healthy; slave morality is sickly. Strength as health is clearly a personal and not a competitive virtue. It has much to do with one's metabolic fund of energy, expressed in a spontaneity that is not so much thoughtless or carefree as robust. Weakness as sickliness is above all a lack of energy, a lethargy caused by exhaustion. But Nietzsche's vision here is often of a very different kind, and it is not health as such but the response to ill-health that is the measure of strength. His famous comment that "what does not overcome me makes me stronger" is emblematic of a certain way of thinking about strength and heroism. One need not speculate or search very far for the personal origins of Nietzsche's concern about health and his rather complex conceptions of the proper response to illness. Nietzsche's own response to his debilitating infirmities was a muscular and aggressive prose, full of vitality, displaying a strength that only the strongest souls can fully comprehend.

One of the most bothersome features of *Genealogy*, even to those who are wholly persuaded by its characterization of "slave morality," is Nietzsche's apparent determinism, as if people are the way they are, and there is little that they can do to change. In this, Nietzsche is starkly at odds with existentialists such as Kierkegaard and Sartre. Personal choice is severely limited by "who we are." Thus he is bitterly sarcastic toward "the 'improvers' of mankind."[8] His analogy of eagles and lambs says explicitly that the difference between the strong and the weak is one of basic biology, not a matter of choice:

> That lambs dislike great birds of prey does not seem strange: only it gives no ground for reproaching these birds of prey for bearing off little lambs. And if the lambs say among themselves: "these birds of prey are evil; and whoever is least like a bird of prey, but rather its opposite, a lamb—would he not be good?" there is no reason to find fault with this institution of an ideal, except perhaps that the birds of prey might view it a little ironically and say: "*we* don't dislike them at all, these good little lambs; we even love them: nothing is more tasty than a tender lamb."[9]

Indeed, at the end of that section, in which Nietzsche is centrally concerned with resentment and the "revaluation of values," he argues that one is not responsible for one's predatory ways, any more than one is responsible for one's weaknesses. That one is responsible and capable of change is an illusion fostered by centuries of Christianity, and more recently by Kant. That view of responsibility in turn justifies the vindictiveness of resentment and the harshness of moral judgments of blame.

> [N]o wonder if the submerged, darkly glowering emotions of vengefulness and hatred exploit this belief [in the Kantian subject] for their own ends and in fact maintain no belief more ardently than the belief that *the strong man is free* to be weak and the bird of prey to be a lamb—for thus they gain the right to make the bird of prey *accountable* for being a bird of prey.[10]

Nietzsche's peculiar brand of fatalism, *amor fati,* is not the same as determinism. It represents a carefree, nonjudgmental attitude, even "a bold recklessness"—something Nietzsche clearly envied. It emerges philosophically in his denial and mockery of "free will" and in his rather restricted insistence on the cultivation of the virtues. His famous instruction "Become who you are" has been read (and read well) as an "existential imperative," and it has been read (equally well) as a mode of discovery and reinterpretation. The dominant impression Nietzsche gives—at least in *Genealogy*—is that one can do very little to change one's basic being, much less to "improve mankind." In particular, whether one is strong and noble or weak and pathetic is not a choice of existential options but a kind of "given," in terms of one's social origins and upbringing, and resides at the core of one's character, perhaps even in one's genes. As he puts it in *Genealogy,* an eagle can no more become a lamb than a lamb can become an eagle. But it is clear to whom Nietzsche is addressing his supposedly neutral descriptions: not to the lambs but to the readers who identify with the "master"-type and suffer from "bad conscience." For them, reading Nietzsche can be a liberating experience.

5

Nietzsche *Ad Hominem*
(Nietzsche's "Top Ten")

ALTHOUGH NIETZSCHE spent most of his career in solitude, he was not one of those hermetic thinkers whose universe wholly consisted of a lonely self with grandiose ideas. He was in the constant company of the great (and some not-so-great) thinkers of his times and of the past. He knew them only through their words, through books and reports, but he was actively engaged with them, even if the engagement was decidedly one-sided. Although he was certainly no "humanist" in the usual sense, Nietzsche delighted in understanding and writing about other people. His most brilliant and biting comments, observations and essays involve a keen insight into people, both as individuals and as types. He wondered what made people "tick," and he rightly suspected that what they thought and said about themselves and their ideals was almost always misleading, mistaken, or just plain fraudulent. In *Ecce Homo* he wrote that "a psychologist without equal speaks from my writings,"[1] but this claim has not always been taken as seriously as it ought to be. Philosophical doctrines carry a strong sense of universality and necessity, while psychological analyses remain inevitably bound to the particular contingencies of a personality or a people. But Nietzsche was suspicious of claims to universality and necessity, and he almost always preferred the witty or dazzling or even offensive psychological insight to the grand philosophical thesis, for example, his comment that Socrates was ugly,[2] that Kant was decadent,[3] that moral leaders are resentful,[4] and "How much *beer* there is in the German intelligence!"[5]

Nietzsche saw himself as a *diagnostician,* and his philosophy consists to a very large extent of speculative diagnoses, concerning the virtues and vices of those whom he read and read about, whose influence determined the temper of the times. His central strategy, accordingly, was the use of the *ad hominem* argument, a rhetorical technique often dismissed as a "fallacy," an attack on the character, the motives, and the emotions of his interlocuters rather than a refutation of their ideas as such. Of Socrates, he writes, "[W]e can still see for ourselves, how ugly he was. But ugliness, in itself an objection, is among the Greeks almost a refutation."[6] Such *ad hominem* arguments pervade Nietzsche's writings. Indeed, much more of Nietzsche's work is devoted to his "skirmishes" with other thinkers than we are usually led to believe, and one might well plot the course of his philosophy by tracing it through his various comments, caustic and otherwise, about other people. With that in mind, we decided to present a short catalogue of those figures on whom Nietzsche lavished the most (though not always the most flattering) attention.

Many years ago, Crane Brinton organized his early book

about Nietzsche under the twin titles, "What Nietzsche Loved" and "What Nietzsche Hated." To be sure, Nietzsche would disapprove of such dichotomous thinking; nevertheless, it is hard to think of this most passionate thinker without thinking in such personal and vehement emotional terms. Nietzsche loved and hated throughout his career—mainly people he knew only through their writings. And to make matters ever more complicated, he both loved and hated some of the same people. The phrase "mixed feelings" has never been more appropriately employed than to describe Nietzsche's attitudes toward his closest competitors, particularly Socrates, who was (at one and the same time) both Nietzsche's role model and nemesis.

So here are Nietzsche's two "Top Ten" lists, the first his favorites, his role models, his heroes; the second, those he attacked and sometimes despised. Our strategy follows that of Nietzsche's own occasional groupings of "exemplary men." Our task is complicated by the fact that Nietzsche is prone to bursts of enthusiasm that suddenly disappear without a trace. For instance, in an early essay he says of Montaigne, "I know of only one writer whom I would compare with Schopenhauer, indeed set above him, in respect of honesty: Montaigne."[7] But immediately afterward, Montaigne virtually disappears from Nietzsche's view. Schopenhauer, of course, works his way from the "best" list to the "worst" list in the space of a few short years. Despite these peculiarities of his assessments, here are Nietzsche's "best" and "worst."

NIETZSCHE'S "TOP TEN"

The Best:

Socrates	Dostoyevsky
Zarathustra	Emerson
Spinoza	Homer
Goethe	Jesus
Wagner	Shakespeare
Kant	Sophocles
Schopenhauer	

Runners-up:

Apollo	Heine
Dionysus	Thucydides
Luther	Darwin

NIETZSCHE'S "BOTTOM TEN"

The Worst:

Socrates	Descartes
Plato	Luther
Saint Paul	Mill
Wagner	Carlyle
Kant	Euripides
Schopenhauer	

Runners-up:

Hegel	God
Darwin	

The Best

SOCRATES (CA. 470–399 B.C.E.)

To say that Nietzsche admired Socrates may seem rather surprising, in light of the fact that he devotes much of *The Birth of Tragedy* and several long sections of his later works to criticizing him. In *Birth* he accuses Socrates of "murdering tragedy." In his essay "The Problem of Socrates"—in *Twilight of the Idols,* one of his last books—he declared Socrates to be no less than an enemy of life itself. Nevertheless, Nietzsche saw Socrates as one of the decisive figures of Western thought, and this is evident even in his first book. He describes Socrates as "the one turning point . . . of world history," suggesting that Socrates saved humanity from extinction.

> For if we imagine that the whole incalculable sum of energy used up . . . had been used *not* in the service of knowledge, . . . universal wars of annihilation and continual migrations of peoples would probably have weakened the instinctive lust for life to such an extent that suicide would have become a general custom and individuals might have experienced the final remnant of a sense of duty when . . . they strangled their parents and friends. . . .[8]

And then, ". . . it must now be said how the influence of Socrates . . . again and again prompts a regeneration of art."[9]

To understand Nietzsche's mixed feelings about Socrates, one thing we should do is distinguish between Socrates and Socratism (much as one might distinguish between Jesus and Christianity, between Marx and Marxism). Socrates as a person is perhaps Nietzsche's closest companion, from his first writings to his last: "Socrates, to confess it frankly, is so close to me that almost always I fight a fight against him."[10] But this intimacy, when it does not breed contempt, often warrants ridicule. "A married philosopher belongs *in comedy.* . . . [T]he malicious Socrates, it would seem, married *ironically* just to demonstrate *this* proposition."[11] Socratism, by contrast, is the commitment to relying on reason to a degree that Nietzsche considers absurd. Socratism, with its preference for abstract categories that are much more orderly than our experience, also tends toward Platonism, the judgments that life on earth is deficient and that perfection must be sought in another realm. Nietzsche had many harsh words for both of these ideologies. (Socrates is known to us primarily through Plato's dialogues, in which he is the primary protagonist. Although the Socrates of the dialogues is modeled on the historical Socrates [Plato's real teacher], Plato probably extrapolated beyond the original Socrates' teachings when he made his *character* Socrates a spokesman for his own ideas. Nietzsche sometimes takes pains to distinguish Socrates and Plato. However, the two thinkers' views are related, and at various times they both defend positions that Nietzsche attacks.)

Nietzsche (like Hegel before him) delighted in comparing Socrates to Jesus, predictably to the detriment of Jesus:

> Above the founder of Christianity, Socrates is distinguished by the gay kind of seriousness and that wisdom full of pranks which constitutes the best state of the soul of man. Moreover, he had the greater intelligence."[12]

It is amply clear, reading through Nietzsche's many comments about Socrates, that his primary attitude toward the great unpublished Greek thinker was *envy*. But envy is in itself something of a mixed emotion, combining grudging admiration with resentment. Nietzsche envied Socrates' remarkable influence, both in antiquity and throughout the long history of Western philosophy. He envied Socrates' talent for attracting and mesmerizing students. He also envied Socrates' ability to refuse discipleship and the fact that he so successfully forced his students to think for themselves. He even envied Socrates for his buffoonery. How Nietzsche would have loved to share in that *joie de vivre,* and how ironic that Nietzsche's harshest accusation should be that Socrates hated life.

ZARATHUSTRA (628–551 B.C.E)

Nietzsche's book *Thus Spoke Zarathustra* features the famous Persian prophet Zarathustra, or Zoroaster. Nietzsche's choice of Zarathustra as his primary spokesman is often considered a bit capricious. Nietzsche preaches against the twin concepts of good and evil that Zarathustra introduced into Western religion and philosophy. Thus the use of Zarathustra is in part ironic.

However, Nietzsche knew and thought a good deal about the Persian prophet and his teachings, and he himself commented on his readers' failure to consider his relationship to the ancient philosopher:

I have not been asked, as I should have been asked, what the name of Zarathustra means in my mouth . . . Zarathustra was the first to consider the fight of good and evil the very wheel in the machinery of things: the transposition of morality into the metaphysical realm, as a force, cause, and end in itself, is his work. But this question itself is at bottom its own answer. Zarathustra created this most calamitous error, morality; consequently, he must also be the first to recognize it. Not only has he more experience in this matter, for a longer time, than any other thinker . . . what is more important is that Zarathustra is more truthful than any other thinker. . . . The self-overcoming of morality, out of truthfulness; the self-overcoming of the moralist into his opposite—into me—that is what the name of Zarathustra means in my mouth.[13]

Nietzsche suggests that Zarathustra's great achievement was not making the particular distinction between good and evil, but to embark on the *process* of making such discernments. Being subtle and honest, Zarathustra would have moved beyond his own dichotomy of good and evil. Unfortunately, as Nietzsche sees it, Zarathustra's descendants—adherents of the great religions of the West—latched on to his moral categories and used them moralistically. They failed to follow Zarathustra in the practice of examining and reexamining one's situation and formulating new distinctions.

Yet in his own time, claims Nietzsche, Zarathustra's morality has reached a point of self-overcoming. The honesty that drove Zarathustra and continued to be cultivated in subsequent religious traditions has led to the death of God and the current crisis of values. Zarathustra has evolved into the opposite of a moralist—into Nietzsche himself! Zarathustra, in other words, is more than a fictional spokesman for Nietzsche. He is a true kindred spirit.

BARUCH SPINOZA (1632–1677)

One might think that Spinoza, a heterodox Jew whose philosophy was dedicated to the love of God and who wrote in the most inelegant, geometrical style, would be as far from Nietzsche as any philosopher of modern times. And yet, in a postcard to a friend in 1881, at the height of his powers, he enthusiastically declared:

> I am utterly amazed, utterly enchanted! I have a *precursor,* and what a precursor! I hardly knew Spinoza: that I should have turned to him just *now,* was inspired by "instinct." Not only is his over-all tendency like mine—namely to make knowledge the *most powerful* affect—but in five main points of his doctrine I recognize myself; this most unusual and loneliest thinker is closest to me precisely in *these* matters: he denies the freedom of the will, teleology, the moral world order, the unegoistic, and evil. Even though the divergences are admittedly tremendous, they are due more to the difference in time, culture, and science. *In summa*: my lonesomeness . . . is now at least a twosomeness.[14]

Nietzsche reaffirms this judgment in other contexts. "When I speak of Plato, Pascal, Spinoza, and Goethe, then I know that their blood rolls in mine."[15] And once again, he lists "my ancestors: *Heraclitus, Empedocles, Spinoza, Goethe.*"[16] Although he was not always generous toward his precursors, Nietzsche describes Spinoza as "the purest sage"[17] and a genius,[18] his work is "a passionate history of a soul"[19] written in a "simple and sublime" manner.[20]

These two lonely, exiled philosophers do share a surprising number of outlooks in common, several of which Nietzsche mentions in the longer passage above. Spinoza, like Nietzsche, also celebrates (what Nietzsche calls) *amor fati,* "the love of fate." Elsewhere Nietzsche recognizes another commonality between Spinoza and himself, their repudiation of pity.

> For this overestimation of and predilection for pity on the part of modern philosophers is something new: hitherto philosophers have been at one as to the *worthlessness* of pity. I name only Plato, Spinoza, La Rochefoucauld, and Kant—four spirits as different from one another as possible, but united in one thing: in their low estimation of pity.[21]

Even theologically, Nietzsche sees the thinker as his compatriot, for he thinks that his theology commits Spinoza to denying the legitimacy of guilt and moral condemnation. In a note, Nietzsche contends that Spinoza's "rejection of moral value judgments . . . was one consequence of his theodicy!"[22] In *Genealogy* Nietzsche suggests that Spinoza himself was aware that he had little room in his philosophy for "the sting of conscience," even though he wanted to maintain it.

> [T]eased by who knows what recollection, he mused on the question of what really remained to him of the famous *morsus conscientiae* [the sting of conscience]—he who had banished good and evil to the realm of human imagination and had wrathfully defended the honor of his "free" God against those blasphemers who asserted that God effected all things *sub ratione boni* [for a good reason] ("but that would mean making God subject to fate and would surely be the greatest of all

absurdities"). The world, for Spinoza, had returned to the state of innocence in which it had lain before the invention of the bad conscience. . . .[23]

Nietzsche's enthusiasm, of course, is not unqualified. Spinoza's description of making peace with fate, which he describes as "the intellectual love of God," strikes Nietzsche as too abstract in tenor to do justice to real lived experience. Nietzsche considers this an example of a common problem in Western thought, philosophical "vampirism": "[W]hat was left of Spinoza, *amor intellectualis dei,* is mere clatter and no more than that: What is *amor,* what *deus,* if there is not a drop of blood in them?"[24]

JOHANN WOLFGANG VON GOETHE (1749–1832)

Nietzsche is hardly alone among his contemporaries in considering Goethe one of the luminaries of German culture, but he surpasses most of them in his enthusiastic praise.

Goethe—not a German event, but a European one: a magnificent attempt to overcome the eighteenth century by a return to nature, by an *ascent* to the naturalness of the Renaissance. . . . He bore its strongest instincts within himself . . . he disciplined himself, he *created* himself.[25]

Goethe is the last German for whom I feel any reverence.[26]

Johann Wolfgang von Goethe, who died a dozen years before Nietzsche was born, was the exemplary figure of the German man of letters. As a young poet, he became well known as one of the *"Sturm und Drang"* generation, defending a new humanism in Germany. A follower of Herder, he became an ardent defender of German culture. He served as a government minister, practiced law, traveled widely, published popular novels (*The Sorrows of Young Werther*), inspired romanticism, retreated to classicism, and in his last decades composed the greatest literary work in the German language, his man-meets-devil play, *Faust.* He was, perhaps, Nietzsche's only real rival for genius-level mastery of the language, and his multicareer life and many-genre writings surely appealed to Nietzsche's perspectivism and his view that one should say yes to life. Nietzsche also saw Goethe as one of those rare figures who was consciously setting the stage for the future, a European and not merely German future. Among the many figures Nietzsche cites as examples of "higher men," Goethe is mentioned most often (by far). If there were to be a German *Übermensch,* Goethe would be the top candidate.

But as so often, Nietzsche shows his admiration by making a target of Goethe—mainly by directing humorous barbs at the concept "the Eternal Feminine," Goethe's principle of feminine purity that provided salvation to the protagonist of his play *Faust.* Zarathustra's speech about the poets, discussed above in chapter 2, includes some quips about this formulation. Pursuing the theme that the poets lie too much, Zarathustra remarks that

". . . *we* do lie too much. We also know too little and we are bad learners; so we simply have to lie. And who among us poets has not adulterated his wine? . . . And because we know so little, the poor in spirit please us heartily, particularly when they are young females. And we are covetous even of those things which the old females tell each other in the evening. That is what we ourselves call the Eternal-Feminine in us. . . . When they feel tender sentiments stirring, the poets always fancy that nature herself is in love with them. . . ."[27]

But this is very mild criticism, particularly coming from Nietzsche. Zarathustra's criticism is blunted by his inclusion of himself among the besotted. Moreover, the target of Zarathustra's sarcasm is probably not Goethe but the vision that the German populace had in mind when it took up the expression "Eternal-Feminine." This term was used to endorse a prudish ideal of women's social role, typified by some very smug and empty women who considered themselves the "saving grace" of of their husbands, according to Carol Diethe. She points out that Goethe was similarly critical of this ideal and "levelled his own critique at society by making the outcast child-murderess Gretchen his ideal," an irony "lost on a society obsessed with its own need to divide women into categories as 'Eves' and 'Madonnas.' "[28] The only sense in which Nietzsche criticizes Goethe himself is that he popularized a term that ultimately became a weapon in the hands of self-righteous prigs.

RICHARD WAGNER (1813–1883)

Perhaps the best-known hero in Nietzsche's life—and his best-known target—was Richard Wagner, the great opera composer. From Wagner, Nietzsche probably absorbed more than he acknowledged, despite his insistence on his gratitude. The tremendous freedom with which Wagner reworked historical materials and advanced modern mythology, the search for perfect devotion that provided his leading theme, the vast scope of Wagnerian opera—all these were inspiring to the young philosopher. It was also through Wagner that Nietzsche deepened his appreciation for Schopenhauer, and it is not coincidental that he ultimately rejected both men at about the same time. Yet even long after Nietzsche's disillusionment with the composer, he still praised Wagner's psychological savvy. Nietzsche opens *Nietzsche contra Wagner* with a passage from *The Gay Science,* which he now entitles, "Where I Admire."

> There is a musician who, more than any other musician, is a master at finding the tones in the realm of suffering, depressed, and tortured souls, at giving language to every mute misery. . . . He draws most happily of all out of the profoundest depth of human happiness, and, as it were, out of its drained goblet, where the bitterest and most repulsive drops have finally and evilly run together with the sweetest . . . Wagner is one who has suffered deeply—that is his distinction above other musicians. I admire Wagner wherever he puts himself into music.[29]

Similarly, he comments in *Ecce Homo*: "I think I know better than anyone else of what tremendous things Wagner is capable—the fifty worlds of alien ecstasies for which no one besides him had wings. . . . I call Wagner the great benefactor of my life."[30]

IMMANUEL KANT (1724–1804)

In his first book, *The Birth of Tragedy,* Nietzsche described Immanuel Kant (along with Schopenhauer as "tragic" and as having "tremendous courage and wisdom."[31] In *The Gay Science* Nietzsche praises *"Kant's* tremendous question mark that he placed after the concept of causality."[32] Although Nietzsche often castigates Kant in the harshest terms, there is no denying Kant's greatness or stature in the world of German thought. He had a profound influence on Goethe and Schopenhauer, two of Nietzsche's early heroes, and it was said then (as it is still said now) that no philosophy following Kant could possibly avoid the monumental arguments of his three great *Critiques,* in which the whole of human reason had been mapped out and boldly defended.

As perhaps the most original and illustrious philosopher that Germany had ever produced, Kant attracted Nietzsche's admiration. But put his views together with the fact that he had a reputation as a rather bourgeois professor and a good citizen and civil servant with pedestrian tastes in art, and Kant provides an excellent target for some of Nietzsche's most vicious attacks. We will consider the specific Kantian views that inspire Nietzsche's ire in our account below of Kant as a target.

ARTHUR SCHOPENHAUER (1788–1860)

Nietzsche discovered Arthur Schopenhauer's philosophy while he was still attending the university, and Schopenhauer was the topic of one of his *Untimely Meditations*. Although Nietzsche ultimately turned on Schopenhauer, he never really shook off the Schopenhauerian view of the world, and some of its components remain at the center of Nietzsche's philosophy. The will to power, for example, is unmistakably presented as a variation on Schopenhauer's Will, particularly when Nietzsche speculates that the Will (to power) is the drive behind all living things, even the world.[33]

Schopenhauer postulated that the world "in itself" that Kant had theorized is a dynamic, unruly force that manifested itself in the world of our experience. This fundamental reality, the will, is in continual conflict with itself, and this conflict is manifested in the tensions among phenomenal entities, evident in the food chain as well as war and hostility. (Although Nietzsche's conception of will to power resembles Schopenhauer's Will in certain respects, Nietzsche presents this notion as an improvement on Schopenhauer's idea, as we will discuss below, in chapter 7.)

Inevitably, according to Schopenhauer, beings within the world suffer, for they are expressions of a suffering will. Human beings suffer not only by virtue of being in tension with other beings, but also because their lives are a series of desires, each of which seems important while one is conscious of it but becomes unimportant when fulfilled. Aesthetic experience, the contemplation of beauty and awesome forces in the world, provides occasional respites for the turmoil caused by our desires, but these are just temporary. The only ultimate end to suffering in life is an inner act of resignation, a conscious decision based on one's intellectual awareness that pursuing one's desires is unfulfilling. Although resignation solves the problem, this route is rarely taken. The only ones who silence the will within themselves through resignation are the great saints of every tradition.

Schopenhauer was no saint. He was a lively, sometimes overly aggressive man with strong passions and strong dislikes. Nietzsche's vehement *ad hominem*s are modeled on Schopenhauer's prose. Nietzsche admired Schopenhauer's cantakerousness, his independence of thought, his willingness to go against the grain of the then prevalent German idealism (although, technically, he still fell within its territory). In particular, Nietzsche admired Schopenhauer's atheism, his willingness to construct a worldview that took blind impulse, not a benign God, as the cause of the world. "This is the locus of his whole integrity; unconditional and honest atheism is simply the *presupposition* of the way he poses his problem. . . . *Schopenhauer's* question immediately comes to us in a terrifying way: *Has existence any meaning at all?* It will require a few centuries before this question can even be heard completely and in its full depth."[34]

FYODOR DOSTOYEVSKY (1821–1881)

Nietzsche is effusive in his praise for Fyodor Dostoyevsky, whom he describes as "the only psychologist. . . . from whom I had something to learn." Nietzsche claims "he ranks among the most beautiful strokes of fortune in my life. . . ." He applauds Dostoyevsky, "this *profound* human being," for his discovery among Siberian convicts that they were "very different from what he himself had expected: they were carved out of just about the best, hardest, and most valuable wood that grows anywhere on Russian soil."[35]

Nietzsche seems clearly to have read *Notes from Underground* and *The Idiot*. Walter Kaufmann, the scholar responsible for rescuing Nietzsche from his reputation as a proto-Nazi in the English-speaking world, suggests that Nietzsche's vision of Jesus owes something to Dostoyevsky's characterization of Prince Mishkin, the "idiot" of the novel of that name.[36] Similarities in portrayal also suggest that Nietzsche may have had

Raskolnikov, the antihero of *Crime and Punishment,* in mind when he wrote the sketch called "The Pale Criminal," which appears in the first part of *Thus Spoke Zarathustra*. Kaufmann points out, however, that this sketch appeared in 1883, yet Nietzsche reports to Overbeck in a letter of February 23, 1887, that he had only just discovered Dostoyevsky. We might also add, as tragic irony, that Nietzsche's final collapse in Turin, his hugging of the horse being beaten, is reminiscent of Raskolnikov's dream of similarly protecting a horse in *Crime and Punishment.*

RALPH WALDO EMERSON (1803–1882)

Ralph Waldo Emerson is the only American to make the list. Although philosophically one of the "Transcendentalists" and the heir of Kant and Hegel, Emerson was also a powerful voice for American individualism. His essay "Self-Reliance" had already become one of the most celebrated pieces of American nonfiction and obviously struck Nietzsche's fancy as well. Emerson is Nietzsche's precursor in directing attention to the historical Zarathustra (or Zoroaster). Some of Nietzsche's most renowned ideas were developed from important themes in Emerson's essay, such as the "over-soul" (which Kaufmann observes is reconfigured in Nietzsche's *"Übermensch"*), self-reliance, Emerson's "Joyous Science" (which may have been a factor in Nietzsche's titling his book *The Gay Science*), the importance of attending to the details of one's experiences, the cyclical rhythms of time, and even the death of God. Emerson's "Divinity School Address" includes such passages as,

> Men have come to speak of the revelation as somewhat long ago given and done, as if God were dead. . . . [37]

and

> We have contrasted the Church with the Soul. In the soul,
> then, let the redemption be sought. . . . The stationariness of
> religion; the assumption that the age of inspiration is past, that
> the Bible is closed; the fear of degrading the character of Jesus
> by representing him as a man; indicate with sufficient clearness
> the falsehood of our theology.[38]

Like Nietzsche, Emerson had religious motives for rejecting
orthodox theology. Perhaps this is the most fundamental reason
for Nietzsche's enthusiasm for the Transcendentalist.

HOMER (NINTH CENTURY B.C.E.)

Nietzsche no doubt knew as much as anyone about the great
ninth-century poet and epic storyteller, and it is evident that the
Iliad and the *Odyssey,* Homer's famous "children" (as Socrates
calls them in the *Symposium*) are never far from Nietzsche's
mind and mythology.

JESUS (CA. 6 B.C.E.–30 C.E.)

Nor is Jesus ever far from Nietzsche's mind. Together with
Socrates, the first (and Nietzsche says "only"[39]) Christian provided the paradigm that Nietzsche sought to follow throughout
his career—not just a philosopher, not just a moralist, but a
true revolutionary, a voluptuary, a sterling example (if only for
"the few").

WILLIAM SHAKESPEARE (1564–1616)

Nietzsche finds Shakespeare an intriguing psychological case, as well as a psychologist of remarkable sensitivity and courage. He remarks in *Ecce Homo*, "I know no more heart-rending reading than Shakespeare: what must a man have suffered to find it so very necessary to be a buffoon?"[40] Nietzsche particularly admires Shakespeare's willingness to probe the full range of human character without compromising his vision to pacify moral sensibilities. In this respect, Nietzsche identifies with Shakespeare, whom he took to share many of his own insights about the tragic dimensions of human experience. Of the playwright's *Julius Caesar* he remarks,

> I could not say anything more beautiful in praise of Shakespeare *as a human being* than this: he believed in Brutus and did not cast one speck of suspicion upon this type of virtue. It was to him that he devoted his best tragedy—it is still called by the wrong name—to him and to the most awesome quintessence of a lofty morality. Independence of the soul!—that is at stake here. No sacrifice can be too great for that: one must be capable of sacrificing one's dearest friend for it, even if he should also be the most glorious human being, an ornament of the world, a genius without peer—if one loves freedom as the freedom of great souls and he threatens this kind of freedom. That is what Shakespeare must have felt.[41]

Similarly, Nietzsche envisions Shakespeare as having the kind of insight that he described as Dionysian.

> In this sense the Dionysian man resembles Hamlet: both have
> once looked truly into the essence of things, they have gained
> knowledge and nausea inhibits action; for their action could
> not change anything in the external nature of things. . . . Con-
> scious of the truth he has once seen, man now sees everywhere
> only the horror or absurdity of existence . . . he is nauseated.[42]

Shakespeare combines this Dionysian insight with the Apollonian power to create beauty through his plays. In this respect,
Shakespeare manifests the rare achievement that Nietzsche
attributes to the greatest Greek tragedies, of wedding the
Dionysian and Apollonian principles in works that grappled
with the meaning of life.

The depth of Nietzsche's admiration for Shakespeare is evident in Zarathustra's speech "On Poets," where he alludes to the
playwright in a way that contrasts with his lampoon of Plato considered above. "Alas, there are so many things between heaven
and earth of which only the poets have dreamed."[43] The line
recalled is Hamlet's to his Stoic friend, Horatio: "There are more
things in heaven and earth, Horatio, / Than are dreamt of in your
philosophy."[44] Zarathustra's comment is a tribute to Shakespeare
at Plato's expense. While Plato considered philosophy superior
to poetry, Zarathustra suggests just the opposite when he alludes
to Shakespeare. He implies that the Bard was a seer who recognized much that the West's great philosophers fail to notice.

SOPHOCLES (496–406 B.C.E.)

In Nietzsche's eyes, Sophocles was the most illustrious of
ancient Greece's three great tragedians (Aeschylus and Euripi-

des being the other two). Sophocles is best known for his three Theban plays, *Oedipus the King, Oedipus at Colonus,* and *Antigone.* Nietzsche admires Sophocles for many of the same reasons he admires Shakespeare. Sophocles was willing to look into the abyss of the human soul, and to respect the nobility of those individuals who do not operate within the conventional moral sphere, and whose destiny is therefore tragic.

> Sophocles understood the most sorrowful figure of the Greek stage, the unfortunate Oedipus, as the noble human being. . . . The noble human being does not sin, the profound poet wants to tell us: though every law, every natural order, even the moral world may perish through his actions, his actions also produce a higher magical circle of effects which found a new world on the ruins of the old one that has been overthrown. That is what the poet wants to say to us insofar as he is at the same time a religious thinker.[45]

Somewhat surprisingly, Nietzsche contrasts morality and religion in this passage. The moral order, particularly as it is articulated in the Christian schema, attempts to rationalize abominable suffering, usually as something deserved as a consequence of sin. Nietzsche finds this "moral" interpretation of suffering hideous, treating the cruelest fates as simple matters of moral bookkeeping. Sophocles' vision, by contrast, involves an outlook that Nietzsche associates with sincere religious reflection on the problem of evil. Such reflection is characterized by a humane and respectful attitude toward those who suffer, and a sense of the nobility of suffering human beings, who can love their lives despite the pain involved. Nietzsche sees Sophocles as one who took such an extramoral perspective on humanity and as an exemplary because he was profoundly humane.

Runners-up

APOLLO (IMMORTAL)

One is hard put to list mythological figures as personal heroes, but given Nietzsche's lack of interpersonal intimacy with virtually all of his favorite figures, one might say that the Greek gods were as close to him as most of his flesh-and-blood contemporaries. Apollo, the Greek god of flocks, healing, justice, music, archery, and light, figures centrally in Nietzsche's first book, *The Birth of Tragedy*, and the "Apollonian" remains a paradigm for him throughout his career. To be sure, Nietzsche is better known for his celebration of Dionysus, and it is Dionysus he identifies with toward the end of his life; but it would be a mistake to think that he thereby rejects Apollo, or more generally the ideals of clarity and precision. It is the Apollonian *in balance with* the Dionysian that is responsible for the greatness of Greek tragedy.

DIONYSUS (IMMORTAL)

Dionysus was the Greek god and inventor of wine, a substance often celebrated but rarely touched by Nietzsche. He surrounded himself with maenads ("wild women" in more colloquial English) and was famed for his orgiastic rites. Dionysiac (Orphic) cults were numerous in early Greece and had a significant influence on the thinking of Pythagoras and Plato. More importantly for Nietzsche, Greek tragedy evolved out of the Dionysian festivals. Dionysus, who had been plucked unborn from his dead mother and raised in Zeus's thigh, who had been torn to pieces by the Titans in Hera's jealous rage, who had been transformed into a kid and raised by nymphs, represented just that illogical fluidity that Nietzsche saw as the essence of the Dionysian, the drunken sense of merging with the whole, "the Bacchanalian revel" that Hegel before him had also celebrated. "[I]t is only in the Dionysian mysteries . . . that the *basic fact* of the Hellenic instinct finds expression—its 'will to life.' "[46]

MARTIN LUTHER (1483–1546)

In light of the uninhibited frenzy associated with Dionysus, it may seem odd that Nietzsche praises Luther in connection with this Pagan god. Nevertheless, Luther is one of the Dionysian heroes of *The Birth of Tragedy*. "So deep, courageous, and spiritual, so exuberantly good and tender did this chorale of Luther sound as the first Dionysian luring call breaking forth from dense thickets at the approach of spring."[47] Although Nietzsche's later assessments of Luther are more mixed, he continued to display considerable appreciation for the artistic Luther, not only as composer of chorales, but as translator of the Bible. He considered Luther an exemplary writer, although his own sense of rivalry is also evident.

[I]t is my theory that with this Z[arathustra] I have brought the German language to a state of perfection. After *Luther* and Goethe, a third step had to be taken—look and see, old chum of mine, if vigor, flexibility, and euphony have ever consorted so well in our language. . . . My line is superior to his

[Goethe's] in strength and manliness, without becoming, as Luther's did, loutish.[48]

Nietzsche valued Luther for his assertion of German culture as well as the artistic merits of these achievements. He tended to praise Luther more as a cultural hero than a religious one. Nevertheless, Nietzsche also displays consistent admiration for Luther's courage as it was revealed in the actions that launched the Protestant Reformation. In particular, Nietzsche points to Luther's willingness to destroy even the Church, an institution he had loved, in order to be true to his intellectual conscience.

Nietzsche's discussions of the Reformation itself are mostly critical, and given his Lutheran upbringing, he was explicitly rejecting Luther's Church when he abandoned Christianity. Yet Nietzsche continued to employ phraseology from Luther in his own discussions of human liberation, suggesting continued acknowledgment of his own indebtedness even when he could no longer follow Luther's belief. For example, Luther describes the arrival of God's grace in the soul in terms of affirmation and negation. At the height of despair, the sinner's soul discovers "deeper than No, and above it, the deep, mysterious Yes."[49] Nietzsche uses the same terminology in describing the faith that grounds his own opposition to Christianity.

[W]e have also outgrown Christianity and are averse to it— precisely because we have grown out of it, because our ancestors were Christians who in their Christianity were uncompromisingly upright: for their faith they willingly sacrificed possessions and position, blood and fatherland. We—do the same. For what? For our unbelief? For every kind of unbelief? No, you know better than that, friend! The hidden Yes in you is stronger than all Nos and Maybes that afflict you and your age like a disease; and when you have to embark on the sea, you emigrants, you, too, are compelled to this by—a *faith*.[50]

Nietzsche's images of the overflowing soul and of the simultaneously cruel and creative hammer were also used earlier by Luther. Perhaps it is not unfair to say that Nietzsche followed Luther in what he saw as Luther's greatness.

HEINRICH HEINE (1797–1856)

The German-Jewish poet Heinrich Heine makes several of Nietzsche's "exemplary men" lists, not least because he was one of the few scholars who anticipated Nietzsche's "Dionysian" vision of the Greeks. He also admired Heine's masterful use of the German language and his "divine malice without which I cannot imagine perfection." Heine exemplifies "the highest concept of the lyrical poet." "I seek in vain in all the realms of history for an equally sweet and passionate music."[51]

Besides explicit homage, Nietzsche indicated his admiration for Heine by further developing some of the poet's ideas. One example is the notion of the death of God, which Heine considers in *On the History of Religion and Philosophy in Germany*. Walter Kaufmann speculates that Nietzsche may also have been inspired to formulate his doctrine of eternal recurrence because of a passage from Heine that appeared in *Letzte Gedichte und Gedanken von H. Heine*, a book that Nietzsche owned. Heine is also Nietzsche's precursor in treating Judaism and Christianity as essentially the same. Heine wrote of the expressions "Jewish" and "Christian," "both expressions are synonymous for me and are used by me not to designate a faith but a character." Heine also opposed this Jewish-Christian character to the character of the Greeks, an opposition that anchors many of Nietzsche's discussions of the Judeo-Christian tradition.

THUCYDIDES (460–400 B.C.E.)

Thucydides was Nietzsche's "cure for Platonism," first of all because he refused to "see reason in reality." Nietzsche praised Thucydides for having to be read "between the lines," a bit of good advice for readers of Nietzsche as well. He admired "that strong hard severe factuality" that could describe the horrors and human foibles of the Peloponnesian War without moralism or squeamishness. Unlike Plato, Thucydides had courage in the face of reality. "Plato flees into the ideal. . . . Thucydides has control of *himself*, consequently he also maintains control of things."[52]

CHARLES DARWIN (1809–1882)

Nietzsche's relationship with Darwin is particularly complex. *On the Origin of Species by Means of Natural Selection* had been published in English in 1859 and its central thesis was well known by the time Nietzsche launched his writing career. In his early essay on David Strauss, Nietzsche praised Darwin's "dangerous idea" that there is no fundamental difference between animals and human beings.[53] Nietzsche complained that Strauss acquiesced to Darwin's basic theory, even praising Darwin as "one of mankind's greatest benefactors," without noticing the frontal challenge to the moral worldview. This most astonishing idea, that there is no fundamental difference between animals and human beings, contradicted the popular vision that human beings were the apex (not just another ape) in the great chain of being and therefore worthy of special moral consideration and capable of moral responsibility in a way that animals are not.

Even Schopenhauer, who emphasized the similarity between the structure of animals and the structure of human beings, held to the view that human beings were of a different order than animals; indeed, human beings were the only form of life capable of reason and of resisting the will and gaining ethical insight. Of course, Nietzsche also thought that human beings can elevate themselves above the level of "beasts" through art, religion, and philosophy, even if he was skeptical that many human beings could or would do so.[54] But the continuity of man and beast, the place of humanity within nature, is always central to Nietzsche's thinking.

Nietzsche seems to be playing with Darwinian imagery in the speeches that Zarathustra makes about the *Übermensch*. "Man is a rope, tied between beast and overman. . . ."[55] Yet we have noted above that Nietzsche mocks those who accuse him of Darwinism. Walter Kaufmann observes, however, that "his own Zarathustric allegories had plainly invited such misunderstanding."[56] Nietzsche took issue with many aspects of Darwin's theory of natural selection; nevertheless, in 1887 he describes Darwinism as "the last great scientific movement."[57]

The Worst

SOCRATES (CA. 470–399 B.C.E.)

Socrates, more than any other figure, is the target of Nietzsche's attacks. Nietzsche was obsessed with him. Socrates' fame, his

infuence, his buffoonery, all appealed to and appalled the shy
hermit of Sils Maria. But despite Socrates' evident joy in living,
Nietzsche saw in Socrates a profound pessimism, the rejection
of life. In Plato's depiction of Socrates' death, the condemned
philosopher insists, "Crito, I owe Asclepius a rooster" (Asclepius
was the patron of physician, so Socrates was suggesting that
death is a *cure* for life.). Nietzsche translates, "Oh, Crito, *life is a
disease*" and asks, "Is it possible that a man like him, who had
lived cheerfully and like a soldier in the sight of everyone,
should have been a pessimist? Socrates *suffered life!*"[58]

Because of this pessimism, Socrates developed a form of reason run wild, an "absurd" rationality that allowed him to abandon this world for another. Nietzsche thus accuses Socrates
of being implicated in Euripides' "killing" of Greek tragedy:
"Euripides was . . . only a mask: the deity who spoke through
him was neither Dionysus nor Apollo, but . . . Socrates."[59] And
although Nietzsche considered Socrates the great buffoon, he
was also the enemy of comedy—and of music, too. Plato's portraits show Socrates famously banning the poets from his imaginary republic, and condemning flute-playing as licentious.

Yet in an earlier dialogue, the *Phaedo,* where we find Socrates
in prison awaiting death, he decides to take up music as an act of
piety toward an apparition that tells him in dreams to "practice
music." This reflects a glimmer of awareness, says Nietzsche,
that rationality alone was not sufficient, but he adds, "It was his
Apollonian insight that, like a barbaric king, he did not understand the noble image of a god and was in danger of sinning
against a deity—through his lack of understanding. The voice of
the Socratic dream vision is the only sign of any misgivings
about the limits of logic."[60]

Still, Nietzsche's attack is mixed with unmistakable admiration. Socrates' "logical urge," he says, "in its unbridled flood displays a natural power such as we encounter to our awed amazement only in the very greatest instinctive forces."[61] Ultimately, Nietzsche sees Socrates as a marvel, despite his dubious legacy.

PLATO (CA. 428–348 OR 347 B.C.E.)

It is by no means easy to separate Plato from his teacher Socrates. Most of what we know (or think we know) of the latter we know through the former, and there is no doubt that Plato rather freely put words and ideas in Socrates' mouth, dramatizing and systematizing his ideas, taking hints and suggestion from Socrates and spinning them into full-blown philosophy. But what Nietzsche knew about Socrates charmed as well as infuriated him, whereas with Plato there are only rarely any such indications of mixed feelings. Plato was *the* philosopher of hyperrationality, of the otherworldly. For Nietzsche, the Platonic Form of the Good was no different in kind than the transcendent Christian God ("Christianity is Platonism for the masses").

Nietzsche claims not to be charmed by the elegance of Plato's writing, much less by the dialectical experimentalism of his writing. (He also no doubt resented how much Plato had done for Socrates while Nietzsche had no such skillful marketer for his philosophy!) In Nietzsche's view, the twists and turns of the dialogues were not ultimately different in their aim from Kant's academic prose—to establish reason as a tyrant, dialectic as a form of revenge. However, Nietzsche's own literary experiment, *Thus Spoke Zarathustra,* pays homage to the dialogues through extensive parody. And although he wanted to "stand Plato on his head," that very aim gives Plato pride of place in the tradition.

SAINT PAUL (D. 64 C.E.)

If there is a bull's-eye in the target that Nietzsche pins on Christianity, it is Saint Paul, (Saul of Tarsus), not the founder of Christianity but certainly the greatest propagandist that Christianity has ever known. Nietzsche describes Paul as having "a mind as superstitious as it was cunning."[62] What Nietzsche despised about Paul, naturally, was his unflagging war against the instincts, against everything natural. "People like St. Paul have an evil eye for the passions: all they know of the passions is what is dirty, disfiguring, and heartbreaking; hence their idealistic tendency aims at the annihilation of the passions, and they find perfect purity in the divine."[63] Like all Christians, Nietzsche says, Paul spoke of faith but acted from instinct alone.[64] Nietzsche attacks Paul for his "rabbinical impudence," for his "logicizing" the Christian mysteries, for his "obscene" and "impertinent" promise of personal immortality as a reward for self-denial.[65] "On the heels of the 'glad tidings' came the *very worst*: those of Paul, . . . the genius in hatred, in the vision of hatred, in the inexorable logic of hatred." It was Paul, more than anyone else, who rejected and hated life, even the life of Jesus himself. "At bottom, [Paul] had no use at all for the life of the Redeemer—he needed the death on the cross *and* a little more."[66]

RICHARD WAGNER (1813–1883)

Wagner was a problematic hero. He was arrogant in the extreme, egotistical, and irresponsible. Nietzsche's "break" with Wagner is one of the most celebrated philosophical cat fights in modern history. From admiring flunky to embittered apostate, Nietzsche did a complete one-eighty on his former hero; and if early in his career Wagner was one of Nietzsche's major influences and role models, by the end of his career he was his *bête noire,* a sellout, a charlatan. Nietzsche came to consider Wagner, even at the pinnacle of his success, "in truth a decaying and despairing decadent, suddenly sunk down, helpless and broken, before the Christian cross." Nietzsche confesses, "I was sick . . . weary from the . . . disappointment, about the universally *wasted* energy, work, hope, youth, love—weary from nausea at the whole idealistic lie. . . ."[67]

We have already considered some of the personal motives that figured in Nietzsche's ending his friendship with Wagner. Here we will consider Nietzsche's more philosophical criticisms, even if these, like all philosophical arguments, are, in Nietzsche's opinion, an unconscious personal memoir.

Even before the end of the friendship, Nietzsche objected to Wagner's notorious anti-Semitism, as well as to his German nationalism. In his later reflections on the relationship, Nietzsche saw these tendencies as basic factors in their eventual parting of the ways.

By the Summer of 1876, during the time of the first *Festspiele,* I said farewell to Wagner in my heart. . . . [S]ince Wagner had moved to Germany, he had condescended step by step to everything I despise—even to anti-Semitism.[68]

What did I never forgive Wagner? . . . that he became *reichs-deutsch*.[69]

Nietzsche also had major disagreements with Wagner's theory of art. In criticizing Wagner, Nietzsche shows his sympathies for the classical aesthetic, which considers the ideal for an artwork to be the unified coordination of parts and the subordination of each part to the life of the whole. By contrast, Wagner (according to Nietzsche) writes music that is an "anarchy of atoms," a chaos of musical elements rather than an integrated structure.[70] Wagner's music, far from achieving unified form, is designed instead to jar and jostle the contemporary audience, which is spiritually exhausted and seeks stimulation wherever it can be found. Because it provides a series of stimulating states without cohesion, says Nietzsche, Wagner's music is decadent, like its era. Indeed, this music made the sick sicker, but it continued to be popular because contemporary tastes themselves were sick.

Nietzsche became convinced that Wagner was ultimately concerned not with creating musical beauty but theatrical gimmicks.

Was Wagner a musician at all? . . . As a musician . . . he became only what he was in general: he *became* a musician, he *became* a poet because the tyrant within him, his actor's genius, compelled him.[71]

. . . his *practice* was always, from beginning to end, "the pose is the end; the drama, also the music, is always merely its means."[72]

. . . he repeated a single proposition all his life long: that his music did not mean mere music . . . "*Not mere* music"—no musician would say that.[73]

Wagner was always eager for nerve-jangling effects, Nietzsche complained. He sought to make music "leap out of the wall and shake the listener to his very intestines."[74] He cast aside the aims of musical form and musical beauty, writing music that jumped from one dramatic event to another, without real coherence.

Wagner lost Nietzsche's favor, ultimately, for the same reason that many became his heroes or objects of his derision: because Wagner, in Nietzsche's view, failed to be true to himself. Wagner did not really respect his own talent. While he excelled as a miniaturist, a master of nuance, he preferred grandstanding. This preference eventually motivated him to abandon his integrity for the sake of the impressive pose, as his music-drama *Parsifal* illustrates. The libretto encourages mindless piety, in Nietzsche's opinion, something that Wagner opposed no less than Nietzsche. It also presents a paean to chastity, a particularly ludicrous message coming from the likes of Wagner, given his adulterous relationship with Cosima and the several children they had before they were married.

Nietzsche was distressed by his break with Wagner throughout the remainder of his creative life. He makes too much of the reasons he had for rejecting Wagner, and the reader is painfully aware of his ambivalence. Even after the break, Nietzsche still admired much that he saw in Wagner, even if Wagner himself recognized it only inconsistently.

> Let us remain faithful in what is *true* and authentic in him—and especially in this, that we, as his disciples, remain faithful to ourselves in what is true and authentic in us. . . . It does not matter that as a thinker he is so often in the wrong. . . . Enough that his life is justified before itself and remains justified—this life which shouts at every one of us: "Be a man and do not follow me . . . !"[75]

Nietzsche seems to be crying out: "See? I am a good friend, after all."

IMMANUEL KANT (1724–1804)

Immanuel Kant is another of those great targets and stumbling blocks in the history of philosophy. Nietzsche recognized that Kant, who had died only forty years before Nietzsche was born, had already established himself as the greatest of German philosophers. Even the briefest overview of nineteenth-century philosophy shows clearly that Kant was the background against which all subsequent philosophers had to define themselves. Nietzsche had no hesitation. Kant is second only to Socrates (and Plato) in the number of times he is abused.

Kant's philosophy can be crudely summarized in terms of three theses to which Nietzsche responds with particular hostility. First and foremost, there is his characterization of morality in terms of rational principles ("categorical imperatives") that apply universally to "all rational beings." Kant proposes such principles of reason in opposition to the "inclinations" (for example, emotions, desires, urges, drives, and instincts), which are of no "moral worth." Nietzsche, by contrast, insists that morality can be understood only in terms of such "inclinations" and that these are always to be understood in terms of particular persons or people and are not matters of universal principle.

Second, Kant defends an elaborate and ingenious conception of reality as "phenomenon," as "constituted" by our mental processes. But the "residuum" of such an analysis is the notion of reality independent of our experience, the world "in itself," a notion that Nietzsche finds unintelligible. "The true world— unattainable, indemonstrable, unpromisable; but the very thought of it—a consolation, an obligation, an imperative." Kant thus harks back to Plato: "At bottom, the old sun, but seen through mist and skepticism. The idea has become elusive, pale, Nordic, Königsbergian." (Kant was from Königsberg.) Nietzsche concludes: "The 'true' world—an idea which is no longer good for anything, not even obligating—an idea which has become useless and superfluous—*consequently*, a refuted idea: let us abolish it!"[76]

Third, Kant believes that God exists not as a being who can be "known" but also as the organizing "teleological" (purposive) principle of the world. Nietzsche does not believe in God and he rejects the idea of a teleological organization of the world. Despite his recognition that Kant was a true revolutionary, Nietzsche also saw Kant as a backslider, who did not have the courage of his convictions:

[T]he old Kant . . . had obtained the "thing in itself" *by stealth* . . . and was punished for this when the "categorical imperative" crept stealthily into his heart and led him *astray—*

back to "God," "soul," "freedom," and "immortality," like a fox who loses his way and goes astray back into his cage. Yet it had been *his* strength and cleverness that had *broken open* the cage![77]

As always, Nietzsche's attack is not without humor. Referring to Kant's notoriously difficult style, Nietzsche notes: "Kant wanted to prove in a way that would dumbfound the 'common man' that the 'common man' was right. . . ." This, Nietzsche submits, was "Kant's joke."[78]

ARTHUR SCHOPENHAUER (1788–1860)

Schopenhauer also suffered (posthumously) Nietzsche's enraged renunciation. Although he had been Nietzsche's early model of an "educator," his guide to the future, Schopenhauer became the exemplar of that pessimism that Nietzsche struggled to reject, often with forced gaiety and the hollow "cheerfulness" that emerge as *amor fati*. In a late comment about Schopenhauer, Nietzsche comments casually that he was wrong "about everything."

Nietzsche takes recurrent potshots at particular features of Schopenhauer's thought. Although initially attracted to the concept of the will, Nietzsche became more and more uncomfortable with Schopenhauer's insistence that we are all one; this was uncomfortably reminiscent of the religion that Nietzsche had discarded, as was Schopenhauer's penchant for mystical language. The notion of a single will also trivializes the individual, in Nietzsche's opinion; Nietzsche defends the importance of individuals, all the more as they are unique. He rejects Schopenhauer's ethic of universal sympathy or pity (the German word, *Mitleid,* denotes both concepts) for the same reasons he considers pity worthless in any context. Schopenhauer's promotion of asceticism and renunciation of the will eventually strike Nietzsche as being just as antilife as Christianity.

Nietzsche never succeeded in throwing off either Schopenhauer's influence or the entirety of his pessimistic worldview. Once again Nietzsche shows that he is never more opposed to anyone than those models whom he once embraced with enthusiasm. In *Ecce Homo* Nietzsche regrets that "the cadaverous perfume of Schopenhauer sticks. . . . to a few [of my own] formulas."[79]

RENÉ DESCARTES (1596–1650)

Nietzsche was not an epistemologist. While he had a great deal to say about the uses and nature of knowledge, he had little to say regarding the great debates of the seventeenth and eighteenth centuries about the origins and justification of knowledge, and so his relation to Descartes is often ignored. He clearly rejected Descartes's mind/body dualism. "[T]he awakened and knowing say: body am I entirely, and the soul is only a word for something about the body."[80] So, too, Nietzsche rejected Descartes's demeaning of the senses, insisting that "we possess scientific knowledge today to precisely the extent that we have decided to *accept* the evidence of the senses." He also delights in emphasizing the importance of the most undervalued of the human senses, smell: "What magnificent instruments of observation we possess in our senses! The nose, for example . . . is actually the most delicate instrument so far at our disposal."[81]

As a defender of a naturalistic philosophy, Nietzsche rejects

Descartes's appeal to the supernatural to defend the most natural and ordinary beliefs (notably, the existence of the "external" world). "Descartes could prove the reality of the empirical world only by appealing to the truthfulness of God and his inability to utter falsehood."[82] But Nietzsche's antipathy for the founder of modern philosophy goes deeper than this. Anticipating Freud's discovery of "the unconscious," Nietzsche praises

> *Leibniz's* incomparable insight . . . against Descartes—that consciousness is merely an *accident* of experience and *not* its necessary and essential attribute; that, in other words, what we call consciousness constitutes only one state of our spiritual and psychic world (perhaps a pathological state) and *not by any means the whole of it*.[83]

With Descartes, by contrast, "consciousness is tyrannized—not least by our pride in it. One thinks that it constitutes the *kernel* of man."[84]

Ultimately, Descartes draws Nietzsche's fire because of his rejection of not only the senses and the false separation of mind and body but his rejection of the body altogether. All of Descartes's method can be viewed as aiming toward this conclusion:

> There must be mere appearance, there must be some deception which prevents us from perceiving that which has being: where is the deceiver? "We have found him," they cry ecstatically; "it is the senses! These senses, which are so immoral in other ways too, deceive us concerning the *true* world. Moral:

let us free ourselves from the deception of the senses, from becoming, from history, from lies. Moral: let us say No to all who have faith in the senses. . . . And above all, away with the body, this wretched *idée fixe* of the senses, disfigured by all the fallacies of logic, refuted, even impossible, although it is impudent enough to behave as if it were real!"[85]

MARTIN LUTHER (1483–1546)

If Lutheranism was deep in Nietzsche's soul, it was also continuously stuck in his craw. Nietzsche's critique of Luther focuses on the latter's religious doctrines and the psychology they express—a belief in the depravity of human beings, the view that faith alone justifies existence. In *The Birth of Tragedy* Nietzsche held that the only justification for existence is an *aesthetic* justification, yet his disagreement goes even deeper: "Faith is a profound conviction on the part of Luther and his kind of their incapacity for Christian works. . . ."[86] If "faith makes blessed," then, Nietzsche suggests, it occurs *instead of* virtue.[87]

Lutheranism, Nietzsche argues, is a religion for the poor in spirit. "The poor in spirit do not know what to do, and if one forbade them their prayer-rattling one would deprive them of their religion—as Protestantism shows us more and more by day."[88] And Luther's Christianity, despite all of its claims to being a philosophy of love, is in fact the hateful invocation of a wrathful God.

As usual, Nietzsche's arguments against Luther ultimately shift to the *ad hominem*:

Luther's disposition was calamitously myopic, superficial, and incautious. He was a man of the common people who lacked everything that one might inherit from a ruling caste; he had no instinct for power. Thus his work, . . . without his knowing or willing it, became nothing but the beginning of a work of destruction. He unraveled, he tore up with honest wrath what the old spider had woven so carefully for such a long time. . . . He smashed an ideal that he could not attain, while he seemed to abhor and to be fighting only against the degeneration of this ideal.[89]

Foremost among Luther's sins, in Nietzsche's opinion, was his anti-Semitism, well documented in Luther's writings, with such passages as the following:

What shall we Christians do now with this depraved and damned people of the Jews? . . . I will give my faithful advice. First, that one should set fire to their synagogues. Then break down and destroy their houses, drive them out of the country.[90]

Nietzsche's response is to turn his sense of humor against Luther, in passages that initially seem to defend him.

"God himself cannot exist without wise people," said Luther with good reason. But "God can exist even less without unwise people"—that our good Luther did not say.[91]

What afterward grew out of his Reformation, good as well as bad, might be calculated approximately today; but who would be naive enough to praise or blame Luther on account of these consequences? He is innocent of everything; he did not know what he was doing.[92]

This latter passage is particularly biting in light of the Scriptural report of Jesus' prayer on the cross, "Father, forgive them, for they know not what they do" (Luke 23:34).

JOHN STUART MILL (1806–1873)

Nietzsche may not have known Mill's works in detail, but in many ways, apart from their very different styles and temperaments, they were kindred spirits. Mill was a strict empiricist and an uncompromising naturalist, as was Nietzsche. Mill decried the appeal of morals to heavenly, or *a priori,* standards. So did Nietzsche. Mill defended the sophistication of "quality" pursuits against the vulgar hedonism of his predecessor, Jeremy Bentham, the same argument that Nietzsche deploys against him.

Although Mill voices many of Nietzsche's favorite themes, Nietzsche nevertheless makes his older English contemporary the target for his own displeasure with British utilitarianism and socialism. To Nietzsche Mill represents the cause of equal rights, a political formula that Nietzsche associated with promoting the lowest common denominator and the shackling of the independent spirit. Nietzsche also rejected the basic theoretical underpinnings of utilitarianism—in particular, the utilitarian presupposition that one should aim to maximize pleasure and minimize pain, which struck Nietzsche as absurd. Pleasure and pain are experienced together, and the most effective strategy for minimizing pain, blunting one's sensibility, makes one ill-equipped to experience pleasure. "Man does not strive for pleasure," Nietzsche famously quips; "only the Englishman does."[93]

As usual, Nietzsche attacks with *ad hominem* arguments: the aspirations of utilitarians, particularly the goal of eliminating pain, are pipe dreams of "the violated, oppressed, suffering, unfree, who are uncertain of themselves and weary," concerned with "enduring the pressure of existence."[94] Nietzsche's countertheses are evident enough, the will to power in place of hedonism, art and creativity in place of the general happiness:

"The general welfare" is no ideal, no goal, no remotely intelligible concept, but only an emetic.[95]

Whether it is hedonism or pessimism, utilitarianism or eudaemonism—all these ways of thinking that measure the value of things in accordance with *pleasure* and *pain,* which are mere epiphenomena and wholly secondary, are ways of thinking that stay in the foreground and naivetés on which everyone conscious of *creative* powers and an artistic consciousness will look down not without derision, nor without pity.[96]

THOMAS CARLYLE (1795–1881)

Like Mill, Carlyle would also seem to be an ally rather than the butt of Nietzsche's sarcasm, with his relentless attacks on hypocrisy, mob democracy, sham idealism, and mindless social legislation, not to mention his celebration of the individual, the strong leader, the hero, the Great Man. Like Nietzsche, he was also an admirer of Goethe and Schiller, a fan of German literature and language, and an explosive, passionate writer. Nevertheless, Nietzsche calls him "this unconscious and involuntary farce, this heroic-moralistic interpretation of dyspeptic states." (Here we see Nietzsche, himself a medical wreck, criticizing a precursor for fighting against his physical frailties with words!) Furthermore, Nietzsche describes Carlyle as "a man of strong words and attitudes, . . . constantly lured by the craving for a strong faith and the feeling of his capacity for it (in this respect, a typical romantic!)." He "drugs something in himself with the *fortissimo* of his veneration of men of strong faith and his rage against the less simple-minded." Nietzsche vents spleen with a further *ad hominem*, one that recalls his spoof on the utilitarians. "Of course, in England he is admired precisely for his honesty. Well, that is English."[97]

EURIPIDES (480–405 B.C.E.)

Nietzsche curiously disdained the younger contemporary of Aeschylus and Sophocles. Where he celebrates the latter two, he abuses Euripides and considers his plays "degenerate." Nietzsche even calls him "the murderer of tragedy." He accuses him of being inspired by Socrates and (what is very different) of giving a voice to "civic mediocrity." Nevertheless, what bothers Nietzsche about Euripides is not at all that evident, and his reasons are demonstrably dubious. Greek scholars have been quick to point out Nietzsche's misinterpretations and misunderstandings. Here, as elsewhere, Nietzsche's preconceived prejudices towards those who in fact seem like kindred spirits is much in evidence.

Indeed, what Nietzsche rejects in Euripides are often just those themes which he himself so often defended, for example, Euripides' more down-to-earth approach to tragedy and his penchant for deep psychological insights. And it is Euripides, above all, who presents us with the best single portrait of Nietzsche's beloved Dionysus, in his play *The Bacchae*, but Nietzsche accuses "sacrilegious" Euripides of abandoning Dionysus, of reducing the tragic hero to a dying myth. (Perhaps that is the source of Nietzsche's jealousy, one lover preempted by another.) To be sure, Nietzsche may have objected to Euripides' defense of the status of women and repudiation of the glory of war. He also used a more vernacular vocabulary, which Nietzsche considered vulgar. On this last point, Nietzsche sides with his hero Sophocles, who complained that Euripides presented men as they are, not as they should be.

Nietzsche criticizes Euripides for being like Socrates—too rational, too reasonable, too keen on finding explanations for the tragic and inexplicable. Reading Euripides' plays, however, one is hard put to defend this accusation. What Nietzsche seems to object to most vehemently, however, is Euripides' eliminating the chorus in Greek tragedy and, according to Nietzsche, replacing its mystical rumblings with rational explanations. This, Nietzsche claimed, amounted to abandoning the classic Hellenic tension between the Apollonian and Dionysian. The Athenian tragedy's subtle response to the problem of evil, which depended on a balance of these principles, was undermined. Euripides' move toward making Greek tragedy more rational was a pivotal step toward the destruction of Athenian culture, on Nietzche's harsh interpretation.

Runners-up (for "Worst")

G. W. F. HEGEL (1770–1831)

It is really quite doubtful that Nietzsche read much Hegel, and he certainly did not read him carefully or sympathetically. Most of what he says about Hegel seems to come from Schopenhauer's prejudices and via the interpretations of the "right" or conservative Hegelians, who had taken over Hegel's legacy after the great dialectician's death in 1831. (The "left" Hegelians, especially Bruno Bauer and young Karl Marx, had more important battles to fight.) The right-wing Hegel—as opposed, one could argue, to the real Hegel of the early antitheological writings and his great *Phenomenology of Spirit*—was profoundly but obscurely Christian. (This was the same Hegel that Kierkegaard in Denmark attacked, but from the point of view of a devout Christian.)

Nietzsche rejects the optimism of Hegel's framework as well as its emphasis on the upward development of collective human self-consciousness ("Spirit"), and, like Kierkegaard, he attacks Hegel's emphasis on the collective (as opposed to the individual) and his pretentious gloss on human history as "rational" and "absolute." Nietzsche also objects to Hegel's effort to systematize philosophy. But, as so often, Nietzsche approaches this nemesis with a mixture of admiration and contempt. He accuses Hegel of exerting "an almost tyrannical influence,"[98] and he complains, in *The Birth of Tragedy*, that his own work "smells offensively Hegelian."[99]

Nietzsche's opposition to Hegel is qualified and intermittant. In one place he refers to "those philosophical laborers after the noble model of Kant and Hegel."[100] Nietzsche even complained about Schopenhauer's "unintelligent wrath against Hegel."[101] In *The Gay Science* Nietzsche describes Hegel as one of the great German philosophers, "the astonishing stroke of *Hegel,* who struck right through all our logical habits and bad habits when he dared to teach that species concepts develop *out of each other*. . . ." Hegel "first introduced the decisive concept of 'development' into science."[102] And yet, the overall verdict is decidedly negative. It is (what Nietzsche takes to be) Hegel's warmed-over Lutheran collective spiritualism, his apparent contempt for the individual and the concrete details of individual life that provide Nietzsche with such a big, attractive target.

CHARLES DARWIN (1809–1882)

Darwin also makes both the "Best" and "Worst" lists (if only as a runner-up in both cases)—the "Worst" list because Nietzsche rejects Darwin's model of natural selection, in particular its premise that species struggle for existence. In *Twilight of the Idols* he contends that this thesis "so far . . . seems . . . to be asserted rather than proved." He acknowledges that such a struggle occurs in some cases, but he thinks these are far from typical. "The total appearance of life is not the extremity, not starvation, but rather riches, profusion, even absurd squandering—and where there is struggle, it is a struggle for *power*."[103]

Nietzsche's argument here is essentially the same as the one he uses against Schopenhauer's doctrine of the "will to existence." (There is some question as to what degree Nietzsche conflates Darwin and Schopenhauer.) The idea of a struggle for existence is at odds with Nietzsche's own model of will to power, which explains the behavior of organisms on the basis of an inner drive to enhance their own vitality and to assert control over their environment.

But most important, Nietzsche has an *ethical* objection to the Darwinian worldview. Nietzsche argues that in those cases in which a struggle for existence does occur "its result is unfortunately the opposite of what Darwin's school desires." Specifically, the result of this struggle is that the less complex forms, which Darwin claims are more common, prevail over the more complex. Nietzsche articulates this point in one of his notes from 1888: "The richer and more complex forms—for the expression 'higher type' means no more than this—perish more easily: only the lowest preserve an apparent indestructibility. . . ." In the human species, the dominance of the weak over the strong is the typical result of such struggles. Nietzsche concludes that the human species is certainly not progressing. "Higher types are indeed attained, but they do not last. The level of the species is *not* raised."[104] He is similarly skeptical of human progress in his early essay, "On the Uses and Disadvantages of History for Life," with an obvious reference to Hegel: "the *goal of humanity* cannot lie in the end but only *in its highest specimens.*"[105]

Nietzsche's notes sketch some biological arguments against Darwin's account of natural selection, for example, the idea of transitional forms: "Every type has its limits: beyond these there is no evolution. . . ."[106] He also questions the extent to which Darwin's model attributes the success and failure of species to external conditions. "The influence of 'external circumstances' is overestimated by Darwin to a ridiculous extent: the essential thing in the life process is precisely the tremendous shaping, form-creating force working from within which utilizes and exploits 'external circumstances.' "[107] Again, Nietzsche favors the account that inner drives rather than outer pressures are decisive in determining forms of life. Nietzsche also defends Lamarck against Darwin, arguing that acquired characteristics can be inherited. Nevertheless, "the brief spell of beauty, of genius, of Caesar, is *sui generis*: such things are not inherited."[108]

But ultimately, as one would expect, Nietzsche's harsh criticisms are often no more than nuances and an advertisement for his own particular emphases: the will to power, the importance of the strong, not the "fittest." "The weak prevail over the strong again and again," he says, and thus evolution is not to be praised or trusted for the betterment of the species. But for the final blow, Nietzsche relies on the familiar *ad hominem*: "Darwin," he says, "forgot the spirit (that is English!). . . ."[109]

GOD (ETERNAL, THOUGH RECENTLY DECEASED)

God the Almighty, according to Nietzsche, has become God the petty, "some petty deity who is full of care and personally knows every little hair on our head. . . ."[110] He has also become God the pitiful.

> Thus spoke the devil to me once: "God too has his hell: that is his love of man." And most recently I heard him say this: "God is dead; God died of his pity for man."[111]

Regardless of whether or not Nietzsche believed in God, it is clear that he thought that the being that most people had come to believe in and pray to was not worthy of the name.

Nietzsche provides a variety of unflattering pictures of God, which describe him as dying because he was no longer godly. In *Zarathustra* the alleged killer of God, the Ugliest Man, insists:

> "But he had to die: he saw with eyes that saw everything; he saw man's depths and ultimate grounds, all his concealed disgrace and ugliness. His pity knew no shame: he crawled into my dirtiest nooks. . . . The god who saw everything, even man—this

god had to die! Man cannot bear it that such a witness should live."[112]

Another character, the Pope, who has been "retired" since God's death, complains:

"He was a concealed god, addicted to secrecy. Verily, even a son he got himself in a sneaky way. At the door of his faith stands adultery.

"Whoever praises him as a god of love does not have a high enough opinion of love itself. Did this god not want to be a judge too? . . .

"When he was young, this god out of the Orient, he was harsh and vengeful and he built himself a hell to amuse his favorites. Eventually, however, he became old and soft and mellow and pitying, more like a grandfather than a father, but most like a shaky old grandmother. Then he sat in his nook by the hearth, wilted, grieving over his weak legs, weary of the world, weary of willing, and one day he choked on his all-too-great pity."[113]

Zarathustra concludes that we are better off without such a deity.

"But why did he not speak more clearly? And if it was the fault of our ears, why did he give us ears that heard him badly? . . . There is good taste in piety too; and it was this that said in the end, 'Away with such a god!' Rather no god, rather make destiny on one's own, rather be a fool, rather be a god oneself."[114]

Zarathustra is not entirely opposed to gods, however. He tells an alternative story to the "twilight of the gods" (alluding again to Wagner's title):

> For the old gods, after all, things came to an end long ago; and verily, they had a good gay godlike end. They did not end in a "twilight," though this lie is told. Instead: one day they laughed themselves to death. That happened when the most godless word issued from one of the gods themselves—the word: "There is one god. Thou shalt have no other god before me!"[115]

6

Nietzsche's Virtues

To "give style" to one's character—a great and rare art!
—from *The Gay Science*[1]

CONTRARY TO THE popular view of Nietzsche as an "immoralist," Nietzsche is very much a moralist. His writings are filled with moral exhortations, practical advice, prescriptions, observations on love and friendship, and warnings about weakness, pity, and Christianity, even along the lines of "don't lie" and "be kind to others," though stated more persuasively and often ironically. He is purposely provocative, provoking not only thought but self-scrutiny. His aim, despite his many pronouncements to the contrary, is *to make us better*, or, at any rate, to get us to appreciate how we might be better, more admirable, more noble.

A quick glance at *Daybreak* or *Human, All Too Human,* for instance, reveals hundreds of such straightforward "Dear Abby" tidbits as "The best means of coming to the aid of people who suffer greatly from embarrassment and of calming them down is to single them out for praise."[2] Nietzsche, like Jesus and Socrates, gave moral advice, even as he denied that he was doing so. His whole philosophy, like theirs, is aimed at provoking self-examination and self-"undergoing."The aim is "to know thyself," to cultivate the virtues, and, ultimately, to "become who you are." But who, in each of our individual cases, should we be or become?

"*Virtue ethics,*" although a recent coinage, describes an approach to ethics that has been well articulated in Western thought since Aristotle and is evident in Nietzsche's ethical thought as well. This is an approach in which personal character—individual excellence—is the primary focus. In the traditional language of moral philosophy, Nietzsche may have appeared to utterly reject Morality. He called himself an "immoralist," even if it is doubtful that he ever did anything truly immoral in his life. And yet, his objection to Morality, Judeo-Christian morality, and even the ethics of Socrates, is that they are "decadent." More to the point, they ignore individual excellence in favor of some supposedly grander concern—pleasing God, serving the public good, obeying the dictates of reason, saving one's immortal soul. But Nietzsche sought to shift the direction of ethics away from God, the Socratic soul, the Kantian rational willing subject, and the utilitarian attention to hedonistic consequences. Nietzsche's ethical outlook directed renewed attention to the character and integrity of the individual, his or her *virtues*. What is ultimately good, according to this viewpoint, is a good person, a person with good character, a person with the right virtues. Thus the central questions of Nietzsche's ethics become: What kind of character? Which virtues?

Aristotle, in answer to the same questions, offered us a neat little list of virtues and one seemingly precise criterion: "a virtue is the mean between the extremes." Aristotle's list and his criterion don't quite fit together, but his list, at least, set the stage for a long history of debate about the virtues. Aristotle's virtues are *courage, temperance, liberality, magnificence, justice, truthfulness, wittiness, friendliness, honor* (an all-embracing virtue), and *shame* (a "quasi-virtue"). Following Aristotle, Thomas Aquinas listed four cardinal virtues—*prudence, fortitude, temperance,* and *justice*—and three theological virtues—*faith, hope,* and *charity.* Nietzsche himself gave us two shorts lists, one in *Daybreak:*

> *Honest*—towards ourselves and whoever else is a friend
> to us
> *courageous*—towards the enemy
> *generous*—towards the defeated (cf. mercy)
> *polite*—always, this is what the four cardinal virtues want
> us to be[3]

and another in *Beyond Good and Evil:*

> courage,
> insight,
> sympathy,
> solitude.[4]

We should not be surprised that the two lists are not consistent (with each other or with what he says elsewhere in his work), and it is never entirely clear how serious Nietzsche may have been. He further insists that the virtues should not be "named" (for that would make them "common"), and he several times insists that each of us has "unique" virtues, which would make any discussion of the "best" virtues self-defeating. Nevertheless, there is more than enough in Nietzsche's various musings, polemics, pronouncements and attacks on the character of others to provide us with a portrait (albeit a multiperspectival cubist portrait rather than a one-dimensional classical one) of the excellent person, the "higher man." When Nietzsche provokes in us an image of ourselves, even a most unflattering image, it is in order to prompt us to reconsider ourselves in terms of our own virtues. Indeed, it may be an image for which we have been searching, perhaps without knowing it, all of our lives, our ignorance based, perhaps, on the fact that we are so often concerned with others' virtues and vices and not our own.

Nietzsche's *ad hominem* arguments also give us clues. His critical and sometimes scathing portrayals of other philosophers, not to mention his condemnations of whole cultures or schools of thought, give us considerable insight into what he valued and what he did not value. It is significant that much of Nietzsche's philosophy consists of personal attacks on others rather than critical comments on their works or ideas as such. Because he insisted that a philosopher should be, above all, an example, the manner in which a philosopher (or a people) lives says a great deal about the worth of their ideas. So, too, philosophical ideas are "proven" by how they manifest themselves in practice.

Nietzsche's positive examples are comparatively few and far

between. The most prominent is Goethe, who is lavishly praised for "creating himself" and making himself "into a whole man." (Yet even Goethe is subject to Nietzsche's sharp pen.) There are positive words for Schopenhauer, Wagner, Socrates, even Jesus, but they are often drowned out in a chorus of subsequent criticism. Nietzsche often praises himself, but that praise, too, is undermined by self-mockery and ridicule. (Is this a virtue?) There are occasional good words for Emerson, Heine, and Dostoyevsky, to name a few, but the personal details are scant at best. Perhaps such writers—for they are virtually all writers—enjoyed the anonymity and safety of distance. Nietzsche never knew, or never bothered to know, much about them. He extrapolated from a few works to an image of what the man himself must have been like. From these examples, however, one can gather—with caution—clues about what virtues Nietzsche most admired and encouraged us to cultivate.

We should probably distinguish between those virtues Nietzsche preached and those he admired. Warrior virtues are often the subject of his exhortations, but there is little doubt that he despised military types. But preaching is itself a part of a person's character, and disdainful preaching, prophetic preaching, ironic preaching, are all relevant to the project of discerning the thesis here. A philosopher who ponderously insists on being careful and serious shows us something important not only about his thesis and the ideals he represents but about himself as well. So, too, when Nietzsche tells us, with multiple exclamation points and italics, with frequent references to the classics and theology, with rhetorical questions and harsh insults, that Christian morality is a "slave" morality, we rightfully conclude not only that he has a problem with Christian morality but that he admires the polemical, offensive, unsympathetic style. Nietzsche's style, and its many variations, tell us what is perhaps the single most important virtue in the Nietzschean canon—"giving style to one's character."

The standard philosophical virtue of consistency, by contrast, has negligible status in Nietzsche's view. Both implicitly and explicitly, Nietzsche asks, "Why do philosophers so praise consistency?" Even without again quoting Emerson on the "hobgoblin of little minds," one may ask, without trying to be merely difficult, why a philosopher should be expected to speak with the same voice, not only in the same book but over his or her entire career. Nietzsche's practice, his tendency toward apparent self-contradiction, suggests that this is not an ideal he sets for himself. His practice even raises the question of why we think in terms of a single authorial identity, "Nietzsche." Is this just because his genius was inextricably bound to one and the same biological organism with that name (an ironic contingency he would have been the first to dismiss)?

Here is a tentative list of traits that Nietzsche considers virtues:

aestheticism	generosity
courage	"hardness"
courtesy	health
depth	honesty
egoism	integrity
exuberance	justice
fatalism (*amor fati*)	playfulness
"the feminine"	"presence"
friendship	pride

responsibility   style
solitude   temperance
strength

aestheticism Aestheticism is a virtue that is most pronounced in Nietzsche's early works, but it would be a mistake to conclude that he came to reject the aesthetic perspective along with its metaphysics. What he clearly came to reject were Schopenhauer's views that life is meaninglessness and that art provides us with an escape from life, from the ineluctable insanity of the Will. The ideal of beauty, however, is one that Nietzsche (like Plato) admired far more obstinately than most philosophers.

Indeed, one would not be wrong in suggesting that beauty remains one of the primary nonmoral evaluative categories of his philosophy. But aestheticism, too, requires cultivation and experience. Nietzsche continually praises the aesthetic virtues of refinement and taste (and employs startling metaphors to suggest their absence). To see the world as beautiful, in spite of suffering—even because of suffering—remains one of the explicit aspirations throughout his philosophy. He describes his aim in *The Gay Science*: "I want to learn more and more to see as beautiful what is necessary in things; then I shall be one of those who make things beautiful."[5] His attack on Socrates as "ugly," by contrast, goes hand in hand with his judgment that Socrates failed to take satisfaction from the beauty of his world or himself. "Whoever is dissatisfied with himself is continually ready for revenge, and we others will be his victims, if only by having to endure his ugly sight. For the sight of what is ugly makes one bad and gloomy."[6]

courage Courage, for Nietzsche, refers not so much to over-coming fear (the standard account) or having "just the right amount" of fear (Aristotle's account), and it certainly doesn't mean having *no* fear (the pathological conception of courage). Rather, as in so many of his conceptions of virtue, Nietzsche has a model of "over-flowing"—overflowing with an assertiveness that overwhelms fear. One imagines one of Homer's Greek heroes, surging with patriotism, warrior gusto, vengeance, or machismo, who, driven by such motives, charges through what-ever fear is surely there. So, too, the inspired artist or philoso-pher pursues his or her ideas despite the dangers of failure and ridicule or, perhaps worse, being utterly ignored—not *without* fear, but *overriding* fear.

Courage, in other words, is not a proper "balance" or "the mean between the extremes." It is an excess, and overwhelm-ing, an overflowing. It is not merely withstanding or enduring (as in all of those made-for-TV movies about "heroes" and "heroines" who suffer through horrible diseases). It is the skill-ful direction of "gung-ho" emotions, incorporating rather than excluding one's sense of honor, which because of its keen focus might too easily be interpreted as calm. But it is passion, not only this apparent calm, that is its virtue. Nietzsche's concep-tion that courage is a passion is evident in his account of the tragic artist in *Twilight of the Idols*:

> What does the tragic artist communicate of himself? Is it not precisely the state without fear in the face of the fearful and questionable that he is showing? . . . Courage and freedom of feeling before a powerful enemy, before a sublime calam-ity, before a problem that arouses dread—this triumphant

state is what the tragic artist chooses, what he glorifies. Before tragedy, what is warlike in our soul celebrates its Saturnalia. . . .[7]

courtesy For those who entertain the thought of Nietzsche-as-barbarian (or the defender of barbarians) his emphasis on courtesy and politeness may come as something of a rude shock. But Nietzsche certainly regarded peaceful relations with others (philosophical polemics notwithstanding) as being of paramount importance. Indeed, this aim is central to his list of "cardinal virtues" in *Daybreak,* cited above. Nietzsche contends that rudeness betrays a lack of style, a lack of self-discipline, and a poverty of perspective. By contrast, more noble individuals are courteous, sometimes even in their thoughts. "He who is of high rank would do well to furnish himself with a courteous memory: that is to say, to notice everything good about other people and after that to draw a line. . . ."[8]

depth The metaphor of "depth" permeates Nietzsche's writings. Sometimes, of course, he can be critical of depth, particularly when he encounters phony profundity ("the crowd believes that if it cannot see to the bottom of something it must be profound"[9]). Profundity, of course, is a cardinal virtue in German scholarship. What is distinctive in Nietzsche's use of the term is that it refers to a *biological* quality in us rather than an intellectual or spiritual quality, to what is *natural* as opposed to what is artifice, pretense, learned sophistication. What is deep is the love of fate, the exploration of the unknown. What is superficial is just what philosophers of the modern period praise most: "clear and distinct ideas," "the light of reason," logic, and (as usually conceived) the scientific method.

egoism Egoism is not usually considered to be a virtue but the very antithesis of the virtues. Suffice it to say that for Nietzsche it is not a vice but a virtue—yet it must be egoism properly understood, not as "selfishness" and not as mere self-aggrandizement. "Whose ego?" is a question Nietzsche always asks, and what are the desires and ambitions that it would satisfy? "Self-interest is worth as much as the person who has it: it can be worth a great deal, and it can be unworthy and contemptible. . . . If he represents the ascending line, then his worth is indeed extraordinary—and for the sake of life as a whole, which takes a step farther through him."[10] What is presupposed here is an utter rejection of the contrast between altruism and self-interest. In a great soul, the satisfaction of self-interest *is* to the benefit of the greater good.

exuberance Exuberance is not only a virtue in itself (in contrast to such traditional virtues as tranquillity and peace of mind) but the core of virtually all of Nietzsche's virtues. Style, for example, while it varies from person to person, nevertheless begins with exuberance, a "yes-saying" to life, enthusiasm, "overflowing . . . abundance," and what he describes in *The Gay Science* as "the great health—that one . . . acquires continually, and must acquire because one gives it up again and again. . . ."[11] Overflowing is a metaphor that derives from Nietzsche's celebration of energy, very much in line (not coincidentally) with the new conception of physics that had become very much in vogue toward the end of the nineteenth century. Exuberance is hardly the same as "effervescence," however, and Nietzsche would have nothing but utter contempt for those personalities that, particularly in the United States, are characterized as "bubbly" or "outgoing."

Like most virtues, exuberance cannot be taken out of context, that is, the context of the other virtues, even if Nietzsche denies that the virtues "fit" together in any unified way (a direct rejection of one of Aristotle's most perplexing theses, "the unity of the virtues"). The virtue of exuberance, in particular, depends upon what it is that is "overflowing." (One can think of several unacceptable candidates, greed and gluttony, for example.) It also depends on the discipline with which it is expressed, or the style of its expression. It is, one might say, *passion,* and being passionate is a virtue.

fatalism *(amor fati)* Nietzsche often writes about the temptations of "living dangerously," although, to be sure, he took few physical risks of the sort that we associate with that phrase today. Nevertheless, there is no doubt that Nietzsche took—and saw himself as taking—many risks in his writing, following his genius wherever it wanted to go. His *Birth of Tragedy,* his first "academic" book, was a conscientious flaunting of academic standards, with no footnotes, no staid philology. His last books, *The Antichrist* and *Ecce Homo,* border on blasphemy and mania, respectively. Taking risks requires accepting the consequences, and this sort of fatalism appeals to Nietzsche. It appealed to him in his analysis of the ancient Greeks, their acceptance of life in the face of absurdity and suffering. It appealed to him in considering his own miserable life, the exultations of genius in the face of his own absurd suffering. "My formula for greatness in a human being is *amor fati*. . . . Not merely to bear what is necessary, still less conceal it . . . but *love* it."[12]

"the feminine" The idea of "the feminine" as a virtue is often overshadowed by the popular (and unfortunate) emphasis on Nietzsche's well-known misogynist comments. Indeed, Nietzsche often expresses a high evaluation of "masculine" virtues. But he also praises some of the values associated with women by his society—perceptiveness, willingness to attend to intuition more than rationality, appreciation of appearances, and bodily gracefulness. Nietzsche expresses such ideals in the voice of Zarathustra:

> And you tell me, friends, that there is no disputing of taste and tasting? But all of life is a dispute over taste and tasting. . . . Gracefulness is part of the graciousness of the great-souled. . . . You shall strive after the virtue of the column: it grows more and more beautiful and gentle, but internally harder and more enduring, as it ascends.[13]

Contemporary feminists frequently oppose the association of women with these qualities, which our culture has usually valued as inferior to masculine traits. Time and again, however, Nietzsche allies himself with these more receptive virtues, as opposed to certain traits he associated with men in his era, such as conformity, clumsiness, insensitivity, and lack of grace.

friendship Reading Nietzsche's letters (not to mention his embarrassing marriage proposals) we get the sense that his personal attempts at friendship were far from calm amiability.

They were rather explosions of desperate affection. Zarathustra's often frustrated search for friends serves as a fair indication of Nietzsche's own attitudes toward friendship. Whatever his celebration of solidtude, Nietzsche clearly agreed with Aristotle, that no one would choose to live without friends; he also agrees with Aristotle that the truest friendship is a rare species of love. "Here and there on earth we may encounter a kind of continuation of love in which . . . possessive craving of two people for each other gives way to . . . a shared higher thirst for an ideal above them. . . . Its right name is *friendship*."[14]

generosity So, too, we can understand Nietzsche's sense of generosity as a virtue not as a mere overcoming of miserliness but as a quite literal overflowing. (In *Zarathustra* generosity is called "the gift-giving virtue.") It is not mere giving, nor the habit of giving. We too often think of generosity in terms of the request "Give till it hurts!" In other words, generosity must overcome resistance. But true generosity, Nietzsche would say, consists in painless giving, even pleasurable giving. Thus Aristotle insists that the performance of a virtue should be pleasurable, not painful, and this is a test of one's virtuousness.

For Nietzsche, generosity resides in what one might simply call one's "overflowing" nature. Having more money than we need, we gladly allow it to flow freely, even indiscriminately. So, too, the other virtues emerge as "overflow" of a great-souled spirit, of one who has an abundance. To object that the virtues are not this but rather a sense of duty that stands in opposition to self-interest and personal need is to fall back into what Nietzsche considers a slavish model of the virtues, the model that emerges in Kant and in Christianity, where it is the poor and not the rich in spirit who become the focus. In short, what constitutes a Nietzschean virtue is first of all a kind of fullness, a sense of oneself on top of the world, unconcerned about preserving one's position. "I love him whose soul squanders itself, who wants no thanks and returns none," says Nietzsche's Zarathustra, "for he always gives away and does not want to preserve himself."[15]

"hardness" Nietzsche's insistence on "hardness" is typically misunderstood—usually as being part of his dubious campaign against compassion and pity. But Nietzsche put a strong emphasis on self-discipline. (A Buddhist proverb: "If a man were to conquer in battle a thousand times a thousand men, and another conquer one, himself, he indeed is the greatest of conquerors."[16]) Nietzsche's conception of hardness involves unswerving commitment to one's task, "Why so soft, so pliant and yielding?" Nietzsche's Zarathustra asks his disciples. "Why is there so much denial, self-denial in your hearts? So little destiny in your eyes? . . . [A]ll creators are hard. . . . Only the noblest is altogether hard. This new tablet . . . I place over you: *become hard!*"[17]

health Health is one of the pervasive themes in Nietzsche's philosophy, as well as in his personal life. The question, of course, is whether good health can sensibly be called a virtue. This question turns, in part, on the degree to which one is responsible for one's health. But the question of responsibility is always ambiguous in Nietzsche, and given his emphasis on instincts and biological constitution it is by no means clear that the virtues have to be directly in one's control.

Nevertheless, health might be understood as the result of certain virtues rather than constitutive of them, or, to the contrary, it might be identified as the central virtue in terms of which all other virtues are measured. For Nietzsche a virtue, in short, is what is healthy; a vice is what is unhealthy. In other words, to see what is wrong with lying, lust, and greed, one need not appeal to the Categorical Imperative or any official list of virtues. It is enough to see what effects these vices have on one's health.

honesty One might also think of honesty as an "overflowing" of the truth, or, more cautiously, of one's most heartfelt opinions. Such honesty characterizes Nietzsche's own writings, a feature that he often proclaims. Honesty is not merely blurting out what one thinks, however, and it is much more than Aristotle's "truthfulness." And it is certainly different from any prohibition against lying that might be derived from the Categorical Imperative. Yet in *Beyond Good and Evil,* after praising honesty as a virtue that even free spirits should not weary of perfecting, Nietzsche warns, "Our honesty, we free spirits— let us see to it that it does not become our vanity, our finery and pomp, our limit, our stupidity."[18] One tells the truth not because it is an obligation, but because one has cultivated truth-telling, and honesty has become a part of one's character. Needless to say, the urge to tell the truth has little to do with the "greatest good for the greatest number." Honesty has more to do with an inner commitment: "I will not deceive, not even myself."[19] Understood in this way, honesty is, as Nietzsche's Zarathustra describes it, the "youngest among the virtues."[20]

integrity Integrity is a virtue, or an integration of the virtues, that is highly prized by Nietzsche. (We see it, notably, in his elaborate praise of Goethe.) Having integrity is not to be confused with any single virtue—for instance, with being honest. One can be ruthlessly or manipulatively honest in a way that betrays one's integrity. Integrity is Nietzsche's version of the unity of the virtues, even when those virtues are at war with one another. The self is a dynamic tension between competing instincts and virtues, and integrity is what holds them, however tenuously, together.

justice Today few philosophers would consider justice to be a personal virtue, as Plato and Aristotle did. Justice today is a rational scheme, a virtue of societies, not individuals. But justice for Nietzsche is very much a personal virtue, not a virtue of proportion (as in Aristotle) nor even "giving each his due" (as in Plato), although Nietzsche often makes comments that could be so construed. Instead, justice involves an open-minded responsiveness to another human being. Nietzsche's Zarathustra remarks, for example, "Where is that justice that is love with open eyes?"[21] Nietzsche seems far less concerned with "distributive" justice than either the ancient or contemporary philosophers. In fact, his philosophy is virtually devoid of any suggestions—much less a theory—concerning the equitable distribution of material goods and honors in distributive justice.

But Nietzsche is greatly concerned with what is sometimes called "retributive" justice—that is, the problems of punishment. In short, he is against punishment. He finds it demeaning, as it is essentially based on resentment, a sign of weakness, a traditional form of decrepitude. This may surprise those who are particularly struck by Nietzsche's frequent references to cruelty—sometimes bordering on an excuse, if not a justification (see chapter 1). But for Nietzsche, justice—which is closely tied to the equally problematic concept of mercy—is, first of all, the *overcoming* of the desire to punish, or, even better, having such a large sense of self that no punishment is even desired. "[T]hat man be delivered from revenge," says Nietzsche's Zarathustra, "that is for me the bridge to the highest hope, and a rainbow after long storms."[22]

playfulness The virtue of playfulness should not be understood in the current rather anemic sense of intellectual self-indulgence (although such verbal fiddling can often be found in Nietzsche), but in terms of the rich, buoyant enthusiasm of a child. In *Zarathustra,* Nietzsche gives us the child as the culmination of "The Three Metamorphoses," representing this exuberant playfulness. (First the camel, then the lion, finally, the child) Nietzsche was not a fan of innocence or childhood as such, but the fresh openness and intense inquisitiveness of a child's approach to the world obviously appealed to him. "A man's maturity—consists in having found again the seriousness one had as a child, at play."[23]

"presence" "Presence," of course, makes no sense except as an interpersonal phenomenon. Nietzsche admires those with the *je ne sais quoi* that we all recognize in certain people who command (not just "attract") attention. He suggests that Zarathustra has it, despite his failure to command much attention on his entrance to the marketplace; the first human being he encounters remarks, "Yes, I know Zarathustra. . . . Does he not walk like a dancer?"[24] Goethe certainly had it, but here again we face difficult questions about whether or not "presence" can be cultivated, and, even more basically, what is a virtue? Indeed, if health, strength, and presence are considered virtues (and not just natural advantages), then perhaps the whole discussion of the virtues, as carried on since Aristotle, has to be reconsidered.

pride Pride is usually listed as one of the "seven deadly sins" in Christianity. But for Nietzsche, as for the Greeks, it means something more like "self-respect." (Thus David Hume, a self-proclaimed "pagan," took pride to be a virtue as opposed to its "monkish" opposite, humility.) Nietzsche talks about pride as an ultimate motive—for example, in *Daybreak* (section 32), where he analyzes pride as the basis of morality and asks, in closing, whether a new understanding of morality (namely, his own) will require "more pride? A new pride?"[25] He also considers pride to be symptomatic of health and satisfaction in bodily existence. "A new pride my ego taught me," says Nietzsche's Zarathustra, "and this I teach men: no longer to bury one's head in the sand of heavenly things, but to bear it freely, an earthly head, which creates a meaning for the earth."[26]

responsibility Nietzsche is often listed among the "existentialists," together with Søren Kierkegaard and Jean-Paul Sartre, both defenders of a strong sense of freedom and responsibility. But Nietzsche's views on freedom are complex and confusing. He rejects "free will" as an illusion. He sees much of what is understood as responsibility—for example, the Kantian sense of obligation—as just another aspect of slave morality. He sarcastically attacks "the improvers of mankind," suggesting that many of the causes that responsible reformers engage in are futile. We cannot change ourselves.

Nevertheless, it would be difficult to read Nietzsche and not conclude that self-cultivation and self-transformation "Become who you are!"—are not central to his thinking. Nietzsche may express his share of skepticism about many of the conceptual presuppositions of autonomy and free choice, but he properly belongs to that group of philosophers with whom he is so often associated, for whom non-self-deceptive individual choice is an essential ingredient in "authentic" existence. Nietzsche does not see responsibility as being evenly distributed throughout the human species, however. He considers the few who are the natural leaders to have profound responsibility for the development of society. In *Beyond Good and Evil* he describes "the philosopher as we understand him, we free spirits" as being "the man of the most comprehensive responsibility who has the conscience for the over-all development of man." [27]

solitude Nietzsche's repeated emphasis on solitude (and not only by way of Zarathustra's example) indicates a virtue very different from those celebrated by most authors, especially by Aristotle and the Greeks. Aristotle clearly conceives of the virtues as essentially social. They have to do with getting along with other people. In Nietzsche, by contrast, the virtues are better understood in an extremely individual context, even the life of a solitary hermit. Indeed, many of his traditional virtues (such as courtesy) reflect the *necessity* of acting properly in the presence of other people. Nietzsche's most distinctive virtues, by contrast, are exemplified in solitude, sometimes existing *only* in solitude. This is true, we would suggest, even of virtues that might more usually be taken as obviously social virtues. The image of a dancing Zarathustra, for example, is not set in a ballroom or a disco. The virtues exemplified by dancing are, to the contrary, very much the virtues of a hermit, dancing alone.

strength Strength is a pervasive theme in Nietzsche, but the same sorts of questions about constitution and responsibility apply. This is complicated, of course, by some of Nietzsche's comments about "natural" strength, as in his brilliant but discomforting parable of lambs and eagles in *Genealogy*. And then there are Nietzsche's frequent references to the will to power. It is not at all clear to what extent strength and the will to power are correlated, and Nietzsche presents all sorts of conflicting views about this. His suggestions that "increase in power" or "the feeling of power" is the ultimate motivation for all things (not to mention his often quoted but unpublished note to the effect that everything is *nothing but* the will to power) makes it somewhat unclear to what extent we are talking about a state of character in any sense.

Nevertheless, if strength is taken to be a virtue, it is clear enough why Nietzsche would take it to be such, given his repeated accusations of "weakness" in virtually everything he opposes. The contrast with Christianity ("The meek shall inherit the earth") is obvious, but the idea that strength is a virtue presents us with many more questions than answers. What kind of strength? Strength as good health? Strength as discipline? Strength as will power? Strength as spirituality? Nietz-

sche characterizes his conception of strength as a virtue in his
description of Goethe's ideal.

> Goethe conceived a human being who would be strong, highly
> educated, skillful in all bodily matters, self-controlled, rever-
> ent toward himself, and who might dare to afford the whole
> range and wealth of being natural, being strong enough for
> such freedom; the man of tolerance, not from weakness but
> from strength, because he knows how to use to his advantage,
> even that from which the average nature would perish; the man
> for whom there is no longer anything that is forbidden—unless
> it be weakness, whether called vice or virtue.[28]

style Style, the heart of Nietzsche's "new" values, should not be
conceived as a "superficial" virtue, except in the sense in which
he described the Greeks as "superficial—out of profundity." It is
not just a way of "dressing" oneself, a way of talking or acting, a
way of "coming on." It reflects an essential "inner" drive, sometimes expressed by Nietzsche in terms of the instincts, which
manifests itself in every aspect of a person's self-presentation. If
Nietzsche says that every virtue is unique, then it certainly follows that style, in particular, is or should be unique to a person.

Most of what passes for style, however, might better be clas-
sified as mere "fashion," which is the very antithesis of style.
Fashion is the attempt to live in conformity with others' expectations, in neglect of one's own virtues. Style, by contrast, is
distinctly one's own.

temperance Temperance should not be construed as "moder-
ation" but rather as *self-discipline*. (In the end, one might say,

Nietzsche was German and not Greek.) Avoiding gluttony, greed, and lust is not a matter of limiting desires but cultivating self-control in the name of *style*. Noting that beauty is no accident but the consequence of sustained effort, Nietzsche insists that the "supreme rule of conduct" is: "before oneself, too, one must not 'let oneself go.' "[29]

Nietzsche's
Affirmative Philosophy

NIETZSCHE IS OFTEN portrayed as the most critical and destructive of philosophers. He attacks Christianity. He savages Socrates. He wages war on morality. One of Nietzsche's contemporaries rejected his philosophy as "waging war on every decent human feeling." In *Thus Spoke Zarathustra,* Nietzsche has his Persian prophet urge his followers to push what is falling. But pushing and destroying are a way of clearing the ground on which an affirmative philosophy can be built. Thus Nietzsche declares (in *Beyond Good and Evil*) that there must be new philosophers, philosophers who will "legislate values." Throughout *Zarathustra,* there is the buoyant ecstasy of worship, but for *this* world, this life, not another one. Nietzsche rejects Judeo-Christian morality not because he rejects all values but because he rejects the nihilism of Judeo-Christian morality. Christianity, like Socrates before, judges life itself to be "no good." Nietzsche aims, accordingly, to get us to appreciate a very different conception of morality, one that is born within us and not imposed upon us, one that celebrates life and doesn't promise another one, one that acknowledges the unavoidability of suffering in life but without drawing the pessimist conclusion: life is no good. And while Nietzsche attacks Christianity in many of its manifestations he does not attack either Jesus or spirituality. Indeed, we tend to see Nietzsche as among the most spiritual philosophers, so long as we do not conflate spirituality with the herd sentimentality of organized religion.

The purpose of philosophy—and of life—is to create, not to destroy. And so in this chapter we have put together some of Nietzsche's most exuberant, "life-affirming" theses. They include his celebrated love of fate, his doctrine of the "eternal recurrence," and the very idea of philosophy as "the gay science." Doctrines and approaches that are elsewhere used to attack are here viewed as celebrations, of moral psychology as a way of appreciating what is deep and marvelous about our moral existence, our passions, desires, ideals, and values, of perspectivism as a realm of open possibilities, of the revaluation of values not as a trick of slave morality but as the most important project facing humanity, and facing the "philosophers of the future," whom Nietzsche anticipates with unbridled glee and enthusiasm. Then there is spirituality, considered not in terms of the superficialities and hypocrisies of slave morality but as a cosmic acceptance of life and a sense of "godlike power." Thus the *Übermensch* as an ideal and the Will to Power itself, considered not as a diagnostic tool but as a celebration of the passionate life.

Amor Fati

The love of fate can be understood in many ways, depending on which of Nietzsche's several perspectives one adopts. It can simply refer to a free and easy attitude toward life—free of anxiety and worry, that is, easy in one's acceptance of circumstances and other people. Not to be judgmental is one of Nietzsche's most constant moral injunctions, whether in spite of or because of the fact that he was (like many of us) quite judgmental himself. "I do not want to wage war against what is ugly. I do not want to accuse; I do not want to accuse those who accuse. *Looking away* shall be my only negation."[1] To love fate, in this view, means to accept with equanimity and even enthusiasm whatever happens, whatever people do, whatever happens to one. It is a judicious outlook for a writer wracked with infirmity, wholly ignored by the public, to dream of a generation of future readers, "philosophers of the future," who would appreciate him.

Looking back to the Greeks, aesthetic acceptance would seem to be the meaning of *amor fati*. To reiterate a passage in which Nietzsche defines this expression, "[O]ne wants nothing to be different, not forward, not backward, not in all eternity. Not merely bear what is necessary . . . but *love* it."[2] The love of fate is rather the love of necessity, a keen eye for *essences*. But, then, what is necessary can also be understood historically and personally in terms of what Spinoza and others have called "destiny," the necessary path to the future.

But destiny, like fate for the ancients, also allows multiple interpretations. In the Greek tragic theater, fate sometimes seemed like a mandatory plot outline, engraved in the heavens. Oedipus had no alternative but to kill his father and marry his mother, despite the fact that he had many apparent choices along the way to doing so. Antigone, inheriting Oedipus's curse, was also destined for destruction, although she, too, had critical choices to make along the way. By contrast, the pre-Socratic philosopher Heraclitus insisted that "character is fate," and so fate is not so much a narrative imposed from the outside but an itinerary determined from the inside, by the person and his or her heredity, upbringing, situation, and response. Nietzsche does not seem to mean any one of these meanings; rather, he implies all of them at once. Like so many of Nietzsche's affirmative doctrines, *amor fati* is perhaps best understood as something of a mantra, part of a continuous pep-talk he gave to himself—and to us, too. Do not regret or resent. Do not worry or live in fear. Do not curse your life but accept it, whatever it may be. For it is life itself, not the pleasures and successes that are enjoyed in life, that gives life its ultimate meaning.

Eternal Recurrence

Near the end of *The Gay Science* Nietzsche gives us his best description of what he calls "eternal recurrence":

> What if some day or night a demon were to steal after you into your loneliest loneliness and say to you: "This life as you now live it and have lived it, you will have to live once more and innumerable times more; and there will be nothing new in it, but every pain and every joy and every thought and sigh and

everything unutterably small or great in your life will have to return to you, all in the same succession and sequence—even this spider and this moonlight between the trees, and even this moment and I myself. The eternal hourglass of existence is turned upside down again and again, and you with it, speck of dust!"

Would you not throw yourself down and gnash your teeth and curse the demon who spoke thus? Or have you once experienced a tremendous moment when you would have answered him, "You are a god and never have I heard anything more divine." If this thought gained possession of you, it would change you as you are or perhaps crush you. The question in each and every thing, "Do you desire this once more and innumerable times more?" would lie upon your actions as the greatest weight. Or how well disposed would you have to become to yourself and to life *to crave nothing more fervently* than this ultimate confirmation and seal?[3]

The same proposition is repeated in *Zarathustra:* "not . . . a new life or a better life or a similar life" but "this same, selfsame life."[4] This phrase, "this same, selfsame life," can be interpreted in a variety of ways. It certainly seems to mean, *in every minute detail.* We have all noticed, perhaps to our dismay, that changing even one small event in the past might have resulted in any number of dramatic alterations of the present. Indeed, if one had been born only five minutes earlier, so the argument goes, one would have been *a different person.* And so, if one regrets having gone to business school instead of pursuing one's true love of literature, or wishes he or she had not gotten married and had children so young, the sense of who one might be, given those counterfactuals, is truly bewildering.

A different interpretation is this: since eternal recurrence is a thought-experiment, its significance lies not in the details but rather in the general outlines. If one had been born five minutes earlier, one would very likely be very much the same person. But if one had become a poet instead of an accountant, or traveled widely instead of establishing a household at the age of eighteen, the differences would be considerable. Maudemarie Clark gives a nice explanation of eternal recurrence in these terms: after a long marriage, which has recently ended in divorce, would you be willing to do it again? In other words, was it worth it, all things considered? A few minor changes here or there would not affect your view. It is, rather, the whole of the marriage—the whole of your life for that considerable amount of time—that is in question. If you would gnash your teeth and curse the very suggestion, we would have to say that your life has been a waste, to that extent. If, on the other hand, you claim to have no regrets, then that is what we would call a happy marriage, a happy life.

So, too, the question is whether the thought of eternal recurrence is intended only to measure one's attitude, one's evaluation of life, or whether it is an instrument for *changing* one's life. Bernd Magnus once suggested that eternal recurrence served Nietzsche as an "existential imperative," a kind of test—not unlike Kant's Categorial Imperative—to evaluate whether this life, as one is now living it, would pass muster, or whether there are some basic things to be changed. (Magnus has since revised this view.) Nietzsche certainly has mixed feelings about changing, "improving" oneself, but he also insisted that one *becomes who one is,* which indicates change at least in the Aristotelian sense of realizing one's potential. One can easily imagine, considering one's life as one is living it—and here the present is much more important than the past that trails behind it—that one does not want to continue doing what one is doing. One's life work—or one's life—may not be painful or demeaning (in which case the decision would be more straightforward). Nevertheless, it may be, on reflection, meaningless or devoid of real interest.

The metaphor of *weight* here becomes an important piece in the puzzle. The idea of repetition is not to be taken literally but figuratively, as giving weight and substance to what otherwise might seem like no more than a fleeting moment. Thus Milan Kundera writes of "the unbearable lightness of being," borrowing directly from Nietzsche the idea that an event that happens many times has more substance than one that happens only once. And yet Kundera, like Nietzsche, combines the idea of eternal recurrence with the equally heavy idea of fate, "*es muss sein*" ("It must be!"),[5] and not for the trivial reason that something repeated innumerable times must be the same each time. To give such weight to the moment is to focus one's attention, to block distracting projections into the distant future or the merely nostalgic past.

As presented, the eternal recurrence is not a theory about the basic structure of time, but a psychological test, "How would you feel if . . . ?" To be sure, it is a model of time that has ancient and illustrious roots, back to the Indian Vedas and the pre-Hellenic Greeks, but there is little evidence that Nietzsche seriously intended to embrace the metaphysical systems of which this view of time is a part. He did not accept the distinction between appearance and reality on which the Vedic system is based, nor would he accept the doctrine that the world is an illusion. Nietzsche's notebooks include some sketches for a "scientific" proof of eternal recurrence, but they are not well supported, even within the physics and mathematics of Nietzsche's era. (Nietzsche's basic "proof" supposes that time is infinite but the number of possible "energy states" is finite, and that therefore the sequence of energy states must eventually repeat itself. This might be interpreted as requiring the infinite linear extension of time, the very claim that Nietzsche seeks to disprove. More charitably, one might see this initial premise as supposing that from within time, the future stretches infinitely forward. On the assumption of cyclical time, the trajectory proceeding from the present moment would eventually circle back to the course that it had previously run.) Nietzsche did not, however, publish any of his scientific "proofs" of recurrence.

The core notion behind eternal recurrence—that the sequence of events recurs again and again—quite brilliantly underscores Nietzsche's insistence on the "affirmation of life." (The placement of the passage from *The Gay Science,* cited above, supports this emphasis, for it is positioned between an attack on Socrates' claim that "life is a disease" and the introduction of life-affirming Zarathustra, which ends the first edition of the book.) Relishing one's life, with all of its pains as well as its pleasures, is the affirmation of life. Resentment, regret, and remorse, by contrast, suggest an unwillingness to live one's life again, exactly as it has been. There is a difference implied here between loving one's life because of its achievements and enjoyments and loving one's life for the sake of life itself. This is a theme that goes through Nietzsche's philosophy from his beginnings in classical philology and tragedy to his last autobiography. Life is suffering, Nietzsche asserts (with Schopenhauer), but the proper response to this is not resentment or disengagement (as Schopenhauer proposed), but instead wholehearted "Dionysian" acceptance.

Gay Science

Perhaps no other thesis in Nietzsche is as appealing or as captivating as the usually unstated theme which defines how Nietzsche conceives of and does philosophy: *gay science*. To state this concept in contemporary terms (which neither Nietzsche nor any respectable German philosopher would have used): *philosophy is fun*. This is not to say that it does not deal with the most sobering and serious of questions: the meaning of life and death; how we should live our lives and how we should think of and treat other people; whether or not we should believe in God and what this means; what tragedy and suffering are all about; and what is the future of humanity. But the caution and excessive sobriety of so much of philosophy, not to mention the self-righteousness of so much of moral theory and theology, is not only unnecessary but counterproductive. Philosophy requires Apollonian clarity, to be sure, but it also demands Dionysian gaiety and intoxication.

One never misses this when reading Nietzsche: he is *in love with* what he is doing, in love with the words, in love with the ideas, in love with the way that the sentences and the segments flow together, in love—as he once said of Spinoza—with his own wisdom. In philosophy as in science, he encourages experimentation, flirtation now with this hypothesis, now with that one. So, too, with moral "theories." The question is not so much

"Are they true?" It is, rather, "What kind of life results from them?"—and the only way to find out is to *try* them. What Nietzsche calls "gay science" (*fröliche Wissenschaft,* or *gaya scienza*) refers directly to the singing of the troubadours in twelfth-century Provence, and what he displays in his writing is no less passionate. As Nietzsche says, what a philosopher does is ultimately more important than—and indeed the test of—.what he says.

Moral Psychology

To call himself "the first philosopher who is a psychologist" was an outrageous claim, writing at the same time as John Stuart Mill and after La Rochefoucauld and Montaigne. But one of Nietzsche's themes was to appreciate the "deep" psychology that underlay even the most banal of actions and feelings. Like Freud, who followed him, Nietzsche often argued that these deep impulses were hateful and humiliating. His diagnosis of morality and Christianity in terms of *ressentiment* is a case in point. But by no means is all motivation ignoble, according to Nietzsche, and his inspirational appeal is based on the fact that he so often suggests that there is something *great* in us, waiting to be realized. (Thus some suffering is a disease, "but as pregnancy is a disease.") Unfortunately, Nietzsche suggests that this is true of only a "few" of us: still, we (the millions of Nietzsche's readers and fans) nurture the fantasy that he is, of course, talking about *us.*

Apart from the vague grand promises, however, what Nietzsche has bequeathed to moral psychology is a keen sense of the analyzable unconscious, a sense in ourselves of complex and sometimes suspicious motivation, even when we believe our motives to be most commendable. Much of what Nietzsche says about pity is quite outrageous, but at least some of what he says strikes us as exactly on the mark. How often is our supposed compassion a mask for our sense of superiority, or at least, our relief that the victim wasn't us? At what point does our love turn into possessiveness and our admiration into envy? To what extent is our morality motivated by self-righteousness rather than by "duty for its own sake," and how often are our judgments based on resentment rather than moral rectitude? But also, how much heroism, aspiration, idealism, and profound beauty is lurking in the depths of the human mind? These are thorny personal questions, not to be answered (as Nietzsche occasionally seems to do) with broad, generic strokes. But as philosophical ethics once again tends toward the merely formal language of obligation and "ought," the insistence that a moral philosopher should first of all be a keen psychologist has never had so much to recommend it.

Perspectivism

Perspectivism is the view that every "truth" is an interpretation from some particular perspective. There is no neutral, all-comprehending, "God's-eye" view available (even for God). There are only perspectives. There is no world "in itself," and even if there were such a world, we would not know it or even know *of* it. Science accepts this tacitly in its conviction that scientific theory must always follow the evidence that supports it.

Science never claims absolute but only tentative truths, even in its most basic laws—for example, the principles of conservation of matter, energy, and more recently, energy-matter. But science, too, goes wrong when it claims itself as the only perspective for getting at the truth, and Nietzsche gives up his scientific enthusiasm when he realizes that "scientism" can be just another dogmatism. In his middle writings (*Human, All Too Human* to *Gay Science*), where Nietzsche takes science to be the epitome of experimentalism, he is impressed by the fact that science never rests, never reaches a final conclusion. But today we know that in science, too, every theory finds itself immersed in experimental techniques, burdened by a catalogue of prior observations, established dogmas, and other theories, none of them immune to the prejudices of the times. Even "revolutionary" science depends on anomalies and incongruities in existing science. Despite its intrinsic safeguards, science can find itself as much in danger of dogmatism and absolutism as any other discipline.

But science is not the only (or best) perspective for seeking out the truth. Nietzsche suggests that scientific claims to truth can conflict with aesthetic claims to truth, that science and aesthetics are two different perspectives and give rise to two different kinds of truth claims. One can imagine a South Pacific sunset and two very different accounts of it, one in terms of the refraction of light and the other in terms of the brilliant glow of colors. Is one more *true* than the other? To so insist is to become a kind of dogmatist. It depends on your purpose, on the context, on the nature of the demand for "an account." Nietzsche often prefers the aesthetic perspective, if only because it is, he thinks, so often neglected in the modern world. But his perspectivism requires that it, too, be understood to be only one perspective, one set of interpretations, and nothing more.

In the realm of morals, one might juxtapose both the aesthetic and the scientific perspective against what one contemporary ethicist has called "the moral point of view."[6] In the confrontation or conflict between moral and aesthetic perspectives, one might think that something is morally wrong but also find that it is beautiful, breathtaking, awe-inspiring, sublime. A moralist would have no patience with this. Kant suggests that compassion is beautiful even if it is not, strictly speaking, of any "moral worth," but the idea that what is evil or obscene might nevertheless be beautiful would be abhorrent to him. Yet Nietzsche sees that *even in* cruelty and in suffering, there may be a kind of beauty. For example, the cruelty of Brutus toward both Julius Caesar and *himself* strikes Nietzsche as beautiful if also tragic. Indeed, the aesthetic task—exemplified by the Greeks but denied by Christianity—is to find or create beauty in suffering and tragedy. One might say that Nietzsche, like some ancient Chinese philosophers, sought to transform morals into aesthetics, to replace an absolutist perspective with one that was more straightforwardly perspectival.

We have seen that Nietzsche describes in some detail two different perspectives on morality (that of the master and that of the slave) and the two very different moralities that arise from each. But one might say that the perspective of master morality is in fact an aesthetic perspective. It has to do with what is beautiful and excellent rather than what is right or obligatory. Slave morality, by contrast, has only to do with good and evil; aesthetic considerations are ruled out, and the ominousness of evil dominates the conversation. The addition of religious considerations complicates matters even further, adding an absolutist metaphysics to an already defensive ethical perspective. Morality, consequently, cannot but conceive of itself in uncompromising, nonperspectival terms. Morality is not, from its own standpoint, a "point of view" at all. And to see it as such is already to weaken its claims considerably.

Nietzsche's idea is that perspectivism and the excitement of finding and exploring ever new perspectives should replace the dogmatic comforts of a supposedly secure perhaps eternal truth. With the end of an absolute conception of truth, Nietzsche writes, we will face a "new dawn," an open horizon, "the sea, *our* sea, lies open again; perhaps there has never yet been such an 'open sea.' "[7]

Philosophers of the Future

Who are Nietzsche's readers? There is no doubt in his mind who those readers ought to be: his "philosophers of the future," philosophers who would also be "legislators," inventing new values.[8] What these new values might be—apart from the fact that they would be free from resentment—is by no means clear. Indeed, it is not clear what "inventing" or "legislating" new values might mean. After all, what are the values Nietzsche most avidly encourages—the good old-fashioned values of courage, honesty, courtesy, and the like? But, in our own terms, it is clear enough what Nietzsche intends. He is sick and tired of "academic" philosophy, philosophy without a point or any goal other than to enhance the reputation of the philosopher, philosophy without any evident concern for the plight of modernity and the future of humanity. The philosophers of the future, in other words, should once again be philosophers, lovers of wisdom and, despite what Nietzsche says elsewhere, *the improvers of mankind*.

Revaluation of Values

In his later works Nietzsche takes as his central concern what he calls the "revaluation of all values," which, as he works it out, has mainly to do with the revaluation of *moral* values: "What is the value of morality for life?" The language of the revaluation of *all* values is misleading. Some value—say, the value of *life*—must remain steady as a criterion for the evaluation of the others. We might compare this process to the repair of a boat at sea, where we would always be using some stable parts of the structure to repair others, shifting our stance—our perspective—as need be. One might well read Nietzsche this way. He does endeavor to evaluate even the value of life in his work as well as the value of beauty, the value of suffering, the value of health, the value of compassion, the value of happiness.

But the underlying question is one toward which all philosophers should find themselves driven: What is the value of values? If the question is ultimately unanswerable (like the metaphysical puzzle, "Why is there something rather than nothing?"), the effort is nevertheless salutary. It prevents us from becoming dogmatic and opens our eyes to the shifting complexity of our interpretations of our world. It makes us appreciate the inescapability of values and thus protects us from nihilism.

The end of the moral interpretation of the world, which no longer has any sanction after it has tried to escape into some beyond, leads to nihilism. "Everything lacks meaning." . . . What does nihilism mean? That the highest values devaluate themselves. The goal is lacking; the answer is lacking to our "Why?"[9]

Spirituality

Because Nietzsche is so often considered an anti-Christian, and thus an anti-religious, thinker, it is too readily assumed that he had no room in his thinking for spirituality. True, he makes many sarcastic comments about the German spirit, and various references to Hegel's *Geist* and Luther's *heilige Geist;* yet it is also possible to view Nietzsche as the most spiritual of philosophers, and this is how he sometimes views himself. In order to understand this, we have to forgo all tendency to identify spirituality with otherworldliness, or with submersion in one or another organized religion.

One can perhaps get a grasp of what Nietzsche understands by *spirituality* by looking to music, the art form Nietzsche considered the most uplifting, the most in tune with the inner truth of things. One is not speaking only metaphorically when he or she claims to have a spiritual experience while listening to a great piece of music. Indeed, that is what spirituality is all about. It is neither selfless nor selfish; that contrast seems not to apply at all. One reaches beyond oneself; one overcomes one's everyday conception of oneself as one is overcome by the music; one is neither active nor passive (even as performer) but, rather, *enlarged.*

Nietzsche's conception of *this*-worldly spirituality involves a similar enlargement of one's sense of self. A naturalistic spirituality involves an appreciation of one's world and other beings in a manner that transcends the contrast between the self and the not-self. Nietzsche's description of his image of earthly happiness, significantly employing a beautiful image from nature, suggests something of this transformed sense of self.

> Anyone who manages to experience the history of humanity as a whole as *his own history* will feel in an enormously generalized way all the grief of an invalid who thinks of health. . . . But if one endured, if one could endure this immense sum of grief of all kinds while yet being the hero who, as the second day of battle breaks, welcomes the dawn and his fortune, . . . if one could finally contain all this in one soul and crowd it into a single feeling—this would surely have to result in a happiness that humanity has not known so far; the happiness of a god full of power and love, full of tears and laughter, a happiness that, like the sun in the evening, continually bestows its inexhaustible riches, pouring them into the sea, feeling richest, as the sun does, only when even the poorest fisherman is still rowing with golden oars! This godlike feeling would then be called humaneness. [10]

Übermensch

One way to think about the grandness within us is, of course, to think of ourselves as the parent to something greater than ourselves, the *Übermensch*. But although it is one of the best-known features of Nietzsche's philosophy (in part due to George Bernard Shaw's play *Man and Superman*), the *Übermensch,* or "overman" or "super-man," in fact plays a very small and obscure role in Nietzsche's thought. The coming of the *Übermensch* is announced in the prologue to *Thus Spoke Zarathustra.* We have noted (in chapter 1) that the *Übermensch* represents strength and courage but also "nobility," style, and refinement. And that is all. Nietzsche talks much more often about "higher men," but often to lament the fact that even they, too, are "human, all too human." Nevertheless, this, like so many of Nietzsche's other affirmative theses, is more of a regulative ideal—something to inspire and strive for—than a concrete prescription for action or transformative behavior.

The Will to Power

The "doctrine of the Will to Power," says Walter Kaufmann, the dean of American Nietzsche scholarship, is the very core of Nietzsche's philosophy. "Properly understood, Nietzsche's conception of power may represent one of the few great philosophic ideas of all time."[11] *The Will to Power,* according to the influential German philosopher Martin Heidegger, is the *core* of Nietzsche's metaphysics. Recently several analytic philosophers have tried to explicate "Nietzsche's system" in terms of this doctrine, and Gilles Deleuze, to name but one of several prominent French philosophers, took the "play of forces" to be the heart of Nietzschean thought. Unfortunately, once one has taken the dubious text of that name, *The Will to Power,* out of play, there is surprisingly little in Nietzsche's writings to support these views. The phrase, to be sure, recurs with considerable frequency. Nietzsche was clearly struck by it. And the hypothesis—that people often act for the sake of power rather than, say, pleasure—is surely a thesis that ties together a great deal of what Nietzsche says about morality, emotions, politics, and even religion. ("Luke, 18:14 corrected. He that humbleth himself wills to be exalted."[12])

The fact is, most of what Nietzsche says about the will to power is to be found in his unpublished notes, and it is therefore to be regarded with considerable suspicion. Nietzsche sometimes talks as if the will to power is the cornerstone of his philosophy, yet it does not have much to do with that mysterious metaphysical entity called "the will," which Nietzsche's mentor Schopenhauer elevated to the highest place in his rather gloomy philosophy, and which Nietzsche frequently and explicitly rejects as nonsense. If we may be particularly perverse, we might add that the *to* in "the will to power" is quite un-Nietzschean insofar as it suggests a teleological, goal-oriented impulse, something Nietzsche rejected; nor does the definite article, *the,* help much, as it indicates a singularity and uniformity that Nietzsche also rejects. (This is one of his many differences with Schopenhauer). Nevertheless, having thus dissected the phrase, let us go on to say some useful things about it.

What Nietzsche has in mind is, first of all, a rejection of ordinary hedonism, the reduction of all emotions, indeed all human (and animal) behavior, to striving for pleasure and avoidance of pain. Here he rejects a long line of English thinkers who have suggested that, ultimately, pleasure and pain are the most basic emotions, or emotion-components. In Nietzsche's view, pleasure is an accompaniment of satisfaction, not its goal, and what moves us more often are other motives, specifically the need to expand and express ourselves. Nietzsche talks about "will" in order to emphasize "drive" (*Trieb*), which has a strong flavor of the biological, of instinct, of purposive but unthinking behavior. Not surprisingly, Nietzsche adapted a strong predilection for evolutionary explanations (although he was not a Darwinian for a variety of reasons). Nietzsche objected to overly intellectual interpretations of human behavior in which all purposive action was immediately elevated to the status of rationality, articulated or at least articulable plans and strategies. Indeed, since Aristotle (and his concept of the "practical syllogism"), this hyper-intellectualization of human behavior had become the philosophers' bread-and-butter. Nietzsche wanted to remind us, in a philosophical era defined by hyperidealism, that, to put it perhaps too simply, we are still animals, still part of nature, still driven by impulses and instincts not of our choosing and sometimes beyond our understanding. (Freud would become an apt student, needless to say.)

To be sure, in his notes Nietzsche makes some extravangant metaphysical-sounding claims for the will to power; for example: "this world . . . a monster of energy, without beginning, without end. . . . This world is the will to power—and nothing besides!"[13] But to take this and a few other unpublished notes and turn them into the core of Nietzsche's philosophy is perverse, to say the least, and it goes against so much else he says (and *published*) about the mistake of looking for "the true world" behind its various appearances. Even where Nietzsche publishes such claims, they are overwhelmed by his own objections, even in the same book. For example, in *Beyond Good and Evil*:

Suppose, finally, we succeeded in explaining our entire instinctive life as the development and ramification of *one* basic form
of the will—namely, of the will to power, as *my* proposition has
it; suppose all organic functions could be traced back to this
will to power and one could also find in it the solution of the
problem of procreation and nourishment—it is *one* problem—
then one would have gained the right to determine *all* efficient
force univocally as—*will to power.* The world viewed from the
inside, the world defined and determined according to its
"intelligible character"—it would be "will to power" and nothing else.[14]

Even as a general claim about life, given the post-Darwinian
atmosphere of the time, the claim is dubious:

[A] living body and not a dying body . . . will have to be an
incarnate will to power, it will strive to grow, spread, seize,
become predominant—not from any morality or immorality
but because it is *living* and because life simply is will to
power. . . . "Exploitation" . . . belongs to the *essence* of what
lives, as a basic organic function; it is a consequence of the will
to power, which is after all the will of life.[15]

What the will to power means varies too. "A living thing
seeks above all to discharge its strength—life is *will to power;*
self-preservation is only one of the indirect and most frequent
results."[16] In the case of human beings, will to power manifests
itself in every other endeavor. Artists are also among Nietzsche's primary examples of individuals expressing will to
power.

Not need, nor desire—no, the love of power is the demon of man. One may give them everything—health, nourishment, quarters. . . . [T]hey remain unhappy. . . . One may take everything away from them and satisfy this demon: then they are almost happy. . . .[17]

Even love is the will to power:

They are cheered by the sight of another person and quickly fall in love with him; therefore they are well disposed toward him, and their first judgment is: "I like him." What distinguishes these people is a rapid succession of the following states: the wish to appropriate (they do not scruple over the worth of the other person), quick appropriation, delight in their new possession, and action for the benefit of their latest conquest.[18]

But although this *psychological* hypothesis pervades much of Nietzsche's work, any more systematic and metaphysical claims are rather dubious, however ingeniously they might be reconstructed.

The psychological hypothesis in question takes several different forms, thus already undermining claims that Nietzsche defended a single systematic thesis about power. In its most straightforward presentation, it can simply be read to mean that one of the dominant drives (if not *the* dominant drive) in human psychology is the desire for mastery—of its environment, of its social group, of its own drives and instincts. (There is the very real possibility of a circle here, namely, that the will to power might itself be one of the drives demanding mastery. Nietzsche actually embraces this suggestion, thus complicating the picture further.) The need to master one's environment is not a surprise, nor a radical thesis in the climate of German idealism and "expressivism" in the nineteenth century and in the mind-set of the Industrial Revolution. With only slight modification, the Darwinian notion of adaptation might fit here quite comfortably.

More problematic is the notion of power within one's social group. On the one hand, one thinks immediately of power *over* other people and power institutionalized as *Reich*. It is worth noting again that the word Nietzsche uses is *Macht*, not *Reich*, and thus might better be understood as personal *strength* rather than political power. It does not mean "power" in the nasty, jackbooted sense that still sends flutters up the European spine. The term means something like effective self-realization and expression. Nietzsche stresses that when a person is successful in pursuing such "power," aggressive and domineering methods are not necessary.

> Be sure you mark the difference: he who wants to acquire the feeling resorts to any means. . . . He who has it, however, has become very fastidious and noble in his tastes. . . .[19]

Nevertheless, the claim that what people want is power in a social context is fraught with ambiguities. Is social status itself to be understood as power? Are respect and admiration to be identified with power? Is manipulating people an expression of the will to power? What about persuading and convincing them with well-formulated rational arguments? At times Nietzsche suggests that logical arguments are straightforward manifestations of the will to dominate, as when he characterizes "logic" as "*compelling* agreement by force of reasons."[20] Indeed, scholarship and philosophy count for Nietzsche as paradigms of the will to power:

> "Will to truth" you call that which impels you . . . ? A will to the thinkability of all being: this *I* call your will. You want to make all being thinkable, for you doubt with well-founded suspicion that it is already thinkable. But it shall yield and bend for you. . . . That is your whole will . . . a will to power—when you speak of good and evil too, and of valuations.[21]

> Philosophy is this tyrannic urge itself, the most spiritual will to power.[22]

What Nietzsche does tell us is tantalizing but obscure. For example, he remarks: "Benefiting and hurting others are ways of exercising one's power upon others; that is all one desires in such cases."[23] "Our love of neighbor—is it not a lust for new possessions?"[24] "The striving for excellence is the striving to overwhelm one's neighbor, even if only very indirectly or only in one's own feelings or even dreams."[25] Here, as often, Nietzsche suggests that one is frequently motivated to pursue the *feeling* of power, not necessarily power itself. "The means of the craving for power have changed, but the same volcano is still glowing . . . and what one did formerly 'for God's sake' one does now for the sake of money . . . which *now* gives the highest feeling of power."[26] But how do we distinguish power from the feeling of power? For instance, Nietzsche condemns pity for a variety of reasons, among these his observation that one who pities is also expressing his *superiority* over the person pitied.

But is this so only when one externally expresses pity, or does a mere feeling of pity involve an expression of superiority?

Perhaps most startling is Nietzsche's claim that even ascetics manifest the will to power: "Indeed, happiness—taken as the most alive feeling of power—has perhaps nowhere on earth been greater than in the souls of superstitious ascetics."[27] Nietzsche sometimes considers the effort to "master" oneself as a special case of the drive for power.

Indeed, self-mastery is, in Nietzsche's opinion, one of the most effective strategies that the will to power employs; and he insists that it is essential to accomplishing anything great. Certainly, a wide range of different practices might be put under the general rubric of "self-mastery," including self-discipline, self-criticism, even self-denial. Many of Nietzsche's examples indicate that self-mastery is not itself the primary goal, but that such self-discipline, and even self-denial, typically aims at some further end, artistry or virtue. This may lead us to wonder whether the will to power is indeed a primary drive or motive in such cases, or whether it is an overly simple name for a wide range of instrumental values.

At the very least, however, the will to power is Nietzsche's expression for whatever it is that human beings fundamentally want (and sometimes for what other living creatures want as well). A human being wants to have an impact on the world, to operate freely within it, and to feel as though he or she is effectively expressing their real nature by doing so. Nietzsche sees all our efforts as having this basic aim in view, diverse though we find their aims and expressions.

Conclusion:
Nietzsche's Opening of
the Modern Mind

NIETZSCHE HAS HAD enormous influence on the twentieth century, and he seems to be starting out as the premier philosopher of the twenty-first. Of all of his various doctrines and images, perspectivism is probably the aspect of his bequest that has been most widely disseminated through Western culture and thought. The position that every outlook is relative to the perspective in which it is formulated has infiltrated the intellectual climate such that even those who still insist that there are absolute and universal values nevertheless tend to avoid the pose of dogmatic assertion, recognizing that dogmatism does not have the ring of authority it once had. Perspectivist assumptions provide the underpinning for several scholarly disciplines that have developed in the aftermath of Nietzsche's thought, including cultural anthropology and the fields of comparative religion, literary theory, and a good deal of philosophy (for example, the discipline of hermeneutics).

More generally, perspectivism has fostered the development of pluralism in the increasingly global intellectual community. It is now generally acknowledged that there is always more than one approach to any given discipline, and such diversity is necessary to the vitality of the field. Some theorists, notably under the banners of "deconstruction" and "postmodernism," emphasize that perspectivism implies that every theoretical outlook is limited and use this position to criticize theoretical dogmatists. These recent strategies are unquestionably influenced by Nietzsche. Ironically, given Nietzsche's own tendency to make outrageous pronouncements, Nietzsche's perspectivism requires us to practice intellectual humility regarding our own theoretical assertions. The polemicists of deconstruction, such as Jacques Derrida, and postmodernists such as Jean-François Lyotard, regularly remind their readers and their targets that they do not have the God's-eye view that their rhetoric sometimes suggests.

The intellectual world is not entirely sanguine about the influence of Nietzsche's perspectivism, however, and this is particularly true in debates about moral values. Nietzsche has been blamed by many cultural commentators (such as Allan Bloom and Alasdair MacIntyre) for the demise of shared values in Western culture. We might note that even these analysts are indebted to Nietzsche, for their critiques depend on the Nietzschean insight that a society's moral values have evolved over time and may even change into its opposites. But Nietzsche, as we have argued, firmly advocated ethical values—even "a more severe morality,"[1] so the complaint that he has personally had a hand in the supposed collapse of moral values is certainly debatable.

Nietzsche's critics are right, however, in claiming that he rejected certain traditional approaches to ethical values, including the focus on moral rules and the elevation of a single type of person as the moral ideal. Nietzsche's alternative approach encourages individual quests for self-realization. This very different nonmoral quest was picked up most famously by the philosophical movement of existentialism, which developed in the middle of the twentieth century. Instead of starting with rules that one attempts to apply to the situation, existentialists insist that ethics should begin by focusing on the concrete moral situation, which is often confusing and rarely ideal. Values are not given in advance by God or society. Instead, human beings create and re-create values. What one values becomes clear through one's concrete moral choices. Thus Jean-Paul Sartre may be viewed as the heir to Nietzsche's insistence that one legislates values through action. Through the choices one makes, one both creates and endorses a way of living.

The existentialists follow Nietzsche in his moral relativism, another consequence of his perspectivism that is sometimes criticized. Nietzsche considers his own willingness to acknowledge a diversity of moral outlooks as healthy and desirable. From his point of view, we would be better off resisting the rigid moralities that make us feel competent to judge others harshly. Instead, we would be better served by making nonjudgmental efforts to understand others as well as ourselves. Nietzsche attempts to put moralities and moralists in their place by stressing that everyone's moral outlook reflects the limitations of a personal perspective. So, too, the existentialists attack in various guises the pretensions of self-righteousness. Sartre attacks the "Champion of Sincerity" in *Being and Nothingness*.[2] Camus, in turn, attacks Sartre for *his* moralizing self-righteousness with such essays as *The Rebel*.

Those who denounce Nietzsche's approach to moral value may be more appreciative of another of his perspectivist claims. Nietzsche considers the scientific worldview to be one perspective among others, however valuable it may be within its own spheres. While he was impressed by the discoveries of science and its potential to help us untangle ourselves from superstitions, Nietzsche is concerned that scientific reductionism, "scientism" (which takes scientific accounts to be the only intelligent accounts), will replace the proper concern about the value of life, the value of our lives. Too often science has become so celebrated that it undermines all religion (not just Judeo-Christianity) and seems to eliminate the need for myth. Nietzsche's enthusiasm for culture and the arts reflects his opposition to scientism, as does his insistence that we still have a psychological need for myth, for imaginative accounts that address our spiritual needs.

Nietzsche's defense of the continuing importance of myth has had an influence in a variety of fields. Writers such as Thomas Mann and artists such as Isadora Duncan have drawn thematic material from Nietzsche's analysis of the myths of Apollo and Dionysus as complementary accounts of the human being's place in the scheme of things. The pioneers of psychoanalytic theory have also taken inspiration from Nietzsche's suggestion that mythic accounts reflect our psychological needs. Sigmund Freud, for example, used the myth of Oedipus to track the individual's development, and C. G. Jung drew widely from the world's mythologies to develop models for the complex activities of the mind. The psychoanalytic movement also drew some of its basic presuppositions from Nietzsche: that we are often not aware of our own objectives, that human motivation is so complex that we may never get to the bottom of it, though it is possible to gain some insight into the motives behind our apparent aims, even when they are distasteful.

Nietzsche himself saw the desire for power as a fundamental drive, at times describing it as *the* fundamental drive in human beings. Psychologist Alfred Adler made this premise the foundation of his own brand of psychoanalytic theory, which postulated that an "inferiority complex" was often the basis for neurotic behavior. French philosopher Michel Foucault drew from Nietzsche's postulation of the will to power, as well as from his account of master and slave morality, in analyzing cultural institutions such as prisons and various practices connected with human sexuality. Martin Heidegger and those influenced by him (for example, French philosopher Gilles Deleuze) tend to give particular prominence to the will to power in Nietzsche's thought. Heidegger himself considered the will to power the central principle in what he takes to be Nietzsche's metaphysical system, and this idea has retained currency among many contemporary Nietzsche scholars, even those who resist Heidegger's contention that the notes compiled as *The Will to Power* was Nietzsche's greatest work.

Although the relative importance of will to power in Nietzsche's thought is still debated, and it is doubtful that he had anything resembling a systematic political philosophy, one cannot dispute the fact that Nietzsche's thought has had considerable influence on political thinkers. In fact, Nietzsche has been claimed as a patron by many diverse, incompatible political movements.[3] Nietzsche has also been attacked as sexist, elitist, anti-Semitic, racist, protofascist, a romantic aestheticist, and an arch-conservative. Fascists, anarchists, social Darwinists, liberals, conservatives, progressives, and feminists have all attempted to appropriate him, as have those who treat the whole political arena with disdain. The tendency of politicos of every stripe to read Nietzsche as endorsing their views is a fascinating phenomenon that requires complex analysis. However, part of the explanation is surely to be found in Nietzsche's defense of the individual against the pressures of prevailing cultural winds. Members of various political movements have various interpretations of the aspects of the status quo that call for change, but many can visualize their own pet peeves as among the targets in Nietzsche's cultural criticism. Nietzsche's contention that one's perspective inevitably conditions one's understanding is certainly apt with respect to the range of politically tinged interpretations of his work.

Attempts to commandeer Nietzsche as part of the support structure for particular political doctrines, however, do seem to fly in the face of another of Nietzsche's own proposals: that we respond to the recognition of the limitations of our outlook by becoming more playful and lighthearted. If we lack the capacity to build conceptual structures on absolutely firm ground, then we may as well treat our theories as artistic creations, meaningful as self-expression and as modes of engagement with reality, but never immune from challenge. Their seriousness is precisely the seriousness of children's play, the sphere of experimentation in responding to the world. This insight, too, is part of Nietzsche's legacy, appreciated by some across the philosophical spectrum, from postmodernism to the best of analytic philosophy.

A century after his death, Nietzsche's influence continues to reverberate. He summarizes the artistic endeavor of his philosophizing in *Twilight of the Idols*: "To create things on which time tests its teeth in vain; in form, in substance, to strive for a little immortality—I have never yet been modest enough to demand less of myself."[4]

Thus far, Nietzsche lives.

Nietzsche's Bestiary:
A Glossary of His Favorite Images

In addition to those broad themes discussed in the body of this book, Nietzsche's works incorporate a variety of images that he uses allusively or symbolically. The following are some of those images and their connotations for Nietzsche.

Animal Imagery

Nietzsche often uses animal images to reflect his belief that human beings are animals and that much of their behavior is no more "rational" than that of other animals. In drawing attention to the "animal" nature of humanity, Nietzsche tries to debunk the tendency of his contemporaries to view humankind as the pinnacle of creation. He also has the more positive agenda of drawing attention to the instinctual nature of humanity and encouraging us to attend to the health of our physical natures. Nietzsche sometimes distinguishes between the strong and the weak by reference to wild and tame animals. Modern human beings take pride in being civilized, Nietzsche notes, but they are actually merely tamed, deprived of strength by calculated means.

Although he uses animals as symbols for aspects of ourselves that we should appreciate, Nietzsche takes issue with those who prefer animals to people. He seems to have Schopenhauer and Wagner in mind in this respect, and he reminds them that it is possible to hate people without loving animals.

Nietzsche also makes reference to particular types of animals, employing common associations with various species to draw attention to specific human traits. The following are among the more prominent animals mentioned in Nietzsche's writing.

birds 1. Birds generally symbolize the unconstrained movement of the free spirit for Nietzsche. The double-edged nature of freedom is indicated in his image of "Prince Free-as-a-Bird" (*Vogelfrei*), the pseudonymous author of the poems that close *The Gay Science,* for the word *Vogelfrei* suggests someone who can be shot on sight. 2. Birds sometimes connote "flightiness," as when Zarathustra compares some women to birds. 3. Birds are capable of a higher point of view than other creatures, and they are able to use this for their own advantage. 4. Birds are also able to carry messages a great distance. Hence, when Nietzsche describes having the insight that he may not matter, he describes this as the message of a "mischievous bird." 5. Birds are also important in the Germanic myth that forms the basis for Wagner's Ring cycle. The hero Siegfried, after slaying the dragon that guarded the golden hoard, burned his finger and touched his tongue to cool it. As a consequence, he could suddenly understand the language of birds, and he learned in this way of a plot to kill him. (Perhaps Nietzsche's hint in the coment about the "mischievous bird" is that the messages of such birds can be urgently important.) See also *eagle.*

buffalo Nietzsche associates the buffalo with the unclean water of swamps in which such creatures bathe. The buffalo is a particularly undignified creature. Zarathustra's description of poets as peacocks who perform before buffalo portrays poets as being too vain to realize the low sensibilities of most of their audience.

bull Nietzsche associates the bull with stubbornness, its lack of self-restraint, and its ability to use its horns in attack. The bull represents unrelenting will.

camel The camel is the quintessential beast of burden. In Zarathustra's "Three Metamorphoses" the camel represents the spirit in its first stage of development, in which it reverently bears the burden (but also the wealth) of the tradition.

cat Nietzsche compares women, or at least some women, to cats. He seems to be associating them with slyness and the potential for ferocity.

cattle Cows are paradigmatic herd animals, prone to following each other without any thought to where they are going. Nietzsche appeals to this association when he describes those who are enthusiastic about democratic institutions as "voting cattle." What they have not noticed, he contends, is that they were only allowed to choose from a few approved candidates, and often follow the lead of others in making their selections. Zarathustra's town, the Motley Cow, is a community of conformists. Despite the implicit critique of some of Nietzsche's references to cattle, however, he seems to have fondness for them. He seems to consider them warm, and he even describes having the impression that the temperature was getting warmer just before he turned a bend and came upon a herd of cattle. Nietzsche also appeals to cows' steadiness, as when he describes a formerly flighty woman becoming content like a cow after marriage in *The Gay Science*.

dog Nietzsche generally refers to dogs in their role as "man's best friend," and the most typical of pets. He also recognizes that dogs are not always well treated by their owners. Thus, when he likens his own pain to a pet dog, he suggests that he can vent his ill-humor on it.

eagle 1. The eagle in *Thus Spoke Zarathustra* represents Zarathustra's pride, we are told. The eagle's capacity to soar and move freely contrasts with the gravity that Nietzsche associates with tradition thus far. If we interpret tradition as having undercut human pride in our own capacities, the eagle represents the buoyant health of the person whose pride has been recovered. 2. The eagle is a bird of prey, hungry for meat, and powerful enough to satisfy its hunger with more docile and less active animals, such as lambs. 3. Nietzsche sometimes uses the eagle to represent solitary nature because eagles hunt as individuals.

fish Nietzsche's allusions to fish and fishing often make reference to the original vocation of some of Jesus' disciples. Jesus promised to make these former fishermen "fishers of men," and Nietzsche himself adopts this image, describing his writings as fishbooks and his potential readers as fish.

lambs Lambs are often emblems of youthful innocence. They are also the image employed in the New Testament to refer to members of Jesus' "flock," with Jesus in the role of the Good Shepherd. Nietzsche gives these associations his own spin. In his references, lambs are neither strong nor very bright. They are also vulnerable to fierce birds of prey. Nietzsche hints that those who feel safe in the flock are unaware of the more powerful who are delighted to prey upon them.

lion 1. The lion in *Zarathustra* symbolizes the strong spirit who has learned how to negate, after an earlier period of simply accepting the teachings of tradition. The lion is characterized by healthy self-assertion and strength. 2. These same characteristics apply to the lion as the "blond beast" in *On the Genealogy of Morals*. In this context, Nietzsche draws upon the image of the lion as king of the jungle, associating the lion with mastery and a master's sense of pride.

snake The snake is one of Zarathustra's animals, and it is associated with his wisdom. This association plays on the Genesis story in which Eve is tempted by a serpent who claims that eating of the tree of good and evil will make human beings as wise as gods. As so often, Nietzsche inverts a traditional image, suggesting that genuine wisdom, not original sin, resulted. As one who crawls into the earth, the snake represents earthly wisdom, as well as insight into the tragic.

spider The spider's characteristic ability to make a web that ensnares its prey is focal in Nietzsche's use of this image. In particular, he associates the spider with the Christian worldview that places God in the center and draws everything else into a web of interpretation. The Christian worldview, Nietzsche contends, renders the believer vulnerable to a fate much like that of the spider's victim.

worm Nietzsche uses the traditional association of the worm with lowliness. He is not flattering the humble when he describes them as being like worms who double up when stepped upon, to make further injury less likely.

Other (Miscellaneous) Images

Ariadne Ariadne helps the Greek hero Theseus, who was imprisoned in the labyrinth along with the children who were to be sacrificed to the Minotaur, her half-brother. Ariadne gave Theseus a ball of twine that he could unfurl along his route and thus be able to retrace his steps. After slaying the Minotaur, he led the children to safety. Taking Ariadne with him, Theseus set sail for Greece along with the children he had rescued. However, he abandoned Ariadne on the island of Naxos, according to one version of the story, where Dionysus discovered her and married her. Nietzsche sometimes appears to use Ariadne as an emblem for the obscure object of desire that leads the lover through a labyrinth. At other times, she appears to represent the human being who, after being abandoned by heroes, is approached by the god. Nietzsche takes inspiration from the idea that human failure may be the preamble to encounter with powers exceeding those known to humanity.

arrow Nietzsche uses this image to indicate unswerving movement toward one's goal and the power to soar above the rest of the world in pursuit of it.

Bayreuth Bayreuth was the location of Wagner's long-planned theater. The theater's inaugural festival, involving the performance of the Ring cycle, signaled the culmination of Wagner's career. This was also the point at which Nietzsche's disillusionment with Wagner and his associates reached a new level, and he did not stay in Bayreuth for the entirety of the premiere festival, as he had planned. Nietzsche's references to Bayreuth, therefore, allude to Wagner after he had lost faith in him.

Blessed Isles The Blessed Isles were the abode of Greek heroes after death, also known as the Elysian Fields. In *Zarathustra* the Blessed Isles are the location in which Zarathustra articulates the possibility of blissful alternatives in the wake of the death of God.

bread When Nietzsche refers to bread, he frequently alludes to the bread used in the Mass, particularly when wine is also mentioned. One case of this is the account of the hermit in the prologue of *Zarathustra,* who gives Zarathustra bread and wine and insists that everyone, even the dead, must eat what he has to offer. Nietzsche is lampooning the Christian insistence that taking what the Church offers (indicated here by the ritual bread and wine) is the only way to attain salvation.

cave Zarathustra's cave in Nietzsche's work is modeled on the reported home of the historical Zarathustra. However, it alludes also to the abode of the population of Plato's mythic account in the *Republic,* a society in which people are chained against cave walls and can see only the shadows of things that pass behind them. The philosopher in this story escapes from the cave, goes outside, and sees what the actual world is like. He returns to tell his community, but they insist that his eyes are faulty and try to kill him. By contrast, Zarathustra's cave is the place where Nietzsche's hero gains spiritual insight, and the challenge for him is to get the people outside the cave to recognize the riches he discovered inside it.

child The child represents three different notions for Nietzsche. **1.** The child stands for innocent, energetic life, unburdened by the past and enthusiastic in trying new things. The child in this sense is the final stage of spiritual development in Zarathustra's "Three Metamorphoses." **2.** The child represents progeny, or the future. Zarathustra pins his hopes on his future child, and Nietzsche hopes to be posthumously appreciated. **3.** The child can also represent immaturity. Nietzsche parodies the New Testament when he suggests that those who urge little children to come to them sometimes ensure that those who approach remain childish.

Columbus Like many Europeans, Nietzsche mythologized Columbus's discovery of the New World. He uses this discovery as an image for the comparable discovery that humanity might make of the new possibilities available after God has died.

(The) Crucified By this term Nietzsche refers to Jesus' mission of appeasing a wrathful God by dying on the cross. He considers this doctrine of atonement a barbaric invention of Saint Paul and essential to institutionalized Christianity but not a part of Jesus' teaching. When Nietzsche uses the expression "Dionysus vs. the Crucified," he counterposes this account against the Dionysus myth. Like Jesus, Dionysus is killed, torn apart by the Titans, a symbol of humanity's being divided through individuation. Followers of Dionysus also believe that their god will be reborn and that humanity will be reunified. The Dionysian myth leaves out the doctrine of sin, and accordingly Nietzsche thinks that it is a superior theological perspective. The Dionysian account treats suffering as being built into the structure of things; yet this suffering is not to be considered punishment for sin but the price of admission to something of incomparable value, life itself.

decadence The decline or corruption of a body, whether that of an individual or a body politic, leads to decadence. Nietzsche suggests that a decadent body seeks its own deterioration, its appetites warped by its basic unsoundness. Not all illness, however, implies decadence. Nietzsche insists that a philosopher must experience various states of health as a means to attaining insight. Moreover, sometimes symptoms of apparent ill health are really manifestations of pregnancy, a condition in which one cannot expend all one's energy because much energy is being used to nurture developing life.

desert The desert is common to the geography of the Middle East, the point of origin of both the Hebrew Bible and the New Testament, as well as the home of the original Zarathustra. For Nietzsche the desert symbolizes the place in which one is completely alone and susceptible to hearing inner voices. In "On the Stillest Hour," Zarathustra is in such a use of the desert image, recalling both the reluctant Hebrew prophet Jeremiah and the temptation of Jesus in the desert. Sometimes, however, Nietzsche uses the image of the desert with Orientalist associations, conjuring an oasis, a garden of delights, complete with wicked dancing girls. *Zarathustra's* "Among Daughters of the Wilderness" is an example of this use.

distance Nietzsche uses distance metaphors to convey the variability of human perspectives, since varying a distance varies optical effects. Vertical distance, specifically, is also used to suggest varying "ranks" of human beings, some being more noble than others. See also *height*.

dragon The Germanic mythology on which Wagner's Ring cycle is based features the story of a hero who kills a dragon that guards the golden hoard, including the golden ring with its special power. Siegfried is the hero in Wagner's version of the myth. Nietzsche casts the dragon as the guardian of traditional Western values in Zarathustra's "Three Metamorphoses." The lion, which represents the second stage of spiritual development, challenges the dragon and eventually kills him. Perhaps Nietzsche is drawing on the Judeo-Christian account as well, for the values based on "good" and "evil" are derived, according to the Genesis account, from Adam and Eve's eating fruit stolen from a forbidden tree. A curse goes with the stolen values, like the curse on the stolen gold in the Germanic myth, even if both confer power.

dwarf In ancient Germanic legend, a dwarf was the rightful owner of the golden hoard. The dwarf put a curse on the ring that was part of the stolen hoard, with the consequence that all who possessed it came to grief, despite the power the ring gave them. The consequences of this theft are elaborated in Wagner's version of the legend, the Ring cycle. Nietzsche considers dwarves vicious, in light of this mythological background. Hence, the dwarf who leaps onto Zarathustra's shoulder and urges him to attempt to assess time from outside of time (a feat that diminishes the apparent importance of life within time) pursues a vicious agenda in doing so. Interestingly, the vision that the dwarf proposes to Zarathustra is the alleged perspective of God in the traditional Judeo-Christian account. The image of the dwarf reflects Nietzsche's conviction that this conception of God in relation to our temporal world is a vicious scheme with harmful consequences for those who accept it.

ears 1. Nietzsche sometimes opposes hearing to seeing, where hearing is a more receptive sensory mode, allowing for more distant communication than does seeing. Hearing also carries the external world into the body, and thus the image of ears represents a more embodied way of encountering reality than Western thought often acknowledges. Nietzsche's privileging hearing over seeing challenges the supremacy of sight as a metaphor for understanding in Western thought. 2. Nietzsche also associates hearing with music, in particular with being captivated by music. 3. Nietzsche frequently utilizes the Scriptural line, "For those who have ears, let them hear," to his own ends. He suggests that only those who are receptive are able to comprehend what he has to offer.

gravity Nietzsche often invokes gravity to suggest weight and heaviness, often with a negative cast. Nietzsche's "gravity" can also mean seriousness, and sometimes he conjoins the two meanings. In calling for a "gay science," or "light-hearted scholarship," for example, he proposes an end to "grave" scholarly pursuits that ultimately serve to weigh one down. Sometimes, however, Nietzsche uses the term to refer, quite literally, to the force that keeps us rooted to the earth and our planet fixed in the solar system. In this respect, gravity is essential to our being at home in the world. The death of God, Nietzsche's Madman reports, unchains the earth from the sun, leaving us lurching through space without a sense of destination. Although this circumstance occasions unprecedented possibilities, the experience itself is terrifying.

hammer In *Twilight of the Idols* Nietzsche speaks of himself as someone who philosophizes with a hammer, and he describes other genuine philosophers in *Beyond Good and Evil* as treating everything they grasp as a hammer. This image is a condensation of a number of ideas. 1. Nietzsche suggests that the hammer is an instrument used to "sound out idols" in order to determine whether or not they are hollow. 2. The second allusion is to the sculptor's hammer. Nietzsche refers to Michelangelo's description of freeing the sculpture from the stone. 3. According to Luther, God employs a powerful hammer to crush the self-righteous pride of the sinner and provoke despair; only after this experience is the soul open to God's grace, which converts the negativity of despair into a condition of affirmation. Nietzsche thus puts himself in the position of God, the hammer-wielder, crushing the self-righteous pride of the moralist in order to provoke a similar condition, in which the affirmative character of the natural world can be recognized. Again, the hammer is a tool of redemption, but a different redemption than that recommended by Luther.

hardness 1. Nietzsche advocates hardness as opposed to the softness of the soft touch, the person who is so moved by pity as to give no thought as to what would be genuinely helpful, or so moved as to be diverted from his or her own work. The hardness here is that of the hard-headed and of the Stoic. 2. Hardness is also an image for strength and muscular power. 3. Hardness also has sexual connotations and represents virility. 4. By contrasting the hard diamond with the soft coal, kin in carbon composition, Nietzsche suggests that hardness is a basis for value. Here, hardness involves resistance to breakage, as well as the beauty of the well-defined edge.

height Various height metaphors in Nietzsche are used to indicate the perspective of someone who stands "above" the crowd, a "lofty" soul. Climbing indicates the strenuous efforts required to attain such a height. Mountains are the home of the lofty, the noble type of person. One who is high up can take a broad view of things. Nietzsche also stresses that the air is clear in the mountains. These images are related to the "pathos of distance," the awareness that human beings have various ranks. One consequence is that the noble person can see lesser souls from above and can recognize that these souls are unable to see very far. Nietzsche warns such a person not to be distracted from important aims by pitying those below him or her. "The abyss," the inchoate gap in the mountains into which the climber might fall, is a related image. Nietzsche describes tragic insight as "abysmal," and reminds climbers that they must always be aware of the abyss, lest they inadvertently plunge to their destruction. See also *under (down)* and *over (up)*.

herd (and flock) See *animals*.

immaculate perception (disinterestedness) Nietzsche lampoons "disinterestedness," one of the doctrines of Kantian aesthetics, in the section of *Zarathustra* focused on "immaculate perception." Kant's influential aesthetic doctrine held that one has a "pure" judgment of beauty only when one is free of all desire in connection with it. Nietzsche thinks, by contrast, that beauty incites one to health and sexuality. He caricatures the "disinterested" thinker as a dirty old man who pretends to be too lofty for sexual interest.

navigation See *water.*

nose The nose is the sense organ least appreciated by Western thinkers, a fact Nietzsche deplores. He sees the low status of the nose as being tied to its associations with earthiness and bodily experience. Sight, the most highly regarded sense, is rarely linked to the body; and its high reputation is based partially on sight's capacity to "get beyond" the body. Nietzsche reminds his readers that the nose and our other bodily means of perception are the sources of information on which all science (typically a source of pride) is based. He describes the nose as a precision instrument, of greater use for knowledge than the most refined pieces of laboratory equipment (which ultimately require refined senses in order to read them). Nietzsche also makes use of the image of the nose to indicate a sensory abhorrence of one's surroundings. Zarathustra, for example, sometimes leaves his company to get some air, for his nose informs him that something stinks.

over (up) The German prefix *Über,* meaning "over," is paired with its opposite, the prefix *Unter* ("under"), in some of Nietzsche's prose. He makes use of such over/under word play in Zarathustra's first speech in *Thus Spoke Zarathustra.* The *Übermensch* is "over" in the sense of being of higher rank than all presently existing human beings. Yet one of the things that marks the *Übermensch* is the willingness to "go under," to risk oneself to the point of perishing in order that something great might be achieved beyond oneself. See also *height.*

overflow Nietzsche uses this image to describe the external manifestations of great health and inner riches. He emphasizes, however, that actions that might initially appear similar may have very different motives, some driven by strength and others by weakness. The overflow of the great soul in creative efforts and generous deeds expresses strength and health, and it represents something of a Nietzschean ideal. Interestingly, here Nietzsche is borrowing an image from his religious background: Luther had emphasized that while good works would not earn one salvation, good works would be the "overflow" of God's grace in the believer's soul.

poison Nietzsche seems to have in mind the slow-acting type of poison that, once ingested, gradually overtakes one's system. He contends that vindictive attitudes—not to mention the conception of human beings as understood in the Judeo-Christian moral vision—are of this sort. The consequence of ingesting such poison is that it invades one's entire system, eventually infecting one's health and one's every thought.

rank See *distance*.

ring Nietzsche's references to a ring always appear against the background of Wagner's account of the *Ring of the Nibelungen,* about a ring that was made from the gold of the Rhine and gave unlimited power to the person who possessed it. The gold used for the ring was cursed because it was stolen. The story of power struggles over the ring, and the successive ruin of everyone who comes to possess it, is the subject matter of Wagner's four-part Ring cycle, comprised of *Das Rheingold, Die Walküre, Siegfried,* and *Götterdämmerung (Twilight of the Gods).* Nietzsche conjoins these Wagnerian associations with the image of the wedding ring in *Zarathustra* as well as with the "ring" shape of time according to the theory of eternal recurrence. Zarathustra weds eternity by conjoining himself with the ring of time; in effect, the human point of connection with eternity *is* this life in time. The ring of eternal recurrence recalls the ring of the Germanic myth in two respects. The person acquiring the "ring" of time gains power, the capacity for action and transformation in the present, but at the same time is assured that time will cause his or her ultimate destruction.

times of day Nietzsche follows the customary employment of times of day to represent distinct periods of an individual's life, or the life of a people. Thus, high noon, or midday, represents the high point of energy and activity. Twilight suggests the imminence of night, when energy is in decline and the importance of the day's concerns recede. Twilight is used with this intent in the title *Twilight of the Idols,* to suggest that the reign of what Nietzsche considers false gods in the West (including the Western conception of God) is about to end. (This title also puns on the title of Wagner's opera *Götterdämmerung, Twilight of the Gods.*)

Midnight represents the silent moment in which one day gives way to another. Nietzsche describes midnight as "the stillest hour," the point at which significant change occurs, even though it is hardly noted. He also uses midnight as a naturalistic image of temporal recurrence. The suggestion seems to be that the moment of midnight, which serves as a gateway between the previous day and the new day, shows us dramatically what is true of every moment: that the present is always new, but always drawn from the life that precedes it.

ugliness Nietzsche associates ugliness with Socrates, and he suggests that the thinker's ugly countenance reflected ugliness of soul. "The Ugliest Man," a character in part IV of *Zarathustra,* is described as the killer of

God, who was moved to his crime because he could not stand God seeing his ugliness in every detail. Nietzsche insinuates that the Christian moral worldview has encouraged human beings to see themselves as hideous, and that God's waning import in Western society may stem from a similar intolerance with our pathetic self-image.

under (down) *Untergehen* has multiple connotations in German. **1.** It literally means "to go down, or under." **2.** *Untergehen* is also the verb used to describe the sun's setting, a "going under" that hints at the sun's reappearance. **3.** It also means "to die" or "to perish." **4.** Nietzsche's use of the term is informed by Wagner's dramatic presentation of the "going-down" of the gods. Wagner's presentation of the god Wotan's self-willed destruction and the triumph of the hero Siegfried (as a representative of humanity) itself drew on Feuerbach's image of the rejuvenation of humanity in the wake of the death of God. In this connection, *Untergehen* brings together Nietzsche's idea of self-overcoming and the hope that humanity will assert its own natural power after the calamity of the death of God.

wandering Nietzsche advocates that the thinker avoid establishing a permanent "camp" with his or her positions. Instead, philosophy and scholarly disciplines generally should aim to keep wandering and exploring. Gilles Deleuze has emphasized this notion when he describes Nietzsche's view as promoting "nomadic" thought.

water Nietzsche uses images of water for various purposes: to suggest the energetic flow of reality, and to characterize the human being's situation, which requires navigation. He makes much of the ongoing movements of ocean waves, which surge forward as if on a mission. He suggests that our own acts of willing are like this, only meaningful inside their projects. Like waves, too, our endeavors dissipate, only to be replaced by new ones. "Water" can also refer to the waters of baptism, although the naturalistic references are more frequent.

weight See *gravity*.

wine Wine has multiple roles in Nietzsche's imagery. **1.** At times, when paired with bread, Nietzsche is alluding to the motif of Christian communion, in which wine, transformed into the blood of Jesus (or a symbol thereof) is ingested along with bread that has been transformed into Jesus' body (or a symbol therof). **2.** Wine is also the drink associated with Dionysus and the intoxicated frenzy of his votaries. Nietzsche associates the creative rapture of the artist with this frenzy. **3.** In Apuleius's book *The Golden Ass,* a satire that chronicles the spiritual development of a man who has misused magic and turned himself into an ass, the ass's fortunes begins to turn around when he is discovered sipping wine from his masters' pantry. In part IV of *Thus Spoke Zarathustra,* an ass is said to drink wine, apparently alluding to Apuleius's satire. **4.** Sometimes Nietzsche mentions wine in the everyday sense of a particular alcoholic beverage, though sometimes used to represent alcoholic beverages in general. In these contexts, he usually describes wine as a narcotic and the use of it as a symptom of declining life. He claims that a real enthusiast (a person filled with spirit) does not need wine.

"Yes and Amen" Nietzsche frequently uses this phrase, drawn from Christian usage, as a formula for expressing affirmation. "Amen" means "So be it," or, in more Nietzschean terms, "Thus I will it." Accordingly, "Yes and Amen" means "That is how it is, and I will it to be so," precisely the state of mind that Nietzsche sees as characteristic of life-affirmation: *amor fati.*

"yes and no" Nietzsche uses this expression to indicate binary thinking. The formulation of any judgment requires some use of "yes and no," in Nietzsche's opinion. He objects, however, to those who are unconditional in their application of these judgments.

Notes

Abbreviations Used in the Notes

A	The Antichrist	HAH	Human, All Too Human
BGE	Beyond Good and Evil	NCW	Nietzsche contra Wagner
BT	The Birth of Tragedy	PN	The Portable Nietzsche
CW	The Case of Wagner	TI	Twilight of the Idols
D	Daybreak	TSZ	Thus Spoke Zarathustra
EH	Ecce Homo	UM	Untimely Meditations
GM	On the Genealogy of Morals	WP	The Will to Power
GS	The Gay Science		

INTRODUCTION: "HOW TO PHILOSOPHIZE WITH A HAMMER"

1. *TI* I, p. 467.

2. Alexander Nehamas, *Nietzsche: Life as Literature* (Cambridge, Mass.: Harvard University Press, 1985).

3. For further commentary on the specific books, beyond what is offered in chapter 2, see Bernd Magnus and Kathleen M. Higgins, "Nietzsche's Works and Their Themes," in *The Cambridge Companion to Nietzsche,* Magnus and Higgins, eds. (New York: Cambridge University Press, 1996), pp. 21–68. For discussions of individual works, see Robert C. Solomon and Kathleen M. Higgins, *Reading Nietzsche* (New York: Oxford University Press, 1988).

1. RUMORS: WINE, WOMEN, AND WAGNER

1. Letter from Nietzsche to Jacob Burckhardt, January 6, 1889, in *PN*, p. 685.

2. Letter from Nietzsche to Franz Overbeck, January 6, 1889, in *PN*, p. 687.

3. *TSZ* I:18, in *PN*, p. 179.

4. *GS* 140, p. 190.

5. *GM* I:7, pp. 33–34. Italics in original.

6. *GM* I:9, p. 36.

7. *GM* I:16, p. 53.

8. *EH* III:1, p. 261.

9. *TI* IX:1, p. 506.

10. This statement and Nietzsche's religious thought generally are discussed below, in chapter 3.

11. *TSZ*, p. 321.

12. *WP* 2, p. 9.

13. *TSZ*, p. 126.

14. *D* 348, p. 165.

15. *GS* 290, p. 232.

16. *EH*, "Why I Am So Clever" 10, p. 258.

17. *TI* IX:7, p. 512.

18. David Farrell Krell and Donald L. Bates, *The Good European: Nietzsche's Work Sites in Word and Image* (Chicago: University of Chicago Press, 1997), p. 47.

19. *EH* II:1, p. 236.

20. *EH* II:1, p. 236.

21. *GM* II:23, p. 93.

22. *D* I:95, p. 54.

23. *GM* II:6, p. 67.

24. *GS* 73, p. 129.

25. *TSZ* I:19, p. 180.

26. Hans von Bülow, 1872 letter to Nietzsche, cited in Ernst Newman, *The Life of Richard Wagner*, vol. 4 (New York: Knopf, 1933–46), p. 324.

27. *EH* II:3, p. 243.

28. Friedrich Nietzsche to Cosima Wagner, beginning of January 1889, in *Selected Letters of Friedrich Nietzsche*, trans. and ed., Christopher Middleton (Chicago: University of Chicago Press, 1969), p. 346.

29. Translated from the records of the asylum at Jena, March 27, 1889; in Walter Kaufmann, *Nietzsche: Philosopher, Psychologist, Antichrist,* 4th edition (Princeton: Princeton University Press, 1974), p. 32.
30. *EH* II:5, p. 247; *EH* II:6, p. 250; and *CW* 1, as discussed in *EH,* p. 317.
31. *EH,* p. 285.
32. *TI* IV:5, p. 483.
33. *TI* IV:2, p. 481.
34. *TI* I, p. 466.
35. *TI* II:8, p. 467.
36. Alexander Nehamas, *Nietzsche: Life as Literature* (Cambridge, Mass.: Harvard University Press, 1985), p. 234.
37. *TI* IX:2, p. 507.
38. Ralph Waldo Emerson, *Self-Reliance* (New York: Wise, 1929), pp. 143–44.
39. *GS* 348, p. 291.
40. See *EH* III:1, p. 261.
41. Marie von Bradke, June 30–September 25, 1886, cited in Sander L. Gilman, *Conversations with Nietzsche: A Life in the Words of His Contemporaries,* trans. David J. Parent (New York: Oxford University Press, 1987), p. 192.

2. FACED WITH A BOOK BY NIETZSCHE

1. *GS* 366, p. 322.
2. *GS* 381, p. 343.
3. *TSZ,* p. 152.
4. *TI* IX:7, p. 512.
5. *EH* III:4, p. 265.
6. *GS* 173, p. 201.
7. *TI* X:51, p. 556.
8. *TSZ* II:17, p. 239
9. See *Sämmtliche Briefe: Kritische Studienausgabe,* 8 vols., G. Colli and M. Moninari, eds. (Berlin: de Gruyter/Deutscher Taschenbuch Verlag, 1975–84), vol. 9, 12 [2], p. 576, our translation.
10. *TI* X:1, p. 513.
11. *GS* 368, p. 326.
12. *EH* IV:1, p. 326.
13. *TSZ* II:6, p. 209.

14. *BT* 5, p. 52; see also *BT* 4 ("Attempt at Self Criticism") p. 22.
15. *GS* 99, p. 155.
16. Nietzsche, "On Truth and Lies in a Nonmoral Sense," in *Philosophy and Truth: Selections from Nietzsche's Notebooks of the Early 1870's*, Daniel Breazeale, trans. and ed. (Highlands, N.J.: Humanities Press, 1979), p. 84.
17. Friedrich Nietzsche, *Beyond Good and Evil*, trans. Walter Kaufman (New York: Random House, 1966), 6, p. 13.
18. *BGE* 187, p. 99.
19. *BGE* 211, p. 136.
20. *BGE* 13, p. 21.
21. *TSZ* IV:13:3, p. 399.
22. *CW* 7, p. 170.
23. *CW* 5, p. 164.
24. Gary Shapiro, "The Writing on the Wall: The Antichrist and the Semiotics of History," in *Reading Nietzsche*, Robert C. Solomon and Kathleen M. Higgins, eds. (New York: Oxford University Press, 1988), p. 200.
25. *A* 62, pp. 655–56.

3. NIETZSCHE SAID, "GOD IS DEAD"

1. *GS* 285, pp. 230.
2. *GS* 136, p. 188.
3. *A* 15, pp. 581.
4. *D* 78, p. 48.
5. *GS* 135, pp. 187–88.
6. *TI* VI:1, p. 486.
7. *D* 60, p. 36.
8. *HAH* 55, p. 41.
9. *GM* II:16, p. 85.
10. *GS* 122, p. 178.
11. *GS* 357, p. 307.
12. *GS* 125, pp. 181–82.
13. *BGE* 116, p. 86.
14. *TSZ* I:13, p. 166.
15. *GS* 109, p. 169.
16. *EH* IV 9, p. 335.
17. *GS* 310, pp. 247–48.

18. *TSZ* III:13, p. 405.

19. *GS* 334, p. 262.

4. NIETZSCHE'S WAR ON MORALITY

1. *BGE* 260, p. 204.

2. *GM* I:7, p. 34.

3. *GM* I:10, p. 36.

4. *GM* I:10, p. 36.

5. *GM* I:11, p. 42.

6. *GM* I:10, p. 38.

7. Simone Weil, "Evil," in *Gravity and Grace* (New York: G. P. Putnam's Sons, 1952), p. 120.

8. *TI* VIII, p. 501.

9. *GM* I:13, pp. 44–45.

10. *GM* I:13, p. 45.

5. NIETZSCHE *AD HOMINEM* (NIETZSCHE'S "TOP TEN")

1. *EH* III:5, p. 266.

2. *TI* III:3, p. 474.

3. *A* 11, p. 578.

4. *GM* I:10, p. 36. The adjective "shabby" comes from *WP* 7, p. 10.

5. *TI* IX:2, p. 507.

6. *TI* III:3, p. 474.

7. "Schopenhauer as Educator" 2, in *UM*, p. 135.

8. *BT* 15, p. 96.

9. *BT* 15, p. 93.

10. Fragment VI, 101, cited in Walter Kaufmann, *Nietzsche: Philosopher, Psychologist, Antichrist*, 4th edition (Princeton: Princeton University Press, 1974), p. 398.

11. *GM* III:7, p. 107.

12. *HAH* 86, p. 332.

13. *EH* IV:3, pp. 327–28.

14. Postcard from Nietzsche to Franz Overbeck, postmarked Sils Engd., July 30, 1881, in Christopher Middleton, trans. and ed., *Selected Letters of Friedrich Nietzsche* (Chicago: University of Chicago Press, 1969), p. 177.

15. Friedrich Nietzsche, *Gesammelte Werke, Musarionausgabe*, 23 vols. (Munich: Musarion, 1920–29), XXI, 98; cited in Kaufmann, *Nietzsche*, p. 306.

16. Nietzsche, *Gesammelte Werke, Musarionausgabe*, XIV, 109; cited in Kaufmann, *Nietzsche*, p. 306.

17. *HAH* 475, p. 175.

18. *D* 497, pp. 202–3.

19. *D* 481, p. 198.

20. *GS* 333, p. 261.

21. *GM* Preface 5, p. 19.

22. *WP* 410, p. 221.

23. *GM* II:15, p. 83.

24. *GS* 372, p. 333.

25. *TI* IX:49, pp. 553–54.

26. *TI* X:51, p. 555.

27. *TSZ* II, p. 239.

28. Carol Diethe, *Nietzsche's Women: Beyond the Whip* (Berlin / New York: De Gruyter, 1996), p. 24.

29. *NCW*, pp. 663–64.

30. *EH* II:6, p. 250.

31. *BT* 18, p. 112.

32. *GS* 357, p. 305.

33. See *WP* 1067, p. 550.

34. *GS* 357, pp. 307–8.

35. *TI* IX:45, pp. 549–50.

36. See Kaufmann, *Nietzsche*, p. 340.

37. Ralph Waldo Emerson, "Divinity School Address" (1838), in *Selected Writings of Ralph Waldo Emerson* (New York: New American Library, 1965), pp. 248–49.

38. Emerson, "Divinity School Address," pp. 253 and 255.

39. *A* 39, p. 612.

40. *EH* II:4, p. 246.

41. *GS* 98, p. 15.

42. *BT* 7, p. 60.

43. *TSZ* II, p. 240.

44. William Shakespeare, *Hamlet*, act 1, scene 5, lines 166–67.

45. *BT* 9, pp. 67–68.

46. *TI* II:4, p. 561.

47. *BT* 23, p. 137.

48. Nietzsche to Erwin Rhode, February 22, 1884, in Middleton, *Selected Letters*, p. 221.

49. "Unter und über dem Nein das tiefe, heimliche Ja." Martin Luther, *Dr. Martin Luthers Werke: Kritische Gesamtausgabe* (Weimar, 1883ff.), 11, 120.

50. *GS* 377, p. 340.

51. *EH* II:4, p. 245.

52. *TI* IX:2, p. 559.

53. The phrase comes from Daniel Dennett, *Darwin's Dangerous Idea: Evolution and the Meanings of Life* (New York: Simon and Schuster, 1995).

54. See Kaufmann, *Nietzsche*, p. 175.

55. *TSZ*, Prologue 4, p. 126.

56. Kaufmann, *Nietzsche*, p. 118.

57. *GS* 357, p. 305.

58. *GS* 340, p. 272.

59. *BT* 12, p. 82.

60. *BT* 15, p. 93.

61. *BT* 13, p. 88.

62. *D* 68, p. 39.

63. *GS* 139, pp. 189–90.

64. *D* 68, p. 39.

65. *A* 41, p. 616.

66. *A* 42, p. 617.

67. *NCW*, "How I Broke Away from Wagner" 1, in *PN*, pp. 675–76.

68. *NCW*, "How I Broke Away from Wagner" 1, p. 676.

69. *EH* II:5, p. 248.

70. *CW* 7, p. 170

71. *CW* 8, p. 172.

72. *NCW*, "Where I Offer Objections," p. 665.

73. *CW* 10, p. 177.

74. *NCW*, "Wagner as a Danger," p. 667.

75. *GS* 99, p. 155.

76. *TI* V, p. 485.

77. *GS* 335, p. 264.

78. *GS* 193, p. 205.

79. *EH* III, pp. 270–71.

80. *TSZ*, p. 146.

81. *TI* IV:3, p. 481.

82. *BT* 12, p. 85.

83. *GS* 357, p. 305.

84. *GS* 11, p. 85.

85. *TI* VI:1, p. 480.

86. *WP* 192, p. 114.

87. *GS* 214, p. 209.

88. *GS* 128, p. 185.

89. *GS* 358, p. 311.

90. Martin Luther, *Sämtliche Schriften* (St. Louis, 1881–1910), XX, 1989ff; cited in Kaufmann, *Nietzsche,* p. 165n. See also "On the Jews and Their Lies," trans. Martin H. Bertram, in *Luther's Works* in 55 vols., Jaroslav Pelikan and Helmut T. Lehmann, eds. (Philadelphia and St. Louis: Concordia Publishing House, 1955ff.), vol. 47: *The Christian in Society* IV, ed. Franklin Sherman, pp. 285–88.

91. *GS* 129, p. 185.

92. *GS* 358, p. 312.

93. *TI* 2:12, p. 468.

94. *BGE* 260, 207.

95. *BGE* 228, p. 157.

96. *BGE* 225, p. 153.

97. *TI* X:12, p. 521.

98. *BGE* 254, p. 193.

99. *EH* III, p. 270.

100. *BGE* 211, p. 136.

101. *BGE* 204, p. 122.

102. *GS* 357, p. 306.

103. *TI* X:14, p. 522.

104. *WP* 684, p. 363.

105. *UM,* "On the Uses and Disadvantages of History for Life" 9, p. 111.

106. *WP* 684, p. 363.

107. *WP* 647, p. 344.

108. *WP* 684, p. 363.

109. *TI* X:14, p. 523.

110. *GS* 277, p. 224.

111. *TSZ* II:3, p. 202.

112. *TSZ* IV:7, pp. 378–79.

113. *TSZ* IV:6, p. 373.

114. *TSZ* IV:6, p. 374.

115. *TSZ* III:8, 2, p. 294.

6. NIETZSCHE'S VIRTUES

1. *GS* 290, p. 232.

2. *HAH* 301, pp. 136–37.

3. *D* 556, p. 224.

4. *BGE* 284, p. 226.

5. *GS* 276, p. 223.

6. *GS* 290, p. 233.

7. *TI*, p. 530.

8. *D* 278, p. 150.

9. *GS* 173, pp. 201–2.

10. *TI* 33, p. 533.

11. *GS* 283, p. 346.

12. *EH* II:10, p. 258.

13. *TSZ* II:13, pp. 230–31.

14. *GS* 14, p. 89.

15. *TSZ* Preface 4, p. 127.

16. Dhammapada, quoted in Freny Mistry, *Nietzsche and Buddhism* (Berlin: De Gruyter, 1981), p. 3.

17. *TSZ* III:12, p. 326.

18. *BGE* 227, p. 156.

19. *GS* 344, p. 282.

20. *TSZ* I:3, p. 145.

21. *TSZ* I:19, p. 211.

22. *TSZ* II:7, p. 180.

23. *BGE* 94, p. 83.

24. *TSZ* Preface 2, pp. 122–23.

25. *D* 32, p. 24.

26. *TSZ* I:3, p. 144.

27. *BGE* 61, p. 72.

28. *TI* X:49, p. 554.

29. *TI* X:47, p. 551.

7. NIETZSCHE'S AFFIRMATIVE PHILOSOPHY

1. *GS* 276, p. 223.

2. *EH* II:10, p. 258.

3. *GS* 341, pp. 273–74.

4. *TSZ* III:13, p. 333.

5. Milan Kundera, *The Unbearable Lightness of Being* (San Francisco: Harper & Row, 1984), pp. 195–96.

6. Kurt Baier, *The Moral Point of View: A Rational Basis of Ethics* (Ithaca: Cornell University Press, 1958).

7. *GS* 343, p. 280.

8. *BGE* 211, p. 136.

9. *WP* 1:3, p. 7, and 1:2, p. 9.

10. *GS* 337, pp. 268–69.

11. Kaufmann, *Nietzsche*, p. xvi.

12. *HAH* I:87, p. 48.

13. *WP* 1067, p. 550.

14. *BGE* 36, p. 48.

15. *BGE* 259, p. 203.

16. *BGE* 13, p. 21.

17. *D* 262, p. 146.

18. *GS* 192, p. 205.

19. *D* 348, p. 165.

20. *GS* 348, p. 291.

21. *TSZ* II:12, p. 225.

22. *BGE* 9, p. 16.

23. *GS* 13, p. 86.

24. *GS* 14, p. 88.

25. *D* 113, p. 113.

26. *D* 204, p. 123.

27. *D* 113, p. 114.

CONCLUSION: NIETZSCHE'S OPENING OF THE MODERN MIND

1. Nietzsche, in a letter to Paul Rée, in 1882.

2. Jean-Paul Sartre, *Being and Nothingness,* trans. Hazel Barnes (New York: Philosophical Library, 1956), pp. 107ff.

3. For discussion, see Steven E. Aschheim, *The Nietzsche Legacy in Germany, 1890–1990* (Berkeley: University of California Press, 1993.

4. *TI* X:51, p. 555.

Bibliography

WORKS BY FRIEDRICH NIETZSCHE

The Antichrist. Translated by Walter Kaufmann. In *The Portable Nietzsche.* Edited by Walter Kaufmann. New York: Viking, 1954.

Beyond Good and Evil. Translated by Walter Kaufmann. New York: Random House, 1966.

The Birth of Tragedy (with *The Case of Wagner*). Translated by Walter Kaufmann. New York: Random House, 1966.

The Case of Wagner (with *The Birth of Tragedy*). Translated by Walter Kaufmann New York: Random House, 1966

Daybreak: Thoughts on the Prejudices of Morality. Translated by R. J. Hollingdale. Cambridge: Cambridge University Press, 1982.

Ecce Homo (with *On the Genealogy of Morals*). Translated by Walter Kaufmann. New York: Random House, 1967.

The Gay Science. Translated by Walter Kaufmann. New York: Vintage, 1974.

Human, All Too Human. Translated by R. J. Hollingdale. Cambridge: Cambridge University Press, 1986.

On the Genealogy of Morals (with *Ecce Homo*). Translated by Walter Kaufmann and R. J. Hollingdale. New York: Random House, 1967.

The Portable Nietzsche. Edited by Walter Kaufmann. New York: Viking, 1954.

Selected Letters of Friedrich Nietzsche. Edited and translated by Christopher Middleton. Chicago: University of Chicago Press, 1969.

Twilight of the Idols. Translated by Walter Kaufmann. In *The Portable Nietzsche.* Edited by Walter Kaufmann. New York: Viking, 1954.

Untimely Meditations. Translated by R. J. Hollingdale. Cambridge: Cambridge University Press, 1983.

The Will to Power. Translated by Walter Kaufmann and R. J. Hollingdale. New York: Random House, 1967.

WORKS BY OTHER WRITERS

Allison, David B., ed. *The New Nietzsche: Contemporary Styles of Interpretation.* New York: Dell, 1977.

Chamberlain, Lesley. *Nietzsche in Turin: An Intimate Biography.* New York: Picador, 1996.

Clark, Maudemarie. "Nietzsche's Misogyny." *International Studies in Philosophy* 26/3 (fall 1994):3–12.

———. *Nietzsche on Truth and Philosophy.* Cambridge: Cambridge University Press, 1990.

Danto, Arthur. *Nietzsche as Philosopher.* New York: Macmillan, 1965.

Diethe, Carol. *Nietzsche's Women: Beyond the Whip.* Berlin/New York: De Gruyter, 1996.

Gillespie, Michael Allen, and Tracy B. Strong, eds. *Nietzsche's New Seas: Explorations in Philosophy, Aesthetics, and Politics.* Chicago: University of Chicago Press, 1988.

Gilman, Sander L. *Conversations with Nietzsche: A Life in the Words of His Contemporaries.* Trans. David J. Parent. New York: Oxford University Press, 1987.

Hayman, Ronald. *Nietzsche: A Critical Life.* New York: Oxford University Press, 1980.

Kaufmann, Walter. *Nietzsche: Philosopher, Psychologist, Antichrist.* Third ed., revised and enlarged. New York: Vintage, 1968.

Krell, David Farrell, and Donald L. Bates. *The Good European: Nietzsche's Work Sites in Word and Image.* Chicago: University of Chicago Press, 1997.

Magnus, Bernd. *Nietzsche's Existential Imperative.* Bloomington: Indiana University Press, 1978.

Magnus, Bernd, and Kathleen M. Higgins. *The Cambridge Companion to Nietzsche.* New York: Cambridge University Press, 1996.

Nehamas, Alexander. *Nietzsche: Life as Literature*. Cambridge, Mass.: Harvard University Press, 1985.

Parkes, Graham. *Composing the Soul*. Chicago: University of Chicago Press, 1994.

Schacht, Richard. *Nietzsche*. London: Routledge and Kegan Paul, 1983.

————. *Nietzsche, Genealogy, Morality: Essays on Nietzsche's "On the Genealogy of Morals."* Berkeley/Los Angeles/London: University of California Press, 1994.

Solomon, Robert, ed. *Nietzsche: A Collection of Critical Essays*. Notre Dame: University of Notre Dame Press, 1980.

Solomon, Robert C., and Kathleen M. Higgins, eds. *Reading Nietzsche*. New York: Oxford University Press, 1988.

Young, Julian. *Nietzsche's Philosophy of Art*. Cambridge: Cambridge University Press, 1992.

Index

About the Authors

Robert C. Solomon is internationally renowned as a teacher and lecturer in philosophy. He is the Quincy Lee Centennial Professor of Philosophy and Distinguished Teaching Professor at the University of Texas at Austin. He has written numerous books, including *From Hegel to Existentialism* and *The Passions: Emotions and the Meaning of Life*.

Kathleen M. Higgins lectures internationally on philosophy and aesthetics. She is professor of philosophy at the University of Texas at Austin and the author of *Nietzsche's Zarathustra* and *Comic Relief: Nietzsche's Gay Science*.

Together, Solomon and Higgins have published *A Short History of Philosophy*, *A Passion for Wisdom: A Very Brief History of Philosophy*, and *Reading Nietzsche*. They have also released, on audio- and videotape, a series of lectures titled *The Will to Power: The Philosophy of Friedrich Nietzsche* (The Teaching Company).